"In a field dominated by Western voices, Mousavian and Kiyaei offer a refreshing perspective as Iranian scholars who understand both worlds. They offer practical ideas for how the Iran nuclear agreement can be a building block to the long-sought goal of a Middle East free of nuclear, chemical, and biological weapons. At a time when the nuclear agreement is under severe pressure, their prescription is another strong reason to preserve the accord."

— *Mark Fitzpatrick, International Institute for Strategic Studies*

"The book makes thoughtful, well-informed, original, balanced, and timely contributions to the academic and policy debates on the challenges of reducing the risks from nuclear weapons and other weapons of mass destruction in the Middle East, focusing particularly in the Persian Gulf region. At a time when we are so close to war as a result of the U.S. confrontation with Iran—nominally over Iran's nuclear program, but at least as much because of regional rivalries—it is an important reminder that there are more creative and positive ways to deal with the situation."

—*Frank von Hippel, Princeton University, USA*

"The dynamics that produce calls for making the Middle East a zone free of weapons of mass destruction are not going away. Neither are the obstacles to creating such a zone. Mousavian and Kiyaei make a fresh and constructive case for why Middle Eastern states and others should more energetically begin efforts to build such a zone and how it could be designed and verified."

—*George Perkovich, Ken Oliver and Angela Nomellini Chair and vice president for studies, Carnegie Endowment for International Peace*

"For over 30 years, the international community has struggled over the goal of freeing the Middle East from weapons of mass destruction. This effort found new impetus in December 2018 when the United Nations agreed to hold an annual conference to develop and conclude a legally binding treaty for such a zone. In this timely and necessary contribution, Mousavian and Kiyaei chart a detailed and compelling path for what such a treaty could include and how it could be achieved."

—*Zia Mian, Princeton University, USA*

A Middle East Free of Weapons of Mass Destruction

The establishment of a Middle East zone free of nuclear weapons, a concept more recently broadened to cover all weapons of mass destruction (WMD), has been before the international community for decades. In this book, two experts from the region explore why the matter remains unresolved and outline a comprehensive yet achievable roadmap to a Middle East free of WMD.

Weapons of mass destruction pose an existential threat to global peace and security. But nowhere is it more urgent to stem their spread than in the Middle East, a region fraught with mistrust and instability. Accounting for these geopolitical realities, including the ongoing talks to curb Iran's nuclear program, the authors present a practical and innovative strategy to a Middle East free of WMD. They outline a phased approach toward disarmament in the region, prescribing confidence-building measures and verification tools to create trust among the region's governments. Their vision also sees the realization of a WMD-free zone within a broader regional agenda for security and cooperation to advance socioeconomic and political progress.

This book will be of great interest to students and scholars of international relations, politics, and security studies in the Middle East.

Seyed Hossein Mousavian is a Middle East security and nuclear policy specialist at the Program on Science and Global Security. He is a former diplomat who served as Iran's ambassador to Germany (1990–1997), head of the Foreign Relations Committee of Iran's National Security Council (1997–2005), spokesman for Iran in its nuclear negotiations with the international community (2003–2005), foreign policy advisor to the secretary of the Supreme National Security Council (2005–2007), vice president of the Center for Strategic Research for International Affairs (2005–2009), general director of foreign ministry for West Europe (1987–1990), chief of parliament administration (1984–1986), and editor-in-chief of the English-language international newspaper *Tehran Times* (1980–1990). Mousavian earned a PhD in international relations from the University of Kent, U.K.

Emad Kiyaei is a principal at the international consulting firm IGD Group, where he provides political, business, and civil society leaders with strategic advice at the intersection of political risk, disarmament, and diplomacy. He is also a director at the Middle East Treaty Organization (METO), which seeks to eradicate all weapons of mass destruction from the Middle East through innovative policy, advocacy, and educational programs.

He lectures and participates at conferences on the Middle East and disarmament issues at various academic and policy institutions. Formerly, he was a researcher for Princeton University's Woodrow Wilson School of Public and International Affairs and an associate at Columbia University's Center for International Conflict Resolution (CICR). Emad served as executive director of the American Iranian Council (AIC), an educational organization that focuses on U.S.–Iran relations. He holds a master's of international affairs from the Columbia University School of International and Public Affairs, USA.

Routledge Advances in International Relations and Global Politics

The Global Politics of Jazz in the Twentieth Century
Cultural Diplomacy and "American Music"
Yoshiomi Saito

South Africa and the UN Human Rights Council
The Fate of the Liberal Order
Eduard Jordaan

Economic Sanctions in International Law and Practice
Edited by Masahiko Asada

Iran in the International System
Between Great Powers and Great Ideas
Edited by Heinz Gärtner and Mitra Strohmaier

International Relations as Politics Among People
Hannes Hansen-Magnusson

Mexico's Drug War and Criminal Networks
The Dark Side of Social Media
Nilda M. Garcia

Transnational Labour Migration, Livelihoods and Agrarian Change in Nepal
The Remittance Village
Ramesh Sunam

A Middle East Free of Weapons of Mass Destruction
A New Approach to Nonproliferation
Seyed Hossein Mousavian and Emad Kiyaei

For information about the series: www.routledge.com/Routledge-Advances-in-International-Relations-and-Global-Politics/book-series/IRGP

A Middle East Free of Weapons of Mass Destruction

A New Approach to Nonproliferation

Seyed Hossein Mousavian and Emad Kiyaei

Routledge
Taylor & Francis Group
LONDON AND NEW YORK

First published 2020
by Routledge
2 Park Square, Milton Park, Abingdon, Oxon OX14 4RN

and by Routledge
605 Third Avenue, New York, NY 10017

First issued in paperback 2022

Routledge is an imprint of the Taylor & Francis Group, an informa business

Publisher's Note
The publisher has gone to great lengths to ensure the quality of this reprint but points out that some imperfections in the original copies may be apparent.

British Library Cataloguing-in-Publication Data
A catalogue record for this book is available from the British Library

Library of Congress Cataloging-in-Publication Data
Names: Musavian, Hossein, author. | Kiyaei, Emad, author.
Title: A Middle East free of weapons of mass destruction : a new approach to nonproliferation / Seyed Hossein Mousavian, Emad Kiyaei. Other titles: Routledge advances in international relations and global politics.
Identifiers: LCCN 2020002589 (print) | LCCN 2020002590 (ebook) | ISBN 9780367489588 (hardback) | ISBN 9781003043676 (ebook)
Subjects: LCSH: Arms control—Middle East. | Weapons of mass destruction—Government policy—Middle East. | Nuclear nonproliferation—Middle East. | Security, International—Middle East.
Classification: LCC JZ6009.M628 M87 2020 (print) | LCC JZ6009.M628 (ebook) | DDC 327.1/7470956—dc23
LC record available at https://lccn.loc.gov/2020002589
LC ebook record available at https://lccn.loc.gov/2020002590

ISBN: 978-0-367-50002-3 (pbk)
ISBN:-978-0-367-48958-8-(hbk)
ISBN:-978-1-003-04367-6-(ebk)

DOI: 10.4324/9781003043676

Typeset in Times New Roman
by Apex Covantage, LLC

Contents

Acknowledgments

We would like to express our sincere thanks to all our colleagues at the Program on Science and Global Security at Princeton University's Woodrow Wilson School of Public and International Affairs for their support, especially Professors Frank von Hippel and Zia Mian, who read the transcript and provided invaluable comments. We are also grateful to Princeton researchers Sina Toosi and Amir Kiyaei for their dedication and assistance throughout the process. Last, we dedicate this book to all victims of weapons of mass destruction in Iran and the Middle East. We hope the proposals outlined in the following chapters will renew efforts to move the region toward banning all such weapons and take a step closer to peace, security, and prosperity.

Foreword

In October 2011, I was appointed by the UN secretary-general as the facilitator for a conference on the establishment of a Middle East zone free of nuclear weapons and all other weapons of mass destruction. This appointment was part of the decision of the 2010 Treaty on the Non-Proliferation of Nuclear Weapons (NPT) Review Conference concluding document, which called for the conference to be held in 2012 with the attendance of all states of the region. In spite of significant efforts by all, the conference in Helsinki has not yet materialized. The goal of a Middle East zone free of weapons of mass destruction thus remains elusive.

It is welcome that discussions and exchanges continue regarding this important topic. The situation on the ground in the Middle East does not bode well for immediate results, but efforts to find workable solutions and, perhaps, new perspectives remain crucial for progress in this important but challenging issue.

I have had the privilege to get to know one of the authors of this book, Ambassador Seyed Hossein Mousavian, during my activities as facilitator. His background as a journalist, politician, diplomat, and scholar gives him an excellent viewpoint from which to evaluate the progress so far, understand the obstacles that until now have prevented the states of the region from making steps toward the goal, and think about the ways forward.

What is remarkable in this book is its fundamental idea to discuss, in the spirit of openness, various new, alternative, or complementary avenues potentially available for the region to try to make progress, including subregional approaches and a wider perspective for security and stability of the Middle East. Perhaps one of the core reasons making progress in this important endeavor has been so difficult is the deep-rooted mistrust that prevails in the region. This has, of course, its reasons, and will be difficult to change. Yet, without an effort to build trust and mutual confidence, chances of success remain low.

I am confident that this interesting book will bring an important contribution to the ongoing discussion regarding ways to improve the perspectives for a more secure and more stable Middle East.

Jaakko Laajava
Finnish ambassador and under secretary of state (Ret.)
Facilitator of WMD-free zone in the Middle East

Introduction

The Middle East might seem to be the last place on earth to establish a geographic area free from all weapons of mass destruction (WMD), but the potential benefits in striving to achieve this goal far outweigh the risks involved. The idea of a weapons of mass destruction-free zone in the Middle East (hereafter WMDFZ, or simply "zone") is decades old and was first proposed by Egypt in 1990 with support from Iran. The primary aim of realizing such a zone is to rid the region of all weapons of mass destruction—chemical, biological, and nuclear. The zone would eventually cover a vast geographic area of about 15 million square kilometers (approximately one and a half times the size of the United States) and include all twenty-two Arab countries in the Middle East and Africa in addition to Iran and Israel (with a total population of more than half a billion), stretching from Iran in the east and north to Mauritania in the west, and as far south as Comoros.

Realizing such a zone in the Middle East is paramount for a region reeling from decades of instability, insecurity, destruction, and WMD proliferation. The scope of the zone should not be limited to ridding the region of these destructive weapons; it should also include the creation of a closer political climate in which it can be achieved, requiring a rare occurrence of collective cooperation in a divided region. This process will require a complete reversal of the current animosity and misunderstanding among regional countries that has decapitated the drive toward improved security and socioeconomic and political advancement in the region. Therefore, the WMDFZ will not only contribute to strengthening nonproliferation efforts; it will inevitably open the discussion to other security-related challenges facing the region. The Middle East has all the ingredients to flourish: strategic location, vast natural resources, millennia-old cultures, and an educated youthful demographic hungry for transformation in their region and eager to be connected to the global community. It also possesses the ingredients for carnage to ensue and hatred to flourish, with an added toxic dose of ethnic, sectarian, national, and religious fanaticism.

The recent history of the region is littered with governments attempting to expand and use weapons of mass destruction, including the use of chemical weapons by Egypt in Yemen (1962–1967); by Iraq on its own citizens (1988) and against Iranians during the eight-year war (1980–1988); and by Syria in multiple cases since 2013.[1] There are also continuing concerns over Israel's opaque nuclear weapons program and the advancement of Iran's nuclear developments. These nonproliferation challenges are further compounded by the lack of global nuclear weapons disarmament; regional proliferation risks as nations develop their own nuclear energy programs; and the increasing threat of WMD acquisition and use by extremists and terrorists. These historical and contemporary WMD proliferation risks impede the realization of the zone and also contribute to the broader security context of threats facing the Middle East. There is no shortage of security challenges, including the role of world powers in the militarization of the Middle East; regional rivalry, particularly between Iran and Saudi Arabia; the unresolved decades-old Israeli–Palestinian conflict; and the origins and ramifications of the Arab Spring, including the ongoing instability in Libya, Syria, and Yemen.

There are, however, encouraging developments that could strengthen the chance of achieving a WMDFZ. Specifically, the breakthrough in nuclear talks between Iran and the EU3 + 3 (the United States, the United Kingdom, Russia, France, China, and Germany) coupled with efforts to rid Syria of its chemical weapons.

Iran and the EU3 + 3 agreed on a Joint Comprehensive Plan of Action (JCPOA) on July 14, 2015, which puts in place unprecedented inspections and transparency measures to ensure Iran's nuclear program remains peaceful. Iran also agreed to limit its nuclear program, which effectively closed the two routes to developing nuclear weapons, namely uranium enrichment to weapons grade and the amassing of plutonium. In return for Iran's full implementation of its nuclear commitments, the United Nations, the European Union, and the United States removed all nuclear-related sanctions imposed on the country.[2] While the JCPOA was a great asset for nuclear nonproliferation, it does face major challenges to its sustainability and full implementation. Chief among them is the unilateral decision by President Trump to withdraw the United States from the deal on May 8, 2018.[3] This move has placed the future of the accord on an unpredictable path, with the risk of the complete collapse of and repercussions for Iran's nuclear program as well as wider regional security implications. Meanwhile, the continuing conflict in Syria and further cases of chemical weapons use have brought into sharp focus the difficulty in verifying the complete removal of Syria's chemical weapons stockpile. It goes without saying that these sobering developments have placed doubt on the longevity of the JCPOA and the complete destruction of Syria's chemical weapons stockpile; however, the limited success thus far, coupled with ongoing international efforts to salvage the JCPOA and bring an end to the Syrian conflict, can ultimately inject needed urgency into achieving a WMDFZ in the Middle East.

More recently, the First Committee of the United Nations General Assembly (UNGA), tasked with addressing disarmament and international security matters, adopted a resolution in October 2018 (introduced by Egypt with support from Arab states) requesting that the UN secretary-general convene an annual regional conference on the zone by the end of 2019 and subsequent conferences each year until an accord on the zone is adopted. Despite explicit opposition from both the United States and Israel, the first "Conference on the Establishment of a Middle East Zone Free of Nuclear Weapons and Other Weapons of Mass Destruction" was convened at the UN Headquarters in New York from November 18 to 22, 2019. The conference was presided over by Jordanian Permanent Representative to the UN Ambassador Sima Bahouz, with facilitation by the UN Office of Disarmament Affairs (UNODA).[4] At the opening session of the conference, UN Secretary-General Antonio Guterres reminded the participants that achieving the zone would not only contribute to WMD nonproliferation but also serve as "means for States to take the initiative and work together to advance their own common regional security."[5] This conference was a watershed moment for advancing the zone, as past attempts had failed to materialize. To the surprise of naysayers, participation in the conference was robust—with the presence of all twenty-two member states of the Arab League, Iran, four nuclear-armed states (China, France, Russia, and the United Kingdom), relevant international institutions, and a handful of civil society organizations. The only ones missing in the room were Israel and the United States, who remain attached to their insistence that the region is not "ready" to discuss the zone, with U.S. Ambassador to the Conference on Disarmament Robert Wood adding that the United States opposes the conference because of its "focus on isolating Israel."[6]

The regional countries participated in good faith, with discussions on key issues facing the realization of the zone (technical and security related), and laid the groundwork for future conferences. At the conclusion of the conference, participating states adopted a political declaration by consensus, which emphasized their intention to "pursue, in accordance with relevant international resolutions, and in an open and inclusive manner with all invited States, the elaboration of a legally binding treaty to establish" the zone.[7] The political declaration leaves the door open for all invited states to participate in subsequent conferences.

Taking advantage of these positive developments, albeit with limitations and challenges, will require implementing innovative initiatives to address WMD and the security challenges that face the realization of the zone. One such initiative would strengthen the nuclear nonproliferation regime by regionalizing the principles of the EU3+3 and the Iran nuclear accord. Furthermore, to remove concerns over national uranium enrichment, which could be weaponized, it is worthwhile to assess the potential for creating the first multinational enrichment facility in the region. As a stepping-stone to the final zone, and to build momentum, another initiative may be to establish a regional cooperation and security arrangement in the Persian Gulf that would include a subregional WMDFZ. This subregional zone would serve as a litmus test for the eventual broader zone by initially addressing both WMD-related and security challenges among a smaller group of participants to boost the chances of reaching a wider consensus. That said, there is a need to think outside the security and nonproliferation paradigm by incorporating the influence of civil society and religion to advance the zone. The role of civil society through activism, advocacy, and public awareness is crucial in pressing governments within the region and beyond to take concrete actions toward the zone. Within the religious domain, working with prominent religious leaders who denounce the production, stockpiling, and use of all WMD will carry enormous weight in achieving popular support for the zone.

While a macro view of the region is necessary to highlight the enormity of the task ahead, there is a need to frame the implementation of the zone within a practical and attainable roadmap. The details of achieving the end state of a WMDFZ in the Middle East through a phased approach will include proposed guidelines and parameters for the zone, with practical, confidence-building measures to shore up trust among all stakeholders and a sequence of steps to achieve universality of all WMD nonproliferation treaties and conventions by regional member states.

With slow progress, political wrangling on the issue, and many setbacks for establishing the zone over the decades, there is a risk that any initiative will be seen as naive and hopeless. Yet, that is exactly why there is an urgent need for advocates of the zone, scholars, and policymakers to refine practical mechanisms to achieve movement toward a WMDFZ in the Middle East. Inaction is not an option, as the region will either continue on its path toward mass destruction or look ahead to the realization of a WMDFZ in the Middle East, which will have wide-ranging socioeconomic, political, security, and nonproliferation benefits. The zone's positive impact will not be limited to the region and will have profound effects on the global WMD nonproliferation regimes. Achieving a WMDFZ will make progress toward a regional security arrangement and cooperation, contribute to the positive influence of religion on nonproliferation, reduce conventional arms expenditure, and bring about a more constructive role for world powers in the region.

The fact that a zone free from all weapons of mass destruction has never existed complicates matters. However, successful examples of nuclear weapons-free zones (which exclude other weapons of mass destruction, such as chemical and biological weapons) could be used as a basis on which to establish the more encompassing WMDFZ. An encouraging sign and notable achievement for nonproliferation of nuclear weapons is that all countries in the region, except Israel, are parties to the Nonproliferation Treaty (NPT).[8] Entered into effect in 1970, the NPT aims to advance disarmament of nuclear weapons already in existence and stem the proliferation of nuclear weapons and related technologies, while at the same time promote peaceful uses of nuclear energy. The NPT established a safeguards arrangement under the auspices of the International Atomic Energy Agency (IAEA) to ensure that nuclear facilities and materials in signatory states are monitored and verified for peaceful purposes. Currently, 191 countries have signed and ratified the NPT, more than any other international arms control and disarmament agreement.[9]

Article VII of the NPT supports establishing nuclear weapon-free zones (NWFZs). The general definition of such a zone is a group of countries in a specified geographic area that agree not to manufacture, acquire, or test nuclear weapons within their respective land and water territories. Once a regional NWFZ is realized, the treaty remains in force indefinitely, though with an option for nations that are party to the zone to withdraw. Currently, there are five NWFZs around the world: Latin America and the Caribbean (2002), the South Pacific (1986), Southeast Asia (1997), Africa (2009), and Central Asia (2009).[10]

The idea for creating an NWFZ in the Middle East dates to the early 1970s, when the UNGA passed a joint Iranian and Egyptian resolution calling for the abolition of nuclear weapons in the Middle East.[11] If realized, the NWFZ would commit regional countries, like other similar zones across the world, to refrain indefinitely from the manufacture, acquisition, testing, or possession of nuclear weapons.[12] A key motivation for the resolution was to constrain the nuclear-weapon capabilities Israel had developed in the late 1960s and to prevent further proliferation in the Middle East.

Since 1980, the UNGA has adopted the resolution and annually called for the NWFZ by consensus, including the official support of all Arab states, Iran, and Israel. The wide support for such a zone, however, has not translated into practical steps toward implementing the resolution, and progress has been slow. The main stumbling block has been the sharp disagreement among countries in the region on the terms and the sequence of steps leading to its establishment. The security concerns in the region are viewed from two perspectives: Israel, as the sole nuclear weapons state, insists on a comprehensive peace agreement with its Arab neighbors before committing to any talks on the zone, while other regional states emphasize the need for the creation of the zone first, before the details of a comprehensive peace agreement are finalized.[13]

Part of the rationale for establishing a WMDFZ is to assuage Israeli concerns that a zone focusing on nuclear weapons would single out Israel and require it to disarm its nuclear weapons. In such a scenario, Israeli nuclear disarmament would be matched by the commitments of other regional countries to dispose of their chemical and biological weapons. Hence, the notion of establishing the wider, encompassing WMDFZ in the Middle East resurfaced during the 1995 NPT Review and Extension Conference. Since the NPT came into force in 1970, all members of the treaty meet every five years at the NPT Review Conference to discuss how to further strengthen global nuclear nonproliferation and to fulfill their obligations.

The 1995 conference had two major outcomes. The first was the indefinite extension of the NPT, and the second was the passing of a resolution (cosponsored by Russia, the United Kingdom, and the United States) calling for the "establishment of an effectively verifiable Middle East zone free of weapons of mass destruction." The resolution also called on all NPT members, in particular the nuclear-weapon states, to "extend their cooperation and to exert their utmost efforts with a view to ensuring the early establishment by regional parties of a Middle East zone free of nuclear and all other weapons of mass destruction and their delivery systems."[14] However, few hard results have materialized.

The NPT Review Conference in 2000 reaffirmed the goal of the 1995 conference and stated that the resolution would be "valid until its goals and objectives are achieved."[15] It was only at the 2010 NPT Review Conference, however, that practical steps were agreed on to make progress toward establishing the WMDFZ. Specifically, it was agreed that, in consultation with regional countries, the UN secretary-general (UNSG) and the three cosponsors of the 1995 resolution would convene a WMDFZ conference in 2012, to be attended by all states in the Middle

East. NPT members also appointed Finland's former ambassador to the United States and United Kingdom, Jaakko Laajava, as the WMDFZ facilitator with "a mandate to support implementation of the 1995 Resolution by conducting consultations and undertaking preparations for the convening of the 2012 conference." It was also agreed that a host country would be selected to convene a conference.[16]

In November 2012, however, the WMDFZ conference was called off by the United States because of ongoing conflicts in the Middle East and because "states in the region have not reached agreement on acceptable conditions for a conference."[17] The American statement also mentioned that the United States could not support a conference "in which any regional state would be subject to pressure or isolation," a clear reference to Israel's objection to participate.[18] With the exception of Israel, all other regional countries had confirmed their intention to attend.[19] Similarly, at the 2015 NPT Review Conference, the final draft document calling to restart the talks on the WMDFZ was derailed by the United States, the United Kingdom, and Canada. This time, the primary objection aired by the United States was that the final draft document set "unworkable conditions" and "arbitrary deadlines" and the agenda set for the conference lacked "consensus and equality."[20] Once again, with only Israel not committing to attend the conference, the U.S. objection alongside those of the United Kingdom and Canada was seen as strong-arming by Israel.[21]

In response, Egypt walked out of the Preparatory Committee (PrepCom) meeting in Geneva for the 2015 NPT Review Conference in protest of the lack of progress on convening the WMDFZ conference. Egypt stated that the purpose of its walkout was "to send a strong message that it does not accept the continued lack of seriousness in dealing with the issue of establishing [the] zone."[22]

The 120 member states of the Non-Aligned Movement (NAM) to the NPT also expressed their regret at the indefinite postponement of the conference and blamed Israel for the hold-up. The NAM was established in 1961 as a group of nations that sought independence not formally aligned with either the United States or the former Soviet Union.[23] The call on Israel went further: "to renounce possession of [its] nuclear weapons, to accede to the NPT without preconditions and further delay, to place promptly all its nuclear facilities under IAEA full-scope safeguards according to Security Council resolution 487 (1981) and to conduct its nuclear related activities in conformity with the non-proliferation regime."[24]

As detailed previously, previous attempts at convening the conference on the zone were intricately tied to the 1995 agreement for the indefinite extension of the NPT. Therefore, with no future date set for the conference, this issue will remain a key point of debate, particularly as nations prepare for the 2020 NPT Review Conference. It is against this bleak background that other avenues to convene the conference outside the NPT process were advanced, specifically the 2018 UNGA resolution that led to the first conference on the zone in November 2019 at the UN Headquarters in New York. While this UN-facilitated conference is independent of the NPT and obligations set by the 1995 indefinite extension, it is an important step toward realizing the zone. An important outcome of the 2019 November conference is that the participating states reached a political declaration in which they reaffirmed their commitment to continue working on the zone issue in an inclusive and consensus-based manner. This positive outcome could also refocus the 2020 Review Conference agenda on the need for nuclear-weapons states under the NPT to deliver on their disarmament obligations.

Notes

1 Cindy Vestergaard, "A Chemical Weapons-Free Middle East?" Center for Strategic and International Studies, May 21, 2013, https://csis-prod.s3.amazonaws.com/s3fs-public/legacy_files/files/publication/130521_Vestergaard_ChemicalWeaponsFreeMidEast.pdf.
2 Dina Esfandiary, "In the Middle East, Get Rid of Chemical Weapons First," Arms Control Association, January 9, 2014, www.armscontrol.org/act/2014_01-02/In-the-Middle-East-Get-Rid-of-Chemical-Weapons-First.
3 New York Times, "Read the Full Transcript of Trump's Speech on the Iran Nuclear Deal," *New York Times*, June 9, 2018, sec. World, www.nytimes.com/2018/05/08/us/politics/trump-speech-iran-deal.html.
4 "Conference on the Establishment of a Middle East Zone Free of Nuclear Weapons and Other Weapons of Mass Destruction," UNODA, accessed December 24, 2019, www.un.org/disarmament/topics/conference-on-a-mezf-of-nwandowomd/.
5 António Guterres, "Remarks at the Conference on the Establishment of a Middle East Zone Free of Nuclear Weapons and Other Weapons of Mass Destruction," United Nations, November 18, 2019, www.un.org/disarmament/wp-content/uploads/2019/11/Opening-Remarks-by-the-Secretary-General.pdf.
6 Alicia Sanders-Zakre, "UN Body Seeks Mideast WMD-Free-Zone Talks," Arms Control Association, December 2018, https://armscontrol.org/act/2018-12/news/un-body-seeks-mideast-wmd-free-zone-talks.
7 "Political Declaration Adopted at the First Session of the Conference on the Establishment of a Middle East Zone Free of Nuclear Weapons and Other Weapons of Mass Destruction," UNODA, accessed December 24, 2019, www.un.org/disarmament/wp-content/uploads/2019/12/A-conf-236-6-annex.pdf.
8 "Disarmament Treaties Database: Treaty on the Non-Proliferation of Nuclear Weapons (NPT)," UNODA, accessed August 24, 2016, http://disarmament.un.org/treaties/t/npt.
9 "Treaty on the Non-Proliferation of Nuclear Weapons (NPT)," UNODA, accessed March 26, 2018, www.un.org/disarmament/wmd/nuclear/npt/.
10 "Nuclear-Weapon-Free Zones (NWFZ) at a Glance," Arms Control Association, May 1, 2015, www.armscontrol.org/factsheets/nwfz.
11 "Establishment of a Nuclear-Weapon-Free Zone in the Region of the Middle East," United Nations General Assembly, January 7, 1997, http://www.un.org/documents/ga/res/51/ares51-41.htm.
12 "Nuclear-Weapon-Free Zones (NWFZ) at a Glance."
13 "Fact Sheets & Briefs," Arms Control Association, June 1, 2015, www.armscontrol.org/factsheets/MEWMDFZ.
14 "History of the NPT 1975–1995," Reaching Critical Will, accessed August 31, 2016, www.reachingcriticalwill.org/disarmament-fora/npt/history-of-the-npt-1975-1995#NPT1995.
15 "2000 Review Conference of the Parties to the Treaty on the Non-Proliferation of Nuclear Weapons," UNODA, May 21, 1999, http://daccess-ods.un.org/access.nsf/Get?OpenAgent&DS=NPT/CONF.2000/1&Lang=E.
16 "Fact Sheets & Briefs."
17 "2012 Conference on a Middle East Zone Free of Weapons of Mass Destruction (MEWMDFZ)," U.S. Department of State, November 23, 2012, www.state.gov/r/pa/prs/ps/2012/11/200987.htm.

18 Patricia M. Lewis, "All in the Timing: The Weapons of Mass Destruction Free Zone in the Middle East," Chatham House, August 2014, https://www.chathamhouse.org/sites/files/chathamhouse/field/field_document/20140805WMDLewis.pdf.
19 Emily B. Landau and Shimon Stein, "The Decision to Call off the 2012 WMDFZ Conference: An Outcome Destined from the Start?" INSS Insight, no. 390, December 5, 2012, www.files.ethz.ch/isn/157165/Insights_390_05Dec2012.pdf.
20 Kelsey Davenport, "WMD-Free Middle East Proposal at a Glance," Arms Control Association, July 2017, www.armscontrol.org/factsheets/mewmdfz.
21 Barak Ravid, "U.S. Blocks NPT Conference Statement Over Israeli Objections," *Haaretz*, May 23, 2015, www.haaretz.com/israel-objects-u-s-blocks-npt-conference-1.5365363.
22 Sameh Aboulenein, "Statement by H. E. Ambassador Dr. Sameh Aboulenein, Deputy Assistant Minister for Disarmament Affairs of the Arab Republic of Egypt Before the Second Session of the Preparatory Committee to the 2015 NPT Review Conference," Reaching Critical Will, April 25, 2013, http://www.reachingcriticalwill.org/images/documents/Disarmament-fora/npt/prepcom13/statements/24April_Egypt.pdf.
23 "Non-Aligned Movement (NAM) | What Is the Non-Aligned Movement," NTI, April 14, 2017, www.nti.org/learn/treaties-and-regimes/non-aligned-movement-nam/.
24 "The Republic of Indonesia on Behalf of the Non-Aligned Movement (NAM) at the Thematic Debate of the First Committee on Regional Disarmament and Security," United Nations Regional Center for Peace and Disarmament in Asia and the Pacific, October 30, 2013, http://unrcpd.org/wp-content/uploads/2013/11/RD30_Oct_indonesia_nam.pdf.

1 Regionalization of the Iran accord

To achieve a zone free of weapons of mass destruction in the Middle East requires measures to enhance transparency and verification in the conventional and peaceful applications of nuclear, biological, and chemical technologies around the region. Luckily, the tremendous international effort to resolve, through diplomatic means, Iran's nuclear ambitions resulted in the extensive Joint Comprehensive Plan of Action (JCPOA) in 2015. The numerous rounds of negotiations and the obstacles encountered in reaching the deal highlight the necessity of sustained political and diplomatic efforts to achieve such an ambitious and wide-ranging endeavor. Ultimately, the historic accord could serve as a foundation in the region for further expansion of the transparency and verification mechanisms created during those negotiations.

The signing of the JCPOA on July 14, 2015, following more than a decade of failed nuclear negotiations between Iran and the EU3+3, marked a peaceful settlement of the Iranian nuclear dispute. The United Nations Security Council (UNSC) unanimously approved the accord on July 20, 2015, ushering in a new era in Iran's relations with the international community.[1] The UNSC is primarily tasked with maintaining international peace and security with the sole power within the United Nations to pass binding resolutions to all 194 UN member states, impose international sanctions, and authorize the use of military force.[2] The JCPOA is the most comprehensive agreement ever achieved on nonproliferation; it contains the most far-reaching transparency and verification mechanisms ever implemented in the history of the NPT. It closes all possible pathways to a nuclear weapon and prevents any covert weapons programs. While the JCPOA represents one of the most important diplomatic and nonproliferation achievements of the last several decades, regrettably, President Trump's withdrawal from the JCPOA in May 2018 has showcased the vulnerability in maintaining such complex multilateral agreements. However, the ongoing international effort to salvage the nuclear deal aims to ensure that its complete unraveling is not contingent on Trump's decision. There are encouraging signs that all other parties to the agreement (United Kingdom, Russia, Germany, France, EU, and Iran), with the notable exception of the United States, are determined to support the full implementation of the JCPOA. Ultimately, the survival of this historic nuclear accord and the process through which the international community succeeds or fails in resolving this current impasse will be paramount to global nuclear nonproliferation and the achievability of any future NWFZ and WMDFZ in the Middle East.

Iran's nuclear negotiations

The achievement of the JCPOA offers a blueprint for multilateral negotiations and provides examples of the concessions and political will required by all sides to move the process forward. It is worth noting that the JCPOA details technical processes that have enabled the international community to render Iran's nuclear program peaceful.

While the JCPOA was aimed specifically at resolving the Iranian nuclear dispute, the composition of the final document can serve as a basis for parts of the final WMDFZ agreement; particularly useful are the sections within the JCPOA that deal with enhanced monitoring and verification tools for nuclear activities and infrastructure. Also, the dispute resolution mechanism and confidence-building measures could be of use in the development process of the WMDFZ. The key to an eventual WMDFZ will be the coupling of multilateralism through diplomacy with the closing of current loopholes in nonproliferation treaties to stem weaponization. For this reason, a closer look at the process that achieved the JCPOA, with details on the key elements of the agreement, provides a realistic and plausible approach to the wider ambition of ridding the region of all weapons of mass destruction. This overview will also illuminate the sheer magnitude of the agreement and the intricate details that had to be ironed out among the negotiating parties. This understanding will be crucial prior to tackling the ramifications arising from President Trump's withdrawal from the JCPOA.

Chronology of important milestones in JCPOA negotiations

The monumental achievement of the JCPOA involved some of the most complex diplomatic negotiations ever undertaken. An examination of these efforts and key milestones detailed subsequently can provide a glimpse into the arduous process necessary to implement a WMDFZ that requires the backing of the entire Middle East.

November 24, 2013. The shift toward a diplomatic resolution, after years of failed attempts to settle the Iranian nuclear issue, accelerated after the EU3+3 and Iran signed an interim nuclear deal called the Joint Plan of Action, and a new round of talks were started to reach a mutually agreed long-term comprehensive solution to ensure Iran's nuclear program would be exclusively peaceful.[3] The Joint Plan of Action represented a serious step toward defusing the long-standing dispute.

February 20, 2014. The EU3+3 and Iran agreed on a framework, a plan of action, and a timetable to conduct negotiations on a comprehensive agreement within four months.[4]

April 9, 2014. Negotiations in Vienna ended on a high note, with the EU foreign policy chief at the time, Catherine Ashton, noting that negotiators "held substantive and detailed discussions covering all the issues which will need to be part of a Comprehensive Agreement," but acknowledging that "a lot of intensive work will be required to overcome the differences which naturally still exist at this stage in the process."[5] They also agreed to start drafting the comprehensive deal in upcoming negotiations.

June 20, 2014. This round of Vienna negotiations ended with key issues unresolved. As a result, the deadline for an agreement was extended to November 24, 2014.

July 19, 2014. Following the extension, further rounds of negotiations were held, with Iran and the EU3 + 3 agreeing to extend the approved provisions in the interim Joint Plan of Action until a final deal could be reached.

November 24, 2014. The negotiations continued in Vienna, with progress made on previous challenges, but it was clear the November 24 deadline to reach a breakthrough was unattainable. Therefore, all sides agreed to a second extension, with an aim to finalize a comprehensive deal by July 2015.[6]

April 2, 2015. The negotiations finally reached a breakthrough in Lausanne. The negotiators agreed to a framework deal for Iran's nuclear activities, with the details presented at a joint press conference held by High Representative of the European Union for Foreign Affairs Federica Mogherini and Minister of Foreign Affairs of Iran Mohammad Javad Zarif. The framework deal addressed key issues that had marred negotiations in the past and accelerated the process toward the final agreement. Primarily, it curtailed Iran's two primary avenues to a possible nuclear weapon: uranium enrichment and the accumulation of plutonium. Therefore, Iran committed to limit its "enrichment capacity, enrichment level and stockpile" while also "redesigning and rebuilding a modernized Heavy Water Research Reactor in Arak that will not produce weapons-grade plutonium." To rule out the possibility of reprocessing the spent fuel from the Arak reactor to amass weapons-grade plutonium, Iran agreed to refrain from future plans to build a reprocessing plant and to export all spent fuel.

Next came the mechanisms to verify Iran would adhere to these limitations. Iran agreed to strict monitoring and inspection by the International Atomic Energy Agency (IAEA), whereby the agency can make "use of modern technologies and will have enhanced access through agreed procedures, including to clarify past and present issues." In return:

> the EU will terminate the implementation of all nuclear-related economic and financial sanctions and the US will cease the application of all nuclear-related secondary economic and financial sanctions, simultaneously with the IAEA-verified implementation by Iran of its key nuclear commitments. . . . A new UN Security Council Resolution will endorse the JCPOA, terminate all previous nuclear-related resolutions and incorporate certain restrictive measures for a mutually agreed period of time.[7]

July 14, 2015. Intense negotiations continued, following the framework agreement reached at the Lausanne talks. With pressure mounting on negotiators from inside and outside their respective countries, the talks were, at times, at risk of collapsing. Ultimately, following seventeen days of negotiations in Vienna, on July 14, 2015, all parties agreed to the final text of the JCPOA.[8]

July 20, 2015. The UNSC unanimously passed a resolution endorsing the JCPOA, which opened the process for UNSC nuclear-related sanctions on Iran to be removed once the steps stipulated in the JCPOA where taken. The JCPOA details a step-by-step approach and reciprocal commitments (by Iran and EU3+3) as laid down in the agreement with endorsement by the UNSC. The JCPOA is composed of a general section addressing the main content of the agreement, the preamble and general provisions, nuclear matters, sanctions, an implementation plan, and a dispute resolution mechanism, and is supplemented with five Annexes (Annex I: Nuclear-Related Measures, Annex II: Sanctions-Related Commitments, Annex III: Civil Nuclear Cooperation, Annex IV: Joint Commission, and Annex V: Implementation Plan).[9]

September 17, 2015. Following official endorsement of the JCPOA by the UNSC, the members of the EU3+3 and Iran had a ninety-day period to pass the legislation in their respective parliamentary bodies. The United States completed its congressional review process on September 17.

October 13, 2015. Iran's parliament, Majlis, passed a bill approving the deal, while Iranian Supreme Leader Ali Khamenei weighed in a week later with a conditional endorsement in which he outlined eight specific concerns over some aspects of the accord.[10] Principal among Ayatollah Khamenei's concerns was his long-held distrust of the intentions of the U.S. government in negotiating with Iran, regardless of the issue at hand. Ayatollah Khamenei alluded to this point in a letter to President Hassan Rouhani regarding the implementation of the JCPOA, in which he wrote "neither in the nuclear issue nor in any other issue, had [the United States] been pursuing no other approach but hostility and disturbance, and [it] is unlikely to do otherwise in the future."[11] He also emphasized that the

> removal of unjust economic and financial sanctions and its enforcement [the lifting of sanctions] is tied to Iran's future actions under the JCPOA, it is necessary that solid and sufficient guarantees be arranged to avoid any infraction by the opposite parties. Written declaration by the US president and the European Union for the lifting of the sanctions is among them. In the statements of the EU and the US president, it must be reiterated that these sanctions will be fully lifted. Any declaration that the structure of the sanctions will remain in force shall imply non-compliance with the JCPOA.[12]

October 18, 2015. This date marked Adoption Day of the JCPOA, upon which all parties to the deal would begin to take concrete steps to turn the agreement into a reality, meaning Iran began taking measures to limit its nuclear program, while the EU3+3 took initial steps to provide Iran with relief from nuclear-related sanctions.[13] In a joint statement marking this milestone, Iranian Foreign Minister Mohammad Javad Zarif and EU Foreign Policy Chief Federica Mogherini said that "all sides remain strongly committed to ensuring" implementation of the deal and "will make all the necessary preparations."[14]

December 15, 2015. The next pivotal moment in the Iran nuclear saga came when the IAEA board of governors passed a resolution endorsing Director General Yukiya Amano's report, *Final Assessment on Past and Present Outstanding Issues Regarding Iran's Nuclear Program*. Amano's report outlined that Iran had conducted feasibility and scientific studies on developing a nuclear explosive device prior to 2003 and that some activities continued thereafter. However, he added that "The Agency has no credible indications of activities in Iran relevant to the development of a nuclear explosive device after 2009. Nor has the Agency found any credible indications of the diversion of nuclear material in connection with the possible military dimensions to Iran's nuclear program."[15] The endorsement by the IAEA was the last step stipulated under the November 2013 Framework for Cooperation between Iran and the IAEA, which was designed to assess issues related to possible military dimensions (PMDs) to Iran's nuclear program by the end of 2015.

January 16, 2016. A major milestone was Implementation Day of the JCPOA, which meant all parties to the agreement (EU3 + 3 and IAEA) were satisfied with Iran's steps, as stipulated under the JCPOA, to curtail its nuclear program for solely peaceful purposes. This indicated that Tehran had completed its nuclear-related commitments under the deal, and nuclear-related sanctions were lifted accordingly.[16] A final report by the IAEA on the same day confirmed that Iran had completed key steps that significantly limited its nuclear program in four major categories (reduction of enrichment capacity and capability, uranium stockpile limits, Arak reactor reconfiguration to avert the possibility of future reprocessing that could produce weapons-grade plutonium, and ending activities related to weaponization) and had adhered to more stringent monitoring and verification provisions. The risk for Iran attempting to pursue a plutonium route to a bomb was centered on the construction of the nuclear reactor at Arak, which would generate spent fuel (irradiated nuclear fuel or used-up nuclear fuel) composed of weapons-grade plutonium. To create weapons-grade plutonium, Iran would have to reprocess the spent fuel, separating the weapons-grade plutonium from the rest of the spent fuel material. To counter this risk, Iran agreed, under the JCPOA, to redesign and rebuild the Arak reactor to not produce weapons-grade plutonium. Iran also agreed to ship all its spent fuel out of the country.[17]

IAEA Director-General Yukiya Amano's statement gave the green light for sanctions to be lifted. "The way is now clear for the Agency to begin verifying and monitoring Iran's nuclear-related commitments under the JCPOA, as requested by the Security Council and authorized by the [IAEA governing] Board," adding "relations between Iran and the IAEA now enter a new phase. It is an important day for the international community. I congratulate all those who helped make it a reality."[18]

Within minutes, former U.S. President Barack Obama signed an executive order lifting nuclear-related economic sanctions on Iran. Then U.S. Secretary of State John Kerry issued a statement confirming that "Iran has undertaken significant steps that many, and I do mean many, people doubted would ever come to pass. And that should be recognized, even though the full measure of this achievement can only be realized by assuring continued full compliance in the coming years."[19]

Simultaneously, the EU began the process of lifting its economic and financial sanctions taken in connection with Iran's nuclear program.[20] Implementation Day, while historic and ushering in a new era for Iran and the international community, was just the beginning of a complex process that has come under threat with Trump's decision to pull out of the agreement, making it more imperative than ever before for the remaining members—Iran, EU3, Russia, China, the EU, and the IAEA—to continue their commitments over the coming years.

Contours of the JCPOA

The following discussion focuses on the provisions of the JCPOA that outline the limitations placed on Iran's nuclear program and the verification, transparency, and monitoring mechanisms to be implemented in exchange for a broad suspension of U.S. nuclear-related sanctions and the lifting of EU and UN sanctions.[21] These provisions, while tailored to the Iranian nuclear program, could play an important role in eventual negotiations for a WMDFZ in the Middle East.

Even with the U.S. withdrawal, it is important to acknowledge five important take-away points from the JCPOA that could apply to broader negotiations on the WMDFZ. First, the success of the negotiations sets a positive precedence for multilateralism and diplomacy, even among states with entrenched mistrust and animosity (such as that which led to the lack of formal diplomatic relations between the United States and Iran since the 1979 revolution). Second, the agreement was not based on trust but verification and monitoring mechanisms that ensured nonproliferation of nuclear weapons. These improved and innovative methods were not limited only to Iran; they were also used broadly in a region fraught with mistrust. Third, the limitations placed on Iran's nuclear program removed the pathways to nuclear weapons. They formed a basis that could apply to an eventual regional agreement on WMDFZ. Fourth, the sanctions placed on Iran came at great economic and political cost, with their removal contingent on Tehran abiding for years to the complex web of commitments under the JCPOA. The lessons learned from this coercive sanctions policy can serve as a warning to other regional countries not to attempt diversion toward weaponization as they develop nuclear capabilities. Finally, the components of the JCPOA, while focused on stemming nuclear weapons proliferation, have many structural parallels to mitigating the spread of other weapons of mass destruction: chemical and biological weapons. Once again, not only can one extrapolate the political will on the Iran nuclear case by world powers to the process of WMDFZ but also the technical aspects of nuclear nonproliferation to the broader range of WMD.

Limits on enrichment

The ability to enrich uranium plays a fundamental role in the production of nuclear power generation but can also, at high levels of enrichment, be used for making nuclear weapons. Since Iran mastered the ability to produce enriched uranium and amass large quantities of the fissile material, the international community grew concerned with the possible diversion towards a nuclear weapons program. The EU3 + 3, therefore, placed great importance on the matter during the nuclear negotiations as it sought to strike the right balance between rights of Iran as a NPT signatory to enrich uranium and the commitments Tehran can provide to ensure non-diversion towards weaponization. The JCPOA achieved this balance through the provisions outlined subsequently, which provide details on the specific limitations on the means, levels, and amount of uranium production and stockpile permitted by Iran.

Centrifuge Limitation. For ten years, Tehran is to use no more than 5,060 first-generation IR-1 centrifuges to enrich uranium, and these will be installed at its Natanz facility.[22] In theory, these centrifuges would produce enough enriched uranium to produce one nuclear bomb per year; however, they are relatively slow compared to more advanced IR-2 centrifuges, which spin three to five times faster than the IR-1. All excess centrifuges are to be used only as replacements for operating centrifuges and equipment.[23]

Level of Enrichment Limitation. Iran agreed to cap its enrichment at 3.67 percent of uranium-235 (U-235) for at least fifteen years. Natural uranium, once mined, is barely radioactive, with less than 1 percent U-235, the specific radioactive isotope that can fuel reactors and also be used in building nuclear bombs. Centrifuges are used to separate the U-235 from the rest of the uranium through a process called *enrichment.* Various levels of uranium enrichment are indicated according to the percent concentration of U-235. Low enriched uranium (LEU) applies to enriched uranium with less than 20 percent U-235, whereas any enrichment beyond that point is considered highly enriched uranium (HEU). For example, most nuclear reactors use enriched uranium up to 5 percent U-235; for weaponization, the uranium enrichment is above 90 percent U-235.[24] Therefore, by Iran limiting its uranium enrichment to 3.67 percent U-235, it will not possess the HEU required for weaponization.

Facility Limitation. Iran agreed to enrich uranium only at the Natanz commercial-scale facility and to refrain for fifteen years from building any new enrichment facilities.

Low-Enriched Uranium Stockpile Limitation. Iran agreed to reduce its LEU stockpile for a fifteen-year period to no more than 300 kilograms of uranium containing 3.67 percent U-235. Iran's LEU, containing between 5 percent and 20 percent U-235, was to be "fabricated into fuel plates, transferred or diluted."

Fordo Conversion. Iran agreed to convert its Fordo enrichment facility into a research and development (R&D) center, and for fifteen years, to maintain no more than 1,044 IR-1 centrifuges at this facility and to not conduct uranium enrichment or R&D related to enrichment there.

Centrifuge Production. Iran would operate only IR-1 centrifuges for ten years, while developing a new generation of centrifuge. After eight years, Iran can begin to manufacture two types of advanced centrifuges; after ten years, Iran can produce complete versions of these centrifuges and store them, under IAEA monitoring, "until they are needed for final assembly."

Research and Development (R&D). The JCPOA contains detailed restrictions on centrifuge and enrichment R&D for at least ten years. The limitations require Iran not to accumulate enriched uranium while undertaking such R&D, while using only one to two centrifuges of type IR-4, IR-5, IR-6, and IR-8. (IR-6 and IR-8 centrifuges are more advanced and have greater speed than the slower first-generation IR-1.) It also requires Iran to conduct R&D at one facility only, the Natanz Pilot Fuel Enrichment Plant (PFEP), monitored by the IAEA.[25]

Arak heavy water reactor

Iran committed to redesign and rebuild the heavy water reactor in the city of Arak to produce only one-tenth as much plutonium as the original design intended. Iran also agreed to export spent fuel from the reactor and manage an international project to redesign and construct the replacement reactor. The JCPOA required Tehran to permanently disable the Arak reactor's original core. To qualify for sanctions relief under the Implementation Day stipulations of the JCPOA, Iran would need to at least begin this redesign process.

U.S. State Department Spokesperson John Kirby confirmed on January 14, 2016, that Iran had taken this step; this was confirmed by the IAEA report of January 16, 2016.[26] Iran also committed to have no plans for fifteen years to reprocess the Arak reactor's spent fuel to extract weapons-grade plutonium. Furthermore, Tehran committed to refrain from accumulating heavy water "beyond Iran's needs" and to "sell any remaining heavy water on the international market for fifteen years."

According to the JCPOA, Iran is required to refrain indefinitely from building additional heavy water-moderated reactors. While Iran committed to refrain from reprocessing and agreed to ship spent fuel outside the country for fifteen years, Tehran also voiced that they are not interested in reprocessing beyond this time limit and will continue to ship their spent fuel. This, in effect, removes the plutonium route to a nuclear bomb for Iran indefinitely.[27]

Verification

The IAEA is to monitor Iranian compliance with the JCPOA provisions concerning its enrichment program and the Arak reactor.[28] To do so, the agency plans to increase its number of inspectors in Iran and to use modern verification technologies. For example, the IAEA will be installing the On-Line Enrichment Monitor (OLEM), a high-tech device that will monitor Iran's uranium enrichment activities around the clock and can send real-time updates to the agency to ensure Iran is keeping to the commitments outlined in the JCPOA, namely limiting uranium enrichment to 3.67 percent.[29]

Iran will also allow a "long-term IAEA presence in Iran" in addition to implementing the Additional Protocol to its safeguards agreements, which ensure that all nuclear activity conducted by the signatory state of the NPT are for peaceful purposes and do not divert toward weaponization. This grants the IAEA the authority to have more intrusive access to information about and inspection of facilities and sites where nuclear activity is declared or suspected. The IAEA is tasked to oversee the implementation of safeguards agreements and to verify the peaceful nature of the nuclear activities in the country.[30]

Iran is also to inform the agency of planned new nuclear facilities and permit the IAEA daily access to "relevant buildings" at the Natanz facilities. For twenty years, Tehran will allow the agency to verify Iran's inventory of certain centrifuge components and the manufacturing facilities for these components. Additionally, Iran is to allow the IAEA to monitor the country's uranium mines and mills for twenty-five years and to monitor Iran's plant for producing heavy water.

Procurement channel

The UNSC resolution endorsing the JCPOA establishes a "procurement channel" for Iran's nuclear program. The JCPOA also indicates that the IAEA will pursue reaching a "broader conclusion that all nuclear material in Iran remains in peaceful activities."[31]

Sanctions relief

JCPOA and IAEA confirmation that Iran had fulfilled the core nuclear requirements triggered the bulk of sanctions relief from the United States, the EU, and the UN. The following details highlight the level and reach of the comprehensive sanctions placed on Iran, the adverse impact on the economy, and the isolation of the country from the global market. They also showcase the complexity of the web of sanctions at all levels, from unilateral action by the United States and the EU to multilateral efforts in the case of the UN. Ultimately, the international sanctions relief is juxtaposed against Iran's commitments to curtail its nuclear program.

United Nations. UNSC Resolution 2231, which endorses the JCPOA, terminates all provisions of the previous UNSC resolutions relating to Iran's nuclear program, including UNSC Resolutions 1696 (2006), 1737 (2006), 1747 (2007), 1803 (2008), 1835 (2008), 1929 (2010), and 2224 (2015).[32] UNSC Resolution 2231, however, places certain restrictions on the sale of conventional arms exports and imports from Iran for five years and restricts ballistic missile technologies for eight years. A decade after Adoption Day (October 2015), Termination Day (October 2025) will usher in the official end to the role of the UNSC in the Iranian nuclear issue.[33] Since many provisions of the JCPOA go beyond a decade, and some stretch out indefinitely, the agreement will remain in place, but the Iranian nuclear program "will be treated in the same manner as that of any non-nuclear weapon state party to the NPT."[34]

European Union. The EU terminated the sanctions first enacted by Council Decision 2010/413/CFSP and Council Regulation 267/2012. The sanctions relief removes restrictions on (1) financial, banking, and insurance: Iran will rejoin the SWIFT electronic payment system that enables the transfer of international funds to and from Iran's central bank and other commercial financial institutions. The EU will also remove most Iranian banks from its sanctions list. Restrictions are removed for (2) oil, gas, and petrochemicals: The EU will resume purchases of Iranian oil and gas. The relief also permits investment in Iranian oil and gas infrastructure: "Investing in the Iranian oil, gas, and petrochemical sectors, by the granting of any financial loan or credit to, the acquisition or extension of and participation in, and the creation of any joint venture with, any Iranian person that is engaged in the oil, gas, and petrochemical sectors in Iran or outside Iran is permitted as of Implementation Day." Sanctions relief also includes (3) shipping, shipbuilding, and civil aviation: This will allow Iran and EU countries to engage in "sale, supply, transfer or export of equipment and technology for ship building, maintenance or refit, to Iran or to any Iranian persons engaged in this sector." It also brings to an end EU inspections, seizures, and disposal of cargo to and from Iran in their territories.

There are also other key sanctions relief, including (4) trading in precious metals, gold, and banknotes; (5) purchasing software through a single procurement channel; and, finally, (6) de-listing persons, entities, and bodies who will "no longer [be] subject to the asset freeze, prohibition to make funds available, and visa ban." This covers UN and EU autonomous listings.[35]

United States. With the U.S. withdrawal from the JCPOA in May 2018, all sanctions relief stipulated under the deal has been reinstated. Yet there is merit in understanding what those sanctions relief entailed, as it highlights the political will necessary to untangle a complex web of U.S. sanctions regime against Iran. Most notably, under the deal the United States suspended all nuclear-related sanctions, in addition to terminating the following executive orders: 13574 (authorizing certain sanctions, mostly in the financial sector as set forth in the Iran Sanctions Act of 1996), 13590 (authorizing certain sanctions with respect to Iran's energy and petrochemical sectors), 13622 (authorizing certain sanctions, expanding extraterritorial sanctions on Iran's petroleum sales as set forth in the Iran Freedom and Counter-Proliferation Act of 2012), 13645 (authorizing certain sanctions, expanding extraterritorial sanctions on Iran's automotive and financial sectors as set forth in the Iran Freedom and Counter-Proliferation Act of 2012), and Sections 5–7 and 15 of Executive Order 13628 (these sections were part of certain sanctions with respect to Iran's petrochemical and financial sectors as set forth in the Iran Threat Reduction and Syria Human Rights Act of 2012).[36] On Implementation Day, then U.S. President Obama issued a new executive order that revoked those previous orders and sections.[37]

The United States, however, is not obligated under the JCPOA to suspend unilateral sanctions on Iran's support for terrorism, its human rights abuses, and arms and WMD-related technology to Iran. Therefore, the majority of U.S. unilateral sanctions on Iran remain in place, even prior to President Trump's decision to reinstate the limited nuclear-related sanctions relief under the JCPOA. Those limited sanctions relief under the nuclear deal focused on the following areas: (1) U.S. secondary sanctions: The bulk of the U.S. sanctions relief are "secondary sanctions," namely those that target and restrict foreign entities and countries trading with Iran and impact the following areas: Iran's financial and banking institutions; energy and petrochemical industries; shipping, shipbuilding, and automotive sectors; port operators; the provision of insurance and re-insurance; trade in gold and other precious metals; trade with Iran in graphite, aluminum, steel, and coal; and certain software with provision of associated services for each of the previous categories; (2) Aviation and Iranian luxury goods: The United States removed the ban on export, re-export, sale, and lease of civilian passenger aircraft and related parts and services while permitting importation of Iranian goods such as carpets, caviar, and nuts; (3) Designated individuals and entities: The United States will also remove, in accordance with the list in Attachment III to Annex II of the JCPOA, "individuals and entities from OFAC's List of Specially Designated Nationals and Blocked Persons (SDN List), Foreign Sanctions Evaders List (FSE List), and/or Non-SDN Iran Sanctions Act List (NS-ISA List)." These constitute mainly shipping and energy-related entities.[38]

President Trump and the Iran nuclear deal

One key determining factor for the longevity of the Iran nuclear accord is the outcome of the 2016 U.S. presidential elections, which ushered in Donald Trump. During the long election campaign, all candidates (with the exception of Senator Bernie Sanders) either ridiculed the Obama administration for signing the accord or vowed to place more sanctions on Iran, thus placing the future of the JCPOA in possible jeopardy.[39] Then Republican Party presidential nominee Donald Trump went a step further at his address to the American Israel Public Affairs Committee (AIPAC) conference on March 21, 2016 (coincidentally falling on the same date as the Iranian new year), where he emphasized that his "number one priority [as president] is to dismantle the disastrous deal with Iran."[40] At the same AIPAC conference, the Democratic Party presidential nominee, Hillary Clinton, while supporting the nuclear deal, did not hesitate to reaffirm that "the United States must also continue to enforce existing sanctions and impose additional sanctions as needed on Iran."[41] In a nutshell, Donald Trump aimed to "tear up" the letter of the Iran nuclear accord, while Hillary Clinton was bent on killing the "spirit" of the deal.

The foreign policy trajectory during the Trump presidency has been both unpredictable and uncertain, and this includes Washington's stance toward Iran and the multilateral Iran nuclear accord. It is no secret that staunch anti-Iranian staff members and opponents of the Iran nuclear accord dominate the Trump administration. This includes then Secretary of Defense General James Mattis, who described Iran as the "single most enduring threat to stability and peace in the Middle East."[42] His views on the nuclear deal, however, were more nuanced during his Senate confirmation hearing, when he called it "an imperfect arms control agreement; it's not a friendship treaty . . . but when America gives her word, we have to live up to it and work with our allies."[43] President Trump's then CIA director and current secretary of state Mike Pompeo has long been one of the fiercest critics of the nuclear deal, eagerly supporting "rolling back this disastrous deal with the world's largest state sponsor of terrorism."[44] Pompeo's strong view on the issue has also softened since his nomination, as he stated during his Senate confirmation hearing that "while as a member of Congress I opposed the Iran deal, if confirmed, my role will change."[45] Then U.S. Secretary of State Rex Tillerson opted to focus on a "full review" of the Iran nuclear accord to ensure Iran was "complying with all the inspections requirements."[46]

On April 9, 2018, then U.S. National Security Advisor General H. R. McMaster was replaced with ultra-hawk John Bolton, completing Trump's war cabinet bent on destroying the nuclear accord and proactively working toward a regime change policy regarding Iran. John Bolton is one of the most radical voices in American foreign policy and as a key architect of the disastrous U.S. invasion of Iraq in 2003 has been calling for similar military actions in Syria, Iran, and North Korea.[47] Shortly before the JCPOA was reached, Bolton penned an op-ed for the *New York Times* titled "To stop Iran's bomb, bomb Iran" in which he insists, "The inconvenient truth is that only military action . . . can accomplish what is required. Time is terribly short, but a strike can still succeed."[48] He has gone on to call the Iran nuclear deal a "massive strategic blunder" and insisted the U.S. policy toward Iran should be based on regime change. Bolton has long backed the Iranian cult-like terrorist organization Mujahideen-e Khalq, or MEK, and identified them as a viable opposition group to replace the current Iranian government. The MEK not only sided with Iraq's Saddam Hussein during the Iran–Iraq war of the 1980s, but was also one of the first groups to be included on the U.S. list of foreign terrorist organizations for murdering American military personnel. While the MEK have been removed from the list since 2012, Bolton's relationship with the shadowy group dates back over a decade, and he has spoken on numerous occasions at MEK's events, in which he has repeatedly called for regime change in Iran.[49] With Bolton and Pompeo having Trump's ear on formulating U.S. foreign and security policy, we are undoubtedly closer to a direct U.S.–Iran confrontation. The revival of failed regime change policy toward Iran since the 1979 revolution closes the brief chapter where President Obama opted for diplomacy during his second term to address bilateral and multilateral challenges involving Iran.

The road to Trump's withdrawal from the JCPOA on May 8, 2018, was littered with discrepancy between harsh rhetoric to dismantle the nuclear deal and actual policy to that end. Instead, there have been contradictory signals from the Trump administration on the issue. For instance, there was an opportunity for the Trump administration to discredit the nuclear accord in the administration's first required quarterly report to U.S. Congress, due on April 20, 2017, on whether Iran was in compliance with the agreement. Yet, on the eve of the ninety-day congressional deadline for the report, then U.S. Secretary of State Rex Tillerson stated that Iran had upheld its commitments and, therefore, the United States would extend the sanctions relief stipulated in the agreement. Tillerson, however, also notified

Congress that the administration was still considering scrapping the agreement and that it would conduct a National Security Council-led interagency review of the nuclear accord to evaluate whether it "is vital to the national security interests of the United States."[50]

In yet another opportunity to "rip up" the nuclear accord, President Trump had the choice to either extend or reverse sanctions relief on Iran, as required every 120 days under the agreement. On May 17, 2017, President Trump opted to sign the sanctions relief waiver that ensured the continuation of the nuclear accord and that previous sanctions would not be reimposed.[51] The administration, however, at the same time, imposed new targeted sanctions against several individuals and organizations involved in Iran's missile program.

Following these two reluctant certifications of Iran's compliance, President Trump moved ahead on his promise to decertify the nuclear deal on October 13, 2017. His decision went against the advice of senior officials, including then Secretary of State Tillerson and then Defense Secretary Mattis, who argued that maintaining the nuclear deal was in the national security interests of the United States. It also went contrary to the position of all other negotiating partners in the deal—the United Kingdom, Russia, France, Germany, China, and the IAEA—who maintained that Iran was abiding by all its commitments under the deal.

Following his earlier decision in October 2017 not to certify the nuclear deal, in January 2018, President Trump reluctantly (for the third time) waived U.S. nuclear-related sanctions on Iran as part of the U.S. commitment under the JCPOA, but warned that it would be the last time. He justified his decision based on giving the Europeans time to "fix the terrible flaws of the Iran nuclear deal," threatening that in the absence of making necessary changes to the JCPOA, "I will withdraw from the deal immediately. No one should doubt my word. I said I would not certify the nuclear deal—and I did not. I will also follow through on this pledge."[52]

On May 8, 2018, President Trump followed through on his promise and announced the unilateral withdrawal of the United States from the JCPOA, calling the landmark agreement a "horrible, one-sided deal that should have never, ever been made," adding that Washington would soon begin "reinstating U.S. nuclear sanctions on the Iranian regime."[53] President Trump warned that the United States would impose "the highest level of economic sanctions" on Iran and followed his statement by signing an executive order reimposing U.S. nuclear-related sanctions that were lifted as part of the JCPOA, with a grace period of three to six months in order for companies to wind down from the Iranian market or face punitive U.S. measures.[54] On November 4, 2018, all previously removed U.S. nuclear-related sanctions as part of the JCPOA are re-imposed and in full effect.[55] Examples of sanctions relief included those on Iran's automotive sector; the central bank; importation of Iranian carpets and foodstuffs; Iran's port operators, ships, and shipbuilding sectors; and Iran's energy sector. Former U.S. President Barack Obama weighed in on Trump's decision, calling it a serious mistake and stating that it "turns our back on America's closest allies . . ., [and] the consistent flouting of agreements that our country is a party to risks eroding America's credibility and puts us at odds with the world's major powers."[56] This decision not only undoes the signature foreign policy achievement of Obama, but also represents an affront to the U.S.'s European allies, which had strongly lobbied the Trump administration to remain in the deal.

Moments after Trump's withdrawal from the JCPOA, Iranian President Rouhani reaffirmed Iran's commitment to continue abiding by the agreement while it negotiates with other signatories (China, France, Germany, Russia, the United Kingdom, and EU) in order to save the agreement. Toward this effort, Iranian Foreign Minister Zarif said that he would "spearhead a diplomatic effort to examine whether remaining JCPOA participants can ensure its full benefits for Iran."[57] Rouhani did, however, warn that in the absence of a satisfactory solution that safeguards the economic benefits Iran is entitled to under the deal, Iran would "start enriching uranium more than before."[58] Iranian Supreme Leader Ayatollah Ali Khamenei, however, voiced his pessimism about the idea of preserving the deal with the existing signatories. "Now they say we can continue with the three European countries, I don't trust these three countries either; don't trust them," he said. "If you want to make arrangements with them get actual guarantees from them or they will also all do the same as America . . . ; if you can't, then we cannot continue the JCPOA."[59]

The international reactions to the U.S. move was also swift, with all other signatories to the JCPOA (United Kingdom, Russia, China, Germany, France, and the EU) resoundingly opposing the decision and reaffirming their commitment to preserve the deal. A statement by then IAEA Director-General Yukiya Amano emphasized that "Iran is subject to the world's most robust nuclear verification regime under the JCPOA," adding that "the IAEA can confirm that the nuclear-related commitments are being implemented by Iran."[60] Iran's closest allies, Russia and China, issued a joint statement declaring their "unwavering support for the comprehensive and effective implementation" of the deal, with the Chinese Foreign Ministry spokesperson Lu Kang stressing that "China will continue with such trade and economic ties with Iran."[61]

Meanwhile, European leaders—German Chancellor Angela Merkel, French President Emmanuel Macron, and then British Prime Minister Theresa May—issued a joint statement emphasizing that "this resolution remains the binding international legal framework for the resolution of the dispute about the Iranian nuclear program. We urge all sides to remain committed to its full implementation and to act in a spirit of responsibility." The statement went further to call on "the U.S. to ensure that the structures of the JCPOA can remain intact, and to avoid taking action which obstructs its full implementation by all other parties to the deal."[62] This unified stance was also echoed by then High Representative of the European Union for Foreign Affairs Federica Mogherini: "As long as Iran continues to implement its nuclear-related commitments, as it has been doing so far and has been confirmed by the International Atomic Energy Agency in 10 consecutive reports, the EU will remain committed to the continued full and effective implementation of the nuclear deal."[63] With looming U.S. sanctions coming into effect, Mogherini asserted that "the European Union is determined to act in accordance with its security interests and to protect its economic investments."[64]

In the absence of continued sanctions relief arising from the JCPOA, Iran has threatened to withdraw from the agreement. To mitigate this possible scenario, Iran has sought concrete actions by the European powers to counter the impact of U.S. renewed sanctions. Ayatollah Khamenei issued three conditions that had to be met by the Europeans for Iran to remain in the nuclear deal. His main demand was for Europe to "guarantee that Iran's oil will be completely sold. If the U.S. can damage the sale of our oil, we must be able to sell as much oil as we want. If the Europeans linger over our demands, Iran has the right to resume its nuclear activities."[65] He also insisted that European banks safeguard trade with Iran and, finally, that European powers not to seek a new agreement on Iran's ballistic missile program or on its regional activities in Yemen, Iraq, and Syria.[66] In the event that the JCPOA collapses and other parties to the deal could not keep their commitments, Ayatollah Khamenei ordered the Iranian Atomic Energy Organization to prepare for resuming large-scale uranium enrichment, while remaining within the confines of the JCPOA. He went on to state that the "Iranian nation and its government will not tolerate to be both subject to sanctions and have its nuclear program restricted and imprisoned."[67]

European powers, meanwhile, have taken steps to shield European business interests from renewed U.S. sanctions and also provide assurances to Iran regarding continued economic benefits by upholding the JCPOA. European foreign and finance leaders wrote a letter to senior Trump administration officials, citing "security interests" in requesting that companies in Europe be granted an exemption from U.S. sanctions, particularly in sectors such as pharmaceuticals, health care, energy, automotive, civil aviation, infrastructure, and banking.[68] While it is unlikely that the current U.S. administration would provide such exemptions to European companies, the letter emphasized that Iranian withdrawal from the nuclear deal would "further unsettle a region where additional conflicts would be disastrous," maintaining that the deal was "the best means through which we can prevent a nuclear-armed Iran," and that there appeared to be "no credible alternatives at this time."[69] In a more concrete move, the European Commission issued a blocking regulation, a mechanism that bans companies in the EU from complying with extraterritorial legislation adopted by a third country. The blocking statute was originally created in 1996 to protect European companies doing business with Libya and Cuba from U.S. sanctions. This updated blocking regulation not only permits European companies to ignore U.S. sanctions, but also stipulates that Europe will not honor foreign court rulings (in this case the United States) based on unilateral sanctions.[70]

The EU also established an independent financial institution that oversees euro-denominated transactions with Iran. This would make such transactions immune to U.S. sanctions, as they would not have any dealings in U.S. dollars or use the U.S. financial system. French Finance Minister Bruno Le Maire emphasized that "we have to work among ourselves in Europe to defend our European economic sovereignty," and that such a move achieves "financial independence" from the United States in response to the sanctions.[71] To garner more support for preserving the JCPOA, Iranian Foreign Minister Zarif went on a whirlwind tour of European capitals and in the aftermath of discussions with then EU Foreign Policy Chief Mogherini, he received assurances that the EU would take measures to ensure continuing purchase of Iran's oil and gas products, maintain mass transportation relations, increase European investment in Iran, and provide financial, insurance, and trade guarantees.[72]

While the remaining signatories to the nuclear deal spearheaded efforts to maintain its survival, staunch opponents—Israel, Saudi Arabia, and the United Arab Emirates—welcomed Trump's decision, with Israel's Prime Minister Netanyahu cheering President Trump's "bold" withdrawal from a "disastrous" deal.[73] He went on to add that "Israel has opposed the nuclear deal from the start because we said that rather than blocking Iran's path to a bomb, the deal actually paves Iran's path to an entire arsenal of nuclear bombs—and this within a few years' time." A Saudi Arabia Foreign Ministry statement echoed Israeli sentiments: "Iran used economic gains from the lifting of sanctions to continue its activities to destabilize the region, particularly by developing ballistic missiles and supporting terrorist groups in the region."[74]

The most enduring impact of President Trump's decision to withdraw from the deal continues to be felt in Tehran. The JCPOA was seen as a litmus test for Iranian leadership in whether the United States could be trusted in negotiations and provide the improve bilateral relations with expanding discussions beyond the nuclear file. That possibility is no longer an option and will shift the policy debate among Iran's elites, who have for several years argued over the merits of dialogue with the United States, toward the skeptic viewpoint of hardline factions.[75] Trump's move has vindicated their long-held mistrust of the United States on the grounds that Washington is fundamentally opposed to Iran's pursuit of an independent political, security, and economic policy and is bent on regime change in Tehran regardless of how much goodwill the Iranians show. Ayatollah Khamenei took this opportunity to bring an end to the debate on the merit of engaging the United States, stating "[The Americans] threatened [us] and went against their commitments. This is an answer to all those who, repeatedly, over time asked me: 'Why don't we negotiate with the U.S., or why don't we develop relations with the U.S.?'"[76]

The uncertainty over the survival of the JCPOA, therefore, has been a major blow to Iranian moderate forces, including the Rouhani administration, who have invested considerable political capital into the landmark nuclear agreement in the hopes to revive Iran's economy and accelerate diplomatic integration with the global community, including the West.[77] The combination of increasing sanctions by the Trump administration and the inability of the European powers to shield Iran from their impact has placed the Iranian government under tremendous pressure to respond more assertively. Iran's patience reached breaking point when in May 2019, the Trump administration ended waivers that permitted several countries to continue importing oil from Iran. This was a tipping point for Iran, with oil exports plummeting and economic conditions worsening for the country (from 2.3 million barrels and 12.5 percent economic growth following the nuclear accord to few hundred thousand barrels and –4.6 percent economic contraction once U.S. reinstated sanctions and removed waivers). Iran insisted that it could no longer continue upholding obligations under the nuclear accord while other signatories were in breach of theirs.[78]

On May 9, 2019, exactly a year after Trump's withdrawal from the nuclear accord, Iran announced it would take its first step in reducing certain commitments under the JCPOA, with President Rouhani stating in a tweet, "starting today, Iran does not keep its enriched uranium and produced heavy water limited. The EU/E3 + 2 will face Iran's further actions if they can not fulfill their obligations within the next 60 days and secure Iran's interests."[79] As the sixty-day ultimatum was approaching, it was clear that the remaining signatories to the nuclear deal, in particular the EU3, would not be able to deliver on their obligations to safeguard Iran's oil and banking sector. On July 1, 2019, Iran took the second step by exceeding the 300-kilogram limit of its stockpile of low enriched uranium and a week later had also begun enriching uranium above the permitted cap of 3.67 percent. Iranian Foreign Minister Zarif reiterated that these incremental steps away from the JCPOA commitments were easily reversible but were conditional on Europeans delivering on their obligations.[80] While European signatories reaffirmed their support for the nuclear accord, in practice they were unable to counter growing coercive U.S. policies toward Iran. Each additional punitive measure taken by the United States on Iran was countered by Tehran reducing its commitment to the JCPOA. In one such case, on September 7, 2019, the United States placed unilateral sanctions on Iran's space agency and oil shipping network, with Tehran responding days later by taking the third step and activating advanced centrifuges at the Natanz nuclear facility to increase its stockpile of enriched uranium.

Meanwhile, the instability facing the region continued to worsen, with Houthi rebels in Yemen claiming responsibility for drone attacks on two major Saudi oil facilities on September 14, 2019. U.S. Secretary of State Pompeo immediately placed the blame on Iran without providing any further evidence, saying that Tehran "has now launched an unprecedented attack on the world's energy supply."[81] Tehran dismissed the claims and warned that the United States was attempting to justify the excessive coercive measures inflicted on Iran. The Trump administration continued to escalate tensions with Tehran on November 4, 2019, by placing targeted sanctions on nine individuals in the inner circle of Iran's Supreme Leader Ayatollah Khamenei, including his chief of staff and the head of judiciary. As expected, Iran responded two days later with its fourth step away from its JCPOA commitments, this time by resuming uranium enrichment at its underground Fordo facility. The U.S.–Iran tensions continued to soar, compounded by series of additional U.S. sanctions on the country (including on Iran's information minister, its largest civilian airline, and its shipping industry). This simmering animosity reached a boiling point on January 3, 2020, when a U.S.-targeted drone attack on Baghdad's airport killed the head of Iran's Islamic Revolutionary Guard Corps' (IRGC) elite Quds Force, Qassem Soleimani, and several Iraqi militia leaders backed by Tehran. This provocative U.S. move prompted Iranian leaders to announce on January 5, 2020, that Iran would take the fifth step by removing limits placed on uranium enrichment, number of centrifuges, and nuclear research and development. Once again, Iran's Foreign Minster Zarif reaffirmed that in a tweet that, "This step is within JCPOA & all 5 steps are reversible upon EFFECTIVE implementation of reciprocal obligations. Iran's full cooperation w/IAEA will continue."[82]

Washington's decision to upend the nuclear deal has been immensely counterproductive for regional and international stability, eliminating the chance for U.S.–Iranian cooperation on the many crises in the Middle East, especially in Syria and Yemen. Notably, several months after the deal was struck, in November 2015, Iran, with the support of the Obama administration, was for the first time invited to the UN's Syrian peace talks. This led to the conflict's first agreement on a cessation of hostilities, which has largely held and expanded to different parts of Syria. Trump's withdrawal from the JCPOA and hostility toward Iran's regional presence will make an enduring political resolution to the multiple regional conflicts an even more distant prospect. Trump's Iran policy is thus strategically self-defeating. It promises to increase U.S. involvement in the Middle East's many entangled conflicts, given Iran's decisive influence in strategic regional theaters—including Afghanistan, Iraq, Syria, and Yemen. Trump has rebuffed the potential for regional cooperation and raised the real possibility of a devastating conflict with Iran.[83] There will also be a proactive shift in Iranian foreign policy toward further strengthening political and economic ties with non-Western powers, including China, India, and Russia, particularly in the event that European powers are unable to preserve the nuclear deal and guarantee the economic benefits from the sanctions relief.

The U.S. withdrawal from the JCPOA brings into question the merits of multilateralism versus unilateralism. The negotiations that led to the JCPOA showcased that multilateralism can be an effective tool in resolving major international disputes rather than resorting to the use of military force or taking unilateral actions. The Trump administration's current policies risk resurrecting old habits of U.S. military adventurism and unilateralism. Former U.S. Secretary of State John Kerry called Trump's move "the biggest strategic mistake," adding that the United States has chosen to pursue a strategy on Iran reminiscent of President George W. Bush's regime change policy against Iraq. Kerry warned that as history has shown, this policy approach does not come out well.[84]

A multilateralism or unilateralism approach has also come into sharp focus following President Trump's unilateral move to bypass international efforts to deal with another nuclear proliferation challenge arising from North Korea. The multilateral discussions to peacefully resolve the North Korean nuclear weapons program, known as the six-party talks (North Korea, South Korea, China, Japan, Russia, and the United States) began in 2003 and had unraveled in 2009, with renewed hopes of resuming in 2018.[85] President Trump, however, went ahead with his meeting with his North Korean counterpart Kim Jong-Un on June 12, 2018, in Singapore, resulting in an agreement toward "the complete denuclearization of the Korean peninsula" and the promise of "new relations" between Washington and Pyongyang.[86] Following the first-ever meeting between a sitting U.S. president and a North Korean leader, President Trump floated the idea that "at the appropriate time, after the sanctions kick in—and they are brutal what we've put on Iran—I hope that they're going to come back and negotiate a real deal because I'd love to be able to do that."[87] While there are few details on the U.S.–North Korea agreement and with its future success still in question, one central question remains—could U.S. unilateralism be an alternative to multilateral efforts to resolve issues of international peace and security, including Iran's nuclear program, disputes throughout the Middle East, and beyond? President Trump's offer of direct talks with Tehran, while shrugged off by the Iranian leadership, may have to be considered more seriously as we enter an era of unilateralism by the sole superpower.

President Trump's disregard for international rule of law, institutions, and agreements, however, will inevitably erode both the legitimacy of U.S. commitment to international cooperation and the institutions tasked with collective peace and security. Such unilateral action will cause the world to view the United States as a belligerent power that is increasingly unreliable and untrustworthy. Trump's latest actions have indeed created a deepening cleavage between the Unites States and the international community, in particular the U.S.'s European allies, who are increasingly growing weary of Trump's obstructionism on global issues—from reneging on the Paris Agreement (on combating climate change), provoking a global trade war with tariff increases on key European and Asian trading partners, and withdrawing from the JCPOA. The Trump administration through these actions has compelled the international community to band together in salvaging the multilateral global order and open up the opportunity for other powers—China, Russia, and the EU—to fill the void left by American unilateralism.

Ultimately, the United States is unlikely to enforce its sanctions as effectively as those applied during the Obama era, because the majority of the international community is committed to preserving the nuclear deal since Iran has upheld its commitments under the deal. The very institutions and global coalition that the Obama administration relied on in applying the most comprehensive sanctions on Iran are those that are being undermined by the Trump administration. Furthermore, the JCPOA was not only signed by the EU3+3, but also unanimously endorsed by the UN Security Council Resolution 2231. The resolution is binding on all UN member states, requiring countries to "take appropriate measures to support the implementation of the JCPOA . . . as well as avoid actions that undermine the fulfillment of the JCPOA-bound obligations."[88] Therefore, such a U.S. unilateral move is in direct violation of the resolution and deemed illegal under international law. For the same reason, the international community as part of their international obligation to comply with the resolution could collectively resist U.S. coercion to broadly apply its unilateral sanctions on Iran.

Trump's decision to withdraw from the JCPOA, therefore, will have wide-ranging implications on the rules-based international system, global nuclear non-proliferation efforts, geopolitical realities in the Middle East, and the political landscape within Iran. There is no doubt that the Trump administration's unrelenting pressure to dismantle the nuclear deal will be detrimental to a robust nuclear non-proliferation agreement that removed Iran's ability to make a nuclear weapon. The

JCPOA was not only a diplomatic breakthrough, but also an important milestone in strengthening nuclear nonproliferation worldwide. Therefore, discrediting the JCPOA will have ramifications beyond the Iranian case and risks weakening the global push for mitigating proliferation of nuclear weapons. In the event of a complete collapse of the nuclear deal, Iran will no longer be bound by the limitations and restrictions to its nuclear program. Under such a scenario, Iranian leadership, having seen no merit in conducting negotiations or respecting agreements, will be compelled to restart, accelerate, and expand their nuclear activities. Such a chain of events could lead to further risk of nuclear proliferation within the Middle East.

The Iran deal as a basis for a regional WMDFZ

The established set of limitations and related transparency measures on Iran's nuclear activities outlined in the JCPOA present an unprecedented opportunity to regionalize limitations, verification, monitoring, and other provisions in the region.[89] There is no doubt that the U.S. withdrawal from the nuclear deal has threatened the very survival of the JCPOA. Nevertheless, the 159-page document is, by far, the most concerted effort by the international community to implement a wide-ranging nonproliferation agreement.[90] More significant is the political will and consensus among all permanent members of the UNSC related to the JCPOA.[91] Since the JCPOA focused on Iran's nuclear program, the direct implications will be on a global nuclear nonproliferation regime that would contribute to the realization of the NWFZ—even without the continued endorsement of the United States. However, since similar challenges are faced in other areas of WMD nonproliferation (chemical and biological weapons), the JCPOA's mechanisms that advance confidence-building, multilateralism, monitoring, and verification methods can be applied more broadly to positively contribute to a WMDFZ in the Middle East.

The JCPOA came into effect at a time when other states in the Middle East, especially Saudi Arabia, the United Arab Emirates (UAE), and Egypt, were planning to establish or expand their own nuclear power programs. To reduce the risk of international conflict and to ensure the safe development of nuclear power programs, the key components of the JCPOA could be used in the region to strengthen the nonproliferation argument.[92]

The long history of covert proliferation in the Middle East has led to a great deal of mistrust in the region, starting with Israel's nuclear program in the 1960s and continuing with the violations by Iraq, Libya, and Syria of their commitments under the nuclear NPT. Additionally, the decade-long confrontation over Iran's nuclear program, coupled with the rise of terrorism, failed states such as Libya and Syria, and civil and sectarian wars necessitates a robust regional regime that promotes safeguards, monitoring, and verification.

In a milestone report, the International Panel on Fissile Materials (IPFM), a body consisting of arms-control and nonproliferation experts from both nuclear weapon and nonnuclear weapon states, detailed the measures that would contribute to realizing a NWFZ (as a major step toward the more encompassing weapons of mass destruction-free zone), such as banning the separation of plutonium; limiting the level of uranium enrichment; capping and reducing Israel's existing stocks of fissile materials available for nuclear weapons; and eliminating its arsenal through a step-by-step process.[93]

Ban on the separation of plutonium

As part of the nuclear deal, Iran agreed that, for fifteen years, it would not carry out any reprocessing and separation of plutonium from spent nuclear fuel (reprocessing separates the weapons-grade plutonium from the rest of the spent fuel, providing an avenue to build a nuclear bomb). In addition, Iran would not build any facility capable of reprocessing spent fuel or carrying out any R&D activities in this field. Moreover, Tehran committed to ship all spent nuclear fuel from all present and future power and research reactors to another country, most likely to Russia.

Among all countries in the region, it is generally agreed that only Israel has separated weapons-grade plutonium from spent nuclear fuel.[94] Its nuclear arsenal is based on plutonium produced by irradiating natural uranium fuel in a reactor that uses heavy water as a neutron moderator (using heavy water means replacing hydrogen molecules in regular water with a heavier isotope called deuterium, which produces more plutonium in the spent fuel of the reactor). The reactor, which France built for Israel in the 1950s, is located at the Negev Nuclear Research Center near Dimona.[95] To separate weapons-grade plutonium from the spent fuel requires a reprocessing plant; the Israelis built one underground adjoining the reactor.[96]

To realize a Middle Eastern NWFZ (with a view to creating the broader WMDFZ) will require Israel to shut down the Dimona reactor and end reprocessing in a manner that is verifiable by the IAEA. Satellite or airborne infrared sensors should be able to verify the operational status of Israel's Dimona plutonium-production reactor, while Israel's declaration of its total production of plutonium could be confirmed through techniques of "nuclear archaeology."[97] Since such reprocessing can be used as a gateway toward weaponization, and since peaceful civilian nuclear programs do not require it, there is no economic or environmental justification for separating and stockpiling plutonium.[98] Other than the five nuclear weapon states, only Japan has a civilian reprocessing plant, which has been the subject of extensive debate over its utility, risks, and cost.[99]

Restrictions on uranium enrichment

Weapons-grade HEU is typically enriched to 90 percent or greater U-235. The IAEA treats uranium enriched above 20 percent as a direct weapons-grade material, and currently only uranium enriched to 5 percent or lower is used to fuel commercial nuclear power reactors worldwide.[100] There are, however, several research reactors in Middle Eastern states—including the U.S.-supplied Tehran Research Reactor—that use fuel enriched to 19.75 percent. Among the Middle

Eastern countries, Iran, Israel, and Syria have research reactors under IAEA surveillance that can use HEU as fuel. The research reactors in Iran and Syria contain only about one kilogram of HEU each, much less than the 25 kilograms of U-235 in uranium enriched to more than 20 percent that is required for a simple nuclear weapon. Iran already has agreed to import such uranium, as other countries do.

Transparency and verification measures

The Additional Protocol represents the maximum level of transparency that NPT member non-weapon states currently agree to. It requires them to declare all their nuclear-related activities and provide IAEA inspectors access to verify those declarations.[101] Like Iran, other regional countries that have not ratified the Additional Protocol—Egypt, Israel, Lebanon, Oman, Palestine, Qatar, Saudi Arabia, Somalia, Sudan, Syria, Tunisia, and Yemen—should agree to bring the Additional Protocol into force pending ratification.[102]

Israel's safeguards agreement, which has been in force since 1975, covers only Israel's U.S.-supplied Soreq reactor (operating since 1960), previously scheduled to be shut down in 2018, but this has yet to occur.[103] The IAEA enters into an "item-specific safeguards agreements" with countries not party to the NPT (in this case, Israel), whereby the IAEA applies safeguards (monitoring, inspections, and verifications regime) to ensure that designated nuclear facilities and material are not diverted toward weaponization and are used only for peaceful purposes.[104] Therefore, once the Soreq reactor is shut down, no IAEA safeguards of any kind will exist in Israel. Ultimately, the IAEA needs to negotiate a new safeguards agreement with Israel that will eventually cover all the country's nuclear materials and facilities if a WMDFZ is to be realized.

In addition to IAEA inspections, the Middle East will need a regional monitoring agency, similar to Europe's Euratom. Another example is the case of Latin America's nuclear weapon-free zone, where Argentina and Brazil have a joint Agency for Accounting and Control of Nuclear Materials (ABACC), through which they monitor each other's nuclear activities. Iran has already given access to the IAEA beyond the stipulations of the IAEA's safeguards agreements and, in the context of a regional monitoring regime, could go further to prolong transparency obligations such as it accepted under JCPOA, which include monitoring of uranium mining and purification, uranium imports, and production of nuclear materials and nuclear-related technology such as centrifuges.

Regional data-sharing system

To maintain a robust monitoring system, the countries of the Middle East can set up a regional data-sharing, analysis, and technical training process focused on existing or planned Comprehensive Nuclear Test Ban Treaty (CTBT) monitoring stations that detect radioxenon and other isotopes and particles leaking from underground nuclear explosive tests. The CTBT bans nuclear explosions and testing on the ground, underwater, and in the atmosphere. To monitor whether a nuclear test has occurred, the CTBT relies on a network of International Monitoring System (IMS) designed to detect seismic activity and distinguish nuclear explosions from natural events (such as earthquakes).[105]

Fissile material under international safeguards

Iran and Israel are the two countries in the Middle East with enrichment capability. If the JCPOA is sustained, international concerns toward the Iranian enrichment facilities will recede and all pathways to a nuclear bomb will be closed for at least ten years. This creates the perfect opportunity for Israel to contribute to a regional confidence-building process and help set the basis for a verifiable WMDFZ in the Middle East by committing to place all its declared fissile material under international safeguards.

Notes

1 Jennifer R. Williams, "A Comprehensive Timeline of the Iran Nuclear Deal," Brookings Institution, July 21, 2015, www.brookings.edu/blog/markaz/2015/07/21/a-comprehensive-timeline-of-the-iran-nuclear-deal/.
2 "United Nations Security Council," United Nations Security Council, www.un.org/en/sc/.
3 Kate Lyons, "Iran Nuclear Talks: Timeline," *The Guardian*, July 14, 2015, sec. World News, www.theguardian.com/world/2015/apr/02/iran-nuclear-talks-timeline.
4 Barbara Slavin, "Study Recommends US Interests Section in Tehran," *Al-Monitor*, February 18, 2014, www.al-monitor.com/pulse/originals/2014/02/iran-us-diplomats-return-nuclear-deal.html.
5 Laura Rozen, "Negotiators at Halfway Point, Move to Drafting Phase of Iran Deal Talks | The Back Channel," *Backchannel*, April 9, 2014, http://backchannel.al-monitor.com/index.php/2014/04/8111/iran-world-powers-move-to-next-phase-of-final-deal-talks/.
6 "Timeline of Nuclear Diplomacy with Iran," Arms Control Association, August 2016, www.armscontrol.org/factsheet/Timeline-of-Nuclear-Diplomacy-With-Iran.
7 "Joint Statement by EU High Representative Federica Mogherini and Iranian Foreign Minister Javad Zarif Switzerland," European External Action Service (EEAS), EU, accessed August 31, 2016, http://eeas.europa.eu/statements-eeas/2015/150402_03_en.htm.
8 Karen DeYoung and Carol Morello, "The Path to a Final Iran Nuclear Deal: Long Days and Short Tempers," *Washington Post*, July 15, 2015, www.washingtonpost.com/world/national-security/long-days-and-short-tempers-the-path-to-a-final-nuclear-deal/2015/07/15/bb90235c-2b1d-11e5-bd33-395c05608059_story.html.
9 "Joint Comprehensive Plan of Action," U.S. Department of State, July 14, 2015.
10 "Ayatollah Khamenei Sends a Letter to President Hassan Rouhani About the JCPOA," Office of the Supreme Leader Grand Ayatollah Sayyid Ali Hosseini Khamenei, October 21, 2015, www.leader.ir/en/content/13791/Ayatollah-Khamenei-sends-a-letter-to-President-Hassan-Rouhani-about-the-JCPOA.
11 Ibid.
12 Ibid.
13 Ben Brumfield, "Iran Nuclear Deal Launches on 'Adoption Day'," *CNN*, October 19, 2015, www.cnn.com/2015/10/18/middleeast/iran-nuclear-deal-adoption-day/index.html.
14 Kelsey Davenport, "Iran, P5+1 Formally Adopt Nuclear Deal," Arms Control Association, accessed August 31, 2016, www.armscontrol.org/ACT/2015_11/News/Iran-and-P5%2B1-Formally-Adopt-Nuclear-Deal.

15 Rodolfo Quevenco, "IAEA Board Adopts Landmark Resolution on Iran PMD Case," International Atomic Energy Agency (IAEA), December 15, 2015, www.iaea.org/newscenter/news/iaea-board-adopts-landmark-resolution-on-iran-pmd-case.
16 Brumfield, "Iran Nuclear Deal Launches on 'Adoption Day'."
17 William Broad and Sergio Pecanha, "The Iran Nuclear Deal—A Simple Guide," *New York Times*, January 15, 2015, www.nytimes.com/interactive/2015/03/31/world/middleeast/simple-guide-nuclear-talks-iran-us.html.
18 Miklos Gasper, "JCPOA Implementation Day Ushers in New Phase for IAEA in Iran: Director General Amano," IAEA, January 19, 2016, www.iaea.org/newscenter/news/jcpoa-implementation-day-ushers-new-phase-iaea-iran-director-general-amano.
19 Don Melvin and Michael Martinez, "Sanctions Lifted After Iran Found in Compliance," *CNN*, January 16, 2016, www.cnn.com/2016/01/16/middleeast/vienna-iran-iaea-nuclear-deal/index.html.
20 "Information Note on EU Sanctions to Be Lifted Under the Joint Comprehensive Plan of Action (JCPOA)," European Union External Action, January 23, 2016, http://eeas.europa.eu/top_stories/pdf/iran_implementation/information_note_eu_sanctions_jcpoa_en.pdf.
21 "Joint Comprehensive Plan of Action."
22 Kenneth Katzman and Paul K. Kerr, "Iran Nuclear Agreement," Congressional Research Service, May 31, 2016, https://fas.org/sgp/crs/nuke/R43333.pdf.
23 Garrett Nada, "Part II: What Would It Take to Build a Bomb?" The Iran Primer, April 9, 2013, http://iranprimer.usip.org/discussion/2013/apr/09/part-ii-what-would-it-take-build-bomb.
24 Broad and Pecanha, "The Iran Nuclear Deal—A Simple Guide."
25 Williams, "A Comprehensive Timeline of the Iran Nuclear Deal."
26 "Joint Statement by EU High Representative Federica Mogherini and Iranian Foreign Minister Javad Zarif Switzerland."
27 "Section 3: Understanding the JCPOA," Arms Control Association, August 10, 2015, www.armscontrol.org/reports/Solving-the-Iranian-Nuclear-Puzzle-The-Joint-Comprehensive-Plan-of-Action/2015/08/Section-3-Understanding-the-JCPOA.
28 Katzman and Kerr, "Iran Nuclear Agreement."
29 Vincent Fournier and Miklos Gaspa, "New IAEA Uranium Enrichment Monitor to Verify Iran's Commitments Under JCPOA," IAEA, January 16, 2016, www.iaea.org/newscenter/news/new-iaea-uranium-enrichment-monitor-verify-iran%E2%80%99s-commitments-under-jcpoa.
30 Kelsey Davenport, "IAEA Safeguards Agreements at a Glance," Arms Control Association, August 2017, www.armscontrol.org/factsheets/IAEAProtoco.
31 "Information Note on EU Sanctions to Be Lifted Under the Joint Comprehensive Plan of Action (JCPOA)."
32 Katzman and Kerr, "Iran Nuclear Agreement."
33 "Resolution 2231 (2015)," United Nations, July 20, 2015, www.un.org/en/ga/search/view_doc.asp?symbol=S/RES/2231(2015).
34 Katzman and Kerr, "Iran Nuclear Agreement."
35 "Information Note on EU Sanctions to Be Lifted Under the Joint Comprehensive Plan of Action (JCPOA)."
36 "Executive Order—Revocation of Executive Orders 13574, 13590, 13622, and 13645 with Respect to Iran, Amendment of Executive Order 13628 with Respect to Iran, and Provision of Implementation Authorities for Aspects of Certain Statutory Sanctions," White House, January 16, 2016, www.whitehouse.gov/the-press-office/2016/01/16/executive-order-revocation-of-executive-orders-with-respect-to-Iran.
37 Katzman and Kerr, "Iran Nuclear Agreement."
38 "Annex II, Attachment 1 of the JCPOA," U.S. Department of State, n.d., www.state.gov/documents/organization/245319.pdf.

39 Barbara Plett Usher, "Trump and Clinton: Where They Stand on Foreign Policy," *BBC News*, November 2, 2016, sec. US Election 2016, www.bbc.com/news/election-us-2016-37830496.
40 "Donald J. Trump Remarks at AIPAC," Trump, accessed September 1, 2016, www.donaldjtrump.com/media/donald-j-trump-remarks-at-aipac.
41 Ryan Teague Beckwith, "Read Hillary Clinton's Speech to AIPAC," *Time*, March 21, 2016, http://time.com/4265947/hillary-clinton-aipac-speech-transcript/.
42 Helene Cooper and Eric Schmitt, "James Mattis, Trump's Choice for Defense, Favors Working with Allies," *New York Times*, December 2, 2016, sec. Politics, www.nytimes.com/2016/12/02/us/politics/james-mattis-donald-trump.html.
43 Austin Wright and Jeremy Herb, "Mattis Breaks with Trump on Iran, Russia," *Politico*, January 12, 2017, www.politico.com/story/2017/01/james-mattis-confirmation-hearing-233530.
44 Geoff Dyer, "Trump's CIA Nominee Mike Pompeo Promises to Roll Back Iran Deal," *Financial Times*, accessed February 7, 2017, www.ft.com/content/e2849b56-ada7-11e6-ba7d-76378e4fef24.
45 Michael Wilner, "Top Trump Cabinet Picks Drop Campaign to Scrap Iran Deal," *The Jerusalem Post*, JPost.com, accessed February 7, 2017, www.jpost.com/American-Politics/Top-Trump-cabinet-picks-drop-campaign-to-scrap-Iran-deal-478281.
46 Laura Rozen, "Tillerson Faces Tough Questions on Iran, Russia," *Al-Monitor*, January 12, 2017, www.al-monitor.com/pulse/originals/2017/01/rex-tillerson-secretary-state-confirmation-iran-trump.html.
47 Zack Beauchamp, "John Bolton, Trump's Ultra-Hawkish New National Security Adviser, Explained," *Vox*, March 22, 2018, www.vox.com/world/2018/3/22/17153338/john-bolton-national-security-adviser-trump-hr-mcmaster.
48 John R. Bolton, "Opinion | To Stop Iran's Bomb, Bomb Iran," *New York Times*, March 26, 2015, www.nytimes.com/2015/03/26/opinion/to-stop-irans-bomb-bomb-iran.html.
49 Robin Wright, "John ('Bomb Iran') Bolton, the New Warmonger in the White House," *The New Yorker*, March 23, 2018, www.newyorker.com/news/news-desk/john-bomb-iran-bolton-the-new-warmonger-in-the-white-house.
50 "Iran Nuclear Deal: Trump Administration Approves Agreement but Review Looms," *The Guardian*, April 19, 2017, www.theguardian.com/world/2017/apr/19/iran-nuclear-deal-trump-administration-approves-agreement-but-review-looms.
51 Gardiner Harris and David E. Sanger, "Iran Nuclear Deal Will Remain for Now, White House Signals," *New York Times*, May 17, 2017, sec. Middle East, www.nytimes.com/2017/05/17/us/politics/trump-iran-nuclear-deal.html.
52 "Statement by the President on the Iran Nuclear Deal," White House, January 12, 2018, www.whitehouse.gov/briefings-statements/statement-president-iran-nuclear-deal/.
53 Mark Landler, "Trump Abandons Iran Nuclear Deal He Long Scorned," *New York Times*, May 14, 2018, sec. World, www.nytimes.com/2018/05/08/world/middleeast/trump-iran-nuclear-deal.html.
54 Julian Borger, Oliver Holmes, and Saeed Kamali Dehghan, "Iran Deal: Trump Breaks with European Allies Over 'Horrible, One-Sided' Nuclear Agreement," *The Guardian*, May 9, 2018, sec. World News, www.theguardian.com/world/2018/may/08/iran-deal-trump-withdraw-us-latest-news-nuclear-agreement.
55 "Frequently Asked Questions Regarding the Re-Imposition of Sanctions Pursuant to the May 8, 2018, National Security Presidential Memorandum Relating to the Joint Comprehensive Plan of Action (JCPOA)," U.S. Department of the Treasury, June 27, 2018, www.treasury.gov/resource-center/sanctions/Programs/Documents/jcpoa_wind-down_faqs.pdf.
56 "Obama Reacts to Trump's Pullout from Iran Nuclear Deal," *Al Jazeera*, May 9, 2018, www.aljazeera.com/news/2018/05/obama-reacts-trump-pullout-iran-nuclear-deal-180509054212330.html.

57 Erin Cunningham and Bijan Sabbagh, "Iran to Negotiate with Europeans, Russia and China About Remaining in Nuclear Deal," *Washington Post*, www.washingtonpost.com/world/middle_east/iran-prepared-for-all-scenarios-if-trump-nixes-nuclear-deal-officials-say/2018/05/08/531047a0-5241-11e8-a6d4-ca1d035642ce_story.html.
58 "Iranian President Slams Trump for Pulling U.S. Out of Nuclear Deal; World Leaders React," *CBS News*, May 8, 2018, www.cbsnews.com/news/iranian-president-hassan-rouhani-slams-trump-nuclear-deal-announcement-today-2018-05-08/.
59 Kay Armin Serjoie, "Iran Reacts to Trump's Decision to Quit Nuclear Deal," *Time*, May 9, 2018, http://time.com/5270821/iran-nuclear-deal-trump-ayatollah-khameini-hassan-rouhani/.
60 "Statement by IAEA Director General Yukiya Amano," Text, IAEA, May 9, 2018, www.iaea.org/newscenter/statements/statement-by-iaea-director-general-yukiya-amano-9-may-2018.
61 David Ramin Jalilvand, "The US Exit from the JCPOA: What Consequences for Iranian Energy?" Oxford Institute for Energy Studies, June 2018, www.oxfordenergy.org/wpcms/wp-content/uploads/2018/06/The-US-Exit-from-the-JCPOA-What-Consequences-for-Iranian-Energy-Comment.pdf.
62 "Joint Statement from Prime Minister May, Chancellor Merkel and President Macron Following President Trump's Statement on Iran," German Missions in the United Kingdom, May 9, 2018, https://uk.diplo.de/uk-en/-/2074760.
63 "Declaration by the High Representative on Behalf of the EU Following US President Trump's Announcement on the Iran Nuclear Deal (JCPOA)," European Council of the European Union, www.consilium.europa.eu/en/press/press-releases/2018/05/09/declaration-by-the-high-representative-on-behalf-of-the-eu-following-us-president-trump-s-announcement-on-the-iran-nuclear-deal-jcpoa/.
64 Jeremy B. White, "Europe Leaders Issue Joint Statement Attacking Trump's Withdrawal from Iran Nuclear Deal," *The Independent*, May 8, 2018, www.independent.co.uk/news/world/iran-nuclear-deal-latest-trump-macron-us-theresa-may-merkel-europe-response-a8342126.html.
65 Saeed Kamali Dehghan, "Iran's Leader: US Pullout from Nuclear Deal Leaves Trump 'Lost in History'," *The Guardian*, May 23, 2018, sec. World News, www.theguardian.com/world/2018/may/23/us-pullout-from-iran-nuclear-deal-leaves-trump-lost-in-history-khamenei.
66 Patrick Wintour, "Iran Lists Demands for Staying in Nuclear Deal," *The Guardian*, May 25, 2018, sec. World News, www.theguardian.com/world/2018/may/25/iran-lists-demands-nuclear-deal-eu-us-sanctions.
67 "Iran's Khamenei Orders Boost in Uranium Enrichment Capacity," *Al-Monitor*, June 5, 2018, www.al-monitor.com/pulse/originals/2018/06/iran-jcpoa-nuclear-deal-khamenei-190000-swu-enrichment.html.
68 "Europe Requests Exemptions from US Sanctions," The Iran Primer, June 6, 2018, http://iranprimer.usip.org/blog/2018/jun/06/europe-requests-exemptions-us-sanctions.
69 Steven Erlanger and Milan Schreuer, "Europe Asks U.S. for an Exemption from Sanctions on Iran," *New York Times*, June 9, 2018, sec. World, www.nytimes.com/2018/06/06/world/europe/iran-europe-us-sanctions.html.
70 Ibid.
71 Zeeshan Aleem, "Europe Is Threatening to Fight Trump on Iran Sanctions," *Vox*, May 11, 2018, www.vox.com/world/2018/5/11/17344242/europe-iran-deal-sanctions-trump.
72 Patrick Wintour and Jennifer Rankin, "EU Tells Iran It Will Try to Protect Firms from US Sanctions," *The Guardian*, May 15, 2018, sec. World News, www.theguardian.com/world/2018/may/15/eu-tells-iran-it-will-try-to-protect-firms-from-us-sanctions.
73 Anthony Zurcher, "Trump Pulls US Out of Iran Deal," *BBC News*, May 9, 2018, sec. US & Canada, www.bbc.co.uk/news/world-us-canada-44045957.
74 White, "Europe Leaders Issue Joint Statement Attacking Trump's Withdrawal from Iran Nuclear Deal."

75 "Strategic Disaster of Leaving Iran Deal," *IFP News* (blog), May 12, 2018, http://ifpnews.com/exclusive/strategic-disaster-of-leaving-iran-deal/.
76 Dehghan, "Iran's Leader: US Pullout from Nuclear Deal Leaves Trump 'Lost in History'."
77 Samanvya Hooda, "Donald Trump and the Art of Ending a Nuclear Deal: Iran's Domestic Politics, India's Interests to Be Hit Hard," *Firstpost*, www.firstpost.com/world/donald-trump-and-the-art-of-ending-a-nuclear-deal-irans-domestic-politics-indias-interests-to-be-hit-hard-4462097.html.
78 Zachary Laub and Kali Robinson, "What Is the Status of the Iran Nuclear Agreement?" Council on Foreign Relations, January 7, 2020, www.cfr.org/backgrounder/what-status-iran-nuclear-agreement.
79 "US-Iran Tensions: Timeline of Events Leading to Soleimani Killing," *Al Jazeera*, January 8, 2020, www.aljazeera.com/news/2020/01/iran-tensions-timeline-events-leading-soleimani-killing-200103152234464.html.
80 Laub and Robinson, "What Is the Status of the Iran Nuclear Agreement?"
81 "US-Iran Tensions: Timeline of Events Leading to Soleimani Killing."
82 Tim Lister, "Iran Drives Another Stake into the Heart of the Nuclear Deal," *CNN*, January 6, 2020, https://edition.cnn.com/2020/01/04/middleeast/iran-soleimani-nuclear-deal-intl/index.html.
83 "Strategic Disaster of Leaving Iran Deal."
84 "Trump Proved Ayatollah Khamenei Was Right: Kerry," *IFP News* (blog), June 10, 2018, http://ifpnews.com/exclusive/trump-proved-ayatollah-khamenei-was-right-kerry/.
85 Kelsey Davenport, "Chronology of U.S.-North Korean Nuclear and Missile Diplomacy," Arms Control Association, www.armscontrol.org/factsheets/dprkchron.
86 "Trump and Kim Make History with a Handshake," *BBC News*, June 12, 2018, sec. Asia, www.bbc.co.uk/news/world-asia-44435035.
87 Holly Ellyatt, "Trump Said He Wants a 'Real Deal' with Iran Now," June 12, 2018, www.cnbc.com/2018/06/12/trump-said-he-wants-a-real-deal-with-iran-now.html.
88 "Iran Urges Other States to Stand Against US Bullying," *IFP News* (blog), June 3, 2018, http://ifpnews.com/exclusive/iran-urges-other-states-to-stand-against-us-bullying/.
89 This initiative was first proposed in an article by Alexander Glaser, Zia Mian, Seyed Hossein Mousavian, and Frank von Hippel, published by *Arms Control Today* in December 2015: www.armscontrol.org/print/7261.
90 "Full Text of the Iran Nuclear Deal," *Washington Post*, July 14, 2015, https://apps.washingtonpost.com/g/documents/world/full-text-of-the-iran-nuclear-deal/1651/.
91 Matthew Bunn, "Beyond Zero Enrichment: Suggestions for an Iranian Nuclear Deal—Harvard—Belfer Center for Science and International Affairs," Harvard University Belfer Center for Science and International Affairs, November 2009, http://belfercenter.hks.harvard.edu/publication/19695/beyond_zero_enrichment.html.
92 Frank N. von Hippel et al., "Fissile Material Controls in the Middle East: Steps Toward a Middle East Zone Free of Nuclear Weapons and All Other Weapons of Mass Destruction," International Panel on Fissile Materials, October 2013.
93 Ibid.
94 Alexander Glaser and Marvin Miller, "Estimating Plutonium Production at Israel's Dimona Reactor," Princeton University, 2011, 10, www.princeton.edu/~aglaser/PU056-Glaser-Miller-2011.pdf.
95 "Negev Nuclear Research Center (NNRC), Facilities, NTI," NTI, November 11, 2011, www.nti.org/learn/facilities/418/.
96 "Global Fissile Material Report 2010: Balancing the Books: Production and Stocks," International Panel on Fissile Materials, December 2010, 107–17.
97 Alex Gasner and Alexander Glaser, "Nuclear Archaeology for Heavy-Water-Moderated Plutonium Production Reactors," *Science and Global Security* 19 (2011): 223–33.
98 "Plutonium Separation in Nuclear Power Programs: Status, Problems, and Prospects of Civilian Reprocessing Around the World," International Panel on Fissile Materials, July 2015.

99 Masafumi Takubo and Frank von Hippel, "Ending Reprocessing in Japan: An Alternative Approach to Managing Japan's Spent Nuclear Fuel and Separated Plutonium," International Panel on Fissile Material, November 2013.

100 Alexander Glaser, "Characteristics of the Gas Centrifuge for Uranium Enrichment and Their Relevance for Nuclear Weapon Proliferation," *Science and Global Security* 16 (2008): 1–28.

101 "Model Protocol Additional to the Agreement Between State(s) and the International Atomic Energy Agency for the Application of Safeguards," IAEA, INFCIRC/540 (corrected), Vienna, 1997.

102 "Status of the Additional Protocol, Status as of 03 July 2015," IAEA, www.iaea.org/safeguards/safeguards-legal-framework/additional-protocol/status-of-additional-protocol.

103 Shlomo Cesana, "Israel's Soreq Nuclear Reactor to Shut Down in 2018," *Israel Hayom*, March 21, 2012.

104 "Safeguards Agreements," IAEA, June 8, 2016, www.iaea.org/topics/safeguards-agreements.

105 "Who We Are: CTBTO Preparatory Commission," Comprehensive Nuclear-Test-Ban Organization, accessed March 26, 2018, www.ctbto.org/specials/who-we-are/.

2 Multiple initiatives to make the zone a reality

There are three interconnected initiatives that could remove major barriers to the WMDFZ through enhancing mutual cooperation, mitigating bilateral security concerns, and using the importance of Islam in the socioeconomic and political fabric of the region. The first initiative aims to reduce proliferation risk arising from national uranium enrichment production by establishing a multinational facility operated and owned by regional countries with participation from the international community. The second initiative focuses on the role religion, in particular Islam, can play in advancing WMD nonproliferation in the region. Specifically, measures to strengthen, expand, and operationalize the religious decree issued by Iranian Supreme Leader Ayatollah Ali Khamenei banning the development and use of WMD. Finally, the third initiative seeks to advance regional nonproliferation efforts by placing them within a broader security arrangement. This approach initially calls for establishing a subregional WMDFZ embedded within a security agreement between Iran, Iraq, and the Gulf Cooperation Council (GCC) states.

Multinational uranium enrichment

As uranium enrichment offers a clear pathway toward building nuclear weapons, it is crucial to have an initiative to address this concern to achieve a WMDFZ. The JCPOA has placed limitations on the Iranian nuclear program, but there are opponents to the agreement (such as Israel and Saudi Arabia). Since there are "sunset clauses" that mean any restrictions will expire in ten to fifteen years and reopen the possibility of Iran producing weapons-grade enriched uranium, opponents argue that the nuclear agreement has only postponed Iranian nuclear activity and has left its nuclear capabilities intact.

According to Behrouz Kamalvandi, spokesman for the Atomic Energy Organization of Iran (AEOI), Iran plans to achieve self-sufficiency in its enrichment capacity to fuel its first civilian nuclear power reactor (Bushehr-1) once the time limitations of the agreement come to an end. Moreover, the country seeks to expand its number of civilian nuclear power reactors to twenty in the future, with nine to be constructed by 2025.[1] Such aspirations, coupled with an increasing interest in nuclear energy by other countries in the Middle East (Egypt, Jordan, Saudi Arabia, Turkey, and the UAE), do not bode well, particularly with the real proliferation risks arising from increased and widely spread enrichment activities.

The JCPOA, while welcomed by the nonproliferation community, has nevertheless exacerbated the regional rivalry between Iran, Saudi Arabia, and Turkey—with the former intelligence chief of Saudi Arabia, Prince Turki bin Faisal, stating, "Whatever the Iranians have, we will have, too."[2] The spread of nuclear energy in the Middle East will bring into focus the significant demand for enrichment supply and the need to mitigate the proliferation of clandestine nuclear weapons programs. According to Princeton University researchers Ali Ahmad and Ryan Snyder, "Even under the conservative low estimate, the region would require about 230 metric tons of low-enriched uranium (LEU) annually, and thus 1.2 million separative work units (SWU) per year. This would increase to 4.4 million SWUs in the high estimate case [by 2025]."[3]

To address the latent proliferation capability of enrichment plants, uranium enrichment in the Middle East and, preferably, globally should be placed under multinational control.[4] There is precedence for such a venture. URENCO is a multinational company established in 1971 following the signing of the Treaty of Almelo (1970) by the governments of the United Kingdom and Northern Ireland, Netherlands, and (West) Germany.[5] Each country has an equal share, and they jointly manage three enrichment facilities (one in each country), with senior management and an oversight body of government officials drawn from all three countries. The respective governments, through a joint committee, assume a supervisory role focusing on security measures, transfer of technology, export of URENCO's products, ownership matters, and nonproliferation issues. The day-to-day operations (commercial and production related), however, are conducted by URENCO.[6] Interestingly, one of the drives for establishing URENCO was to limit Germany's national uranium enrichment capability to develop nuclear weapons.[7] At present, URENCO supplies uranium enrichment products (UEP) to more than fifty utilities in nineteen countries.[8] The company also makes up a third of the global uranium enrichment capacity, including the only commercial enrichment plants currently operating in two of the five NPT nuclear-weapon states, the United Kingdom and the United States.[9]

The Treaty of Almelo established the necessary safeguards, monitoring, transparency, and principles for supervising enrichment technology and operations in accordance with the IAEA, Euratom (the European Atomic Energy Commission), and other nonproliferation regimes. Euratom is a European organization tasked with advancing peaceful uses of nuclear energy among its twenty-eight member states (same as the European Union). A key rationale for establishing Euratom was to encourage a regional (European) cooperation in the nuclear field rather than working on a national level.[10] The Treaty of Almelo can serve as a reference point for developing a sustainable multinational uranium enrichment facility in the Middle East.

A further advantage of multilateral enrichment facilities is the sharing of the high financial burden. To address and balance the demand for nuclear energy, technology acquisition, geopolitical and economic considerations, and proliferation risk, one option is to establish a multinational uranium enrichment facility in Iran. The facility could be modeled on URENCO and could provide nuclear fuel to civilian nuclear power plants throughout the Middle East.

Such an initiative could alleviate regional and international concerns over the nature of Iran's nuclear activities post-JCPOA; build regional confidence and relationships; address regional nuclear fuel needs; and mitigate proliferation risk arising from other possible national enrichment programs in the region. Behrouz Kamalvandi has reiterated Iran's readiness to cooperate in the nuclear sector with regional countries, focusing on the business sense of such cooperation: "As regards industry, this region is an oil and gas region. Our centrifuges can help with the regional development at very reasonable prices. What is called for is to work out a cooperation mechanism among ourselves."[11] In addition, Iran has previously voiced its support for an international consortium for enrichment; former Iranian president Mahmoud Ahmadinejad, addressing the UNGA in 2005, stated that Iran was "prepared to engage in serious partnership with private and public sectors of other countries in the implementation of a uranium enrichment program in Iran."[12]

Ultimately, a multilateral arrangement would be a great confidence-building measure, limiting the risk of proliferation in the region and beyond. The added transparency, joint ownership, and fuel supply would not only contribute to regional cooperation but also be a step toward the wider ambition of creating a zone free from all weapons of mass destruction.

Iran needs to take practical steps over the next decade to ensure its nuclear power industry is operational following the lifting of restrictions on its enrichment activities in 2025. Iran could agree to have the current single national industrial enrichment plant scaled to supply only nuclear fuel for Bushehr-1. The facility is already built, thus avoiding any controversy regarding its construction, and this would guarantee nuclear fuel supply for Iran's sole nuclear power reactor. It would also satisfy geopolitical realities and concerns that have historically blocked Iran's access to the international nuclear fuel market.[13] Such an enrichment facility would need to adhere to the strictest monitoring and verification regime under the IAEA and limit enrichment to 5 percent. In addition, a larger multinational plant would be established in Iran and managed in partnership with regional and international nations to provide fuel for other projected nuclear plants both in Iran and regionally.

The ownership, operation, and management of the enrichment facility would be based on shareholder allocations, with an option for member countries of the NPT—both regional and international—to buy shares. Shares would first be offered to regional countries, then to EU3 + 3, and then opened to other NPT member countries. As an added layer of transparency, Middle Eastern shareholders could form a regional nuclear inspectorate, modeled on the Brazilian–Argentine ABACC, formed after Brazil and Argentina abandoned their nuclear weapons programs.

Finally, the location for the multinational facility, based on feasibility studies, might be positioned within a designated free zone and modeled on the "Free Trade

Zone" concept. Such a designation could alleviate concerns by regional countries over sovereignty and legal matters.

This proposal would be significantly strengthened if a major nuclear power from outside the region were involved as a partner. Russia seems the most obvious choice due to its constructive role in the EU3+3 negotiations and as the key developer of nuclear energy in the region, with agreements to build nuclear plants in Turkey, Egypt, the UAE, and Iran (and it is in talks for a similar agreement with Saudi Arabia).[14] The framework, terms, and conditions for the multinational enrichment facility would be negotiated and agreed upon by EU3+3, Iran, and the regional countries.

To account for the current and most likely continued antipathy from the West toward Russia, an alternative avenue to safeguard the supply of nuclear fuel to the region could be to include Iran within an international nuclear fuel bank. A nuclear fuel bank holds reserves of LEU sourced from countries with uranium enrichment capability and supplies countries without the technology to enrich fuel for their power reactors.[15] An international nuclear fuel bank aims to place uranium enrichment under multinational control to reduce proliferation risks and discourage individual countries from establishing their own enrichment facilities while assuring a supply of nuclear fuel to those countries.

A proposal by the IAEA for the first international nuclear bank was approved in 2009. An agreement between the IAEA and Kazakhstan in 2015 aimed to establish the fuel bank in that country within a few years, under the ownership and control of the IAEA and operated by Kazakhstan.[16] In August 2017, the fuel bank in Kazakhstan passed a major milestone with the completion of the storage facility to house low enriched uranium (LEU).[17] The fuel bank will eventually hold reserves of up to ninety metric tons of low enriched uranium—enough to fuel a 1,000-megawatt (MW) light-water reactor capable of powering a city the size of Boston for three years. The IAEA LEU bank will "act as a supplier of last resort for member states in case the supply of LEU to a nuclear power plant is disrupted due to exceptional circumstances and the member state is unable to secure LEU from the commercial market or by any other means." It will also require member states that need fuel to have the IAEA Comprehensive Safeguard Agreement in force, further strengthening nonproliferation regimes.[18] As the first international fuel bank under the control of the IAEA, it would be an encouraging sign if there were plans to expand the fuel bank with "regional branches," like one in the Middle East, that would receive its reserve nuclear fuel from Iran.

Religious support for the WMDFZ

For millennia, religion has been used to justify acts of good and evil, a fact that is unlikely to change. Extremist and terrorist groups such as Al-Qaeda, and more recently the Islamic State of Iraq and Syria (ISIS), have used distorted Islamic teachings and interpretations to justify acts of violence, including the potential use of WMD, to attract new recruits. Religion is a powerful tool in the region and could play a constructive role in countering the extremist narrative and advancing

WMD nonproliferation in the region. A central role for religion in conjunction with international nonproliferation norms and laws could prove a powerful combination.

The three major monotheistic religions of Judaism, Christianity, and Islam originated in the Middle East and have played a fundamental role in every facet of society there.[19] The Middle East and North Africa region is overwhelmingly Muslim, with 93 percent of the population adhering to Islam.[20] This solidarity can be used to bring the region together.

A clear first step toward an Islamic ban on WMD would be to operationalize the Fatwa (religious decree) issued by Iranian Supreme Leader Ayatollah Ali Khamenei banning the development, possession, and use of WMD. The Fatwa against WMD would need to be endorsed and operationalized by regional Islamic leaders of the two major Muslim sects: Shia and Sunni.[21]

The Fatwa

A Fatwa is a religious-legal opinion or decree handed down by an Islamic religious leader, an expert in Islamic jurisprudence. In Islam, a Fatwa is a judicial ruling concerning Islamic law, stated orally or in written form, by a prominent religious leader referred to by the title of *Marje-taghlid* by Shia or *Mufti* by Sunnis. These authorities base their rulings on the relevant legal proofs deduced from the Qur'an, specifically the practices (Sunnah) or sayings (Hadiths) of the Prophet Muhammad and his successors, reason (in line with the needs and realities of the contemporary world), and consensus (not driven by individual opportunism or political subjugation).[22] Once a Fatwa is issued, it is considered a religious obligation by devout followers, and disregarding it constitutes a sin.[23]

This is where Ayatollah Khamenei's Fatwa on WMD plays a crucial role in building support for nonproliferation. Khamenei's Fatwa leaves no room for doubt over the banning of the production, acquisition, stockpiling, and use of nuclear weapons. He stated the Fatwa during his inaugural address to more than 120 heads of state and officials at the 16th NAM summit in Tehran in 2012:

> The Islamic Republic of Iran considers the use of nuclear, chemical and similar weapons as a great and unforgivable sin. We proposed the idea of a Middle East free of nuclear weapons and we are committed to it. . . . I stress that the Islamic Republic has never been after nuclear weapons but that it will never give up the right of its people to use nuclear energy for peaceful purposes. Our motto is: "Nuclear energy for all and nuclear weapons for none." We will insist on each of these two precepts.[24]

For Muslims, the Qur'an is the main basis for issuing Fatwas, as it is considered to be the word of God.[25] The Qur'an prohibits Muslims from committing transgressions during a war, such as killing civilians, destroying the environment, or any kind of actions that lead to the spread of evil on Earth.[26] According to verse 5:32 of the Qur'an, "Whoever kills an innocent human being, it shall be as if he had killed all mankind, and who so saves the life of one, it shall be as if he had saved the life of all mankind."[27]

Fatwas issued by prominent religious figures in Islam, the ultimate authority in matters pertaining to morals and ethics, play an important role in shaping the rules of war.[28] The destruction caused by WMD fails to distinguish between combatants, noncombatants, and the environment. The cited Qur'an passage is clear in stating the prohibition against killing and destruction, including the use of WMD, in Islamic teachings. This religious foundation makes it possible for a Fatwa to form the basis of a wider ban of such weapons.

The unambiguous nature of the Qur'an's position on WMD means that no Islamic religious leader—Sunni or Shia—can change or issue a ruling against a Fatwa banning WMD. The most prominent members of the Islamic clergy, in both Shia and Sunni sects, agree on these principles. In addition to the Fatwa issued by Shia cleric Ayatollah Khamenei, there have been a number of prominent Sunni clerics who have also condemned the use and production of WMD. The highly respected Grand Mufti of Egypt, Ali Gomaa, issued a comprehensive Fatwa to counter radical clerics who justify the use of WMD. Grand Mufti Gomaa's Fatwa banning WMD as un-Islamic is based on the premise that such weapons are in breach of international agreements and treaties, would bring about widespread destruction for the entire world, and would inevitably kill innocent civilians and damage properties.[29] Those who challenge the credibility of the Fatwa banning WMD in Islam constitute a minority view and lack prominence and followers.

In this context, it is important to point out that the sole Islamic country with a nuclear arsenal, Pakistan, could challenge universal Islamic support for the zone. Nevertheless, overwhelming support for the zone from the Islamic community would halt the further spread of WMD throughout the Islamic world. Such an initiative could revive internal discussions in Pakistan on the merit and utility of having nuclear weapons. It is important to keep in mind that Pakistan does not fall within the eventual boundary of the WMDFZ in the Middle East and, in principal, would not be an obstacle to the zone's creation.

Legitimacy of the Fatwa in Iran

Based on Article 57 of the Iranian constitution, the supreme leader has the ultimate authority over the three branches of government. This fact determines the status of the Fatwa on the issue of WMD in Iran. It carries both legislative and religious importance, leaving it unchallenged and irreversible by other authorities and religious leaders.

This situation lends itself to another key concept, *Hokme Hokumati*, or State Decree, defined as a ruling issued by a religious leader who is also governing the nation (*Vilayat-e Faqih*). Hokme Hokomati is not only binding on the executive branch but also requires support from other religious leaders, who are bound to either agree fully or refrain from issuing any counter-Fatwas. The Fatwa by the supreme leader on WMD serves both as a Fatwa and Hokme Hokomati, making its annulment impossible.[30]

After the 1979 revolution, Imam Khomeini, the founder of the Islamic Republic of Iran, clearly stated his religious opinion on the proliferation and use of WMD:

> If they [two superpowers] continue to make huge atomic weapons and so forth, the world may be pushed into destruction and major loss will afflict the nations. Everybody wherever he is, the writers, intellectuals, scholars, and scientists throughout the world, should enlighten the people about this danger so that the masses of people will stand up against these two powers themselves and prevent the proliferation of these weapons.[31]

Imam Khomeini stood by his words during Iraq's invasion of Iran in 1980–1988. At that time, the United States[32] and the West supported Saddam Hussein with material and technology to build Iraq's chemical weapons capability. As such, the Iraq military used chemical weapons throughout the eight-year war, resulting in over a million Iranians being exposed to chemical agents, 100,000 Iranians injured, and 7,500 killed immediately from their chemical injuries.[33]

The Iraqi military continued to use chemical weapons with impunity, even with the UNSC issuing two statements (in March 1984 and March 1986) and two resolutions (in May 1988 and August 1988) condemning such attacks.[34] As a desperate reaction to such attacks, Iranian military officials requested Imam Khomeini permit them to reciprocate with chemical weapons. Even while on the receiving end of Iraqi chemical weapons, Imam Khomeini did not give permission, as it would transgress Islamic belief. This episode is the most credible evidence for the power and legitimacy of such a Fatwa, where, based on religious grounds, a country, even during wartime, did not respond in kind to an enemy using weapons of mass destruction.[35]

Iran's commitment to the eradication of WMD continued under Imam Khomeini's successor Ayatollah Khamenei. After differences over Iran's nuclear activities emerged during the EU3+3 discussions, Ayatollah Khamenei's own Fatwa was read out by the Iranian representative at the IAEA Emergency Meeting on August 10, 2005: "The Leader of the Islamic Republic of Iran, Ayatollah Ali Khamenei has issued a Fatwa that the production, stockpiling, and use of nuclear weapons are forbidden under Islam and that the Islamic Republic of Iran must never acquire these weapons."[36]

The supreme leader's Fatwa also played an important role in securing the JCPOA, as it added another layer of commitment by Iran to not pursue WMD. President Obama recognized the Fatwa during his UNGA speech on September 24, 2013, when he explicitly stated that "the supreme leader has issued a fatwa against the development of nuclear weapons."[37]

Regionalizing the Fatwa

Proliferation concerns in the Middle East will continue to increase as other countries seek to develop their own nuclear programs. The Fatwa's strong roots in

Islam imbue it with the credibility to play a constructive role in uniting the countries of the region in banning the proliferation of WMD.

The "regionalization" of the Fatwa requires prominent religious leaders within the Sunni and Shia sects to speak with one voice opposing the possession of WMD. As a first step, the fifty-seven member states of the Organization of Islamic Cooperation (OIC), which includes all Muslim majority countries in the proposed WMDFZ in the Middle East, could take the initiative to hold a conference where prominent Shia and Sunni religious leaders could convene, discuss, and collectively endorse a ban on all WMD by issuing a religious decree. Reaching consensus on a Fatwa among the major Islamic sects would go a long way toward building a strong following and marginalizing extremists. While there could be some opposition to such a move by Pakistan, which is also a member of the OIC, the charter of the organization regarding rules of procedure and voting stipulates in Article 33 that "decisions shall be taken by consensus. If consensus cannot be obtained, decision shall be taken by a two-thirds majority of members present and voting."[38]

Such a step would provide leverage for the Islamic religious community in the region to contribute immensely to nonproliferation, putting the region firmly on the path to a WMDFZ in the Middle East. With religious, social, and regional endorsements, all countries in the region would have greater legitimacy and incentives to implement national legislation banning all WMD. Thus, it is an opportune time to utilize the huge potential of Islam and the power of a collectively endorsed Fatwa in combination with the JCPOA as a model for containing proliferation. Such a step would take the region closer to realizing the "nuclear-zero dream" President Obama outlined during a speech at the Brandenburg Gate in Berlin: "Peace with justice means pursuing the security of a world without nuclear weapons."[39]

Subregional security cooperation

The proliferation of nuclear weapons and other WMD is primarily viewed by the countries of the Middle East through the security prism. Any nonproliferation effort, therefore, must be embedded within a security arrangement. Another initiative that could go a long way toward the eventual region-wide zone would be to create a subregional WMDFZ, within a comprehensive cooperation and security package, comprising Iran, Iraq, and the Gulf Cooperation Council (GCC) states.[40]

Multiple developments have made it necessary for Iran, Iraq, and the GCC to engage with one another on issues of security and stability. The first is the reversal of the antagonistic foreign policy of President Mahmoud Ahmadinejad with the election of moderate Iranian president Hassan Rouhani in 2013 and 2017. Soon after his victory, President Rouhani demonstrated his readiness to forge closer relations with regional countries by stating that "the enhancement of relations with regional and neighboring countries is among the priorities of the Islamic Republic of Iran's foreign policy."[41] The second development is the 2015 Iran Nuclear Accord, which removed a major proliferation concern for regional countries, in particular for those in the GCC. Third, as the multiple military theatres in the region (Iraq, Syria, and Yemen) increasingly involve regional powerhouses (Iran and Saudi Arabia), there is a need for more diplomatic approaches to reduce such rivalries.[42] These developments continue to present the need for both a regional engagement and constant recalibration to circumvent obstacles arising from the fluid nature of regional conflagrations.

Prior to realizing the subregional WMDFZ, the first step would be to establish a Persian Gulf Cooperative Security Arrangement (PGCSA) as an instrument to address and provide mechanisms for mitigating conflicts among member states. The PGCSA would eventually evolve into a subregional WMDFZ and address the security needs and proliferation risks of their respective member states, as well as collectively build momentum toward the realization of a wider WMDFZ in the Middle East. The PGCSA initiative should include key principles such as maintaining existing borders, respecting the sovereignty of member states, and noninterference in internal affairs.

The PGCSA could be based on existing models, such as the Shanghai Cooperation Organization (SCO).[43] The SCO was founded in 2001 in Shanghai, and its membership includes China, Kazakhstan, Kyrgyzstan, Russia, Tajikistan, and Uzbekistan—with India and Pakistan joining as full members in 2016. The aim of the SCO is to advance political, economic, and military cooperation among its member states while safeguarding their "national independence, sovereignty, territorial integrity, and social stability."[44] The SCO primarily focuses on its member nations' security-related concerns; chief among them is counterterrorism, separatism, and extremism.[45]

The PGCSA could also revive UNSC Resolution 598 on the Iran–Iraq ceasefire, which requested the secretary-general examine measures to enhance the security and stability of the Persian Gulf in consultation with Iran, Iraq, and other states of the region.[46] This was a key task for the UNSG. Unfortunately, to date, little has been done to implement this essential mandate. The security arrangement would, however, facilitate regional cooperation to stabilize Iraq; provide security reassurances for Arab allies of the United States; engage Iran's extensive regional clout more constructively; and promote wider peace in the Middle East. The challenges facing Iraq, such as the security threats arising from transnational terrorist organizations, are not limited to its border, as demonstrated by the rise of ISIS in Iraq and Syria. In addition, the sectarian nature of conflicts within Iraq have been framed within the wider regional rivalry between Saudi Arabia and Iran, which are aiming to outmaneuver one another in orienting Baghdad into their sphere of influence. Therefore, the PGCSA would open the door to multinational cooperation to stem the spread of terrorism and, this would, by extension, allow a rapprochement between Iran and Saudi Arabia to limit their proxy wars played out in other countries in the region, chiefly in Iraq, Yemen, and Syria.

To initiate the process toward the PGCSA, a joint security committee would be established to deal with common security concerns including terrorism, extremism, sectarianism, organized crime, asymmetric warfare, drug smuggling, and interferences in the internal affairs of other member states.[47] Gradual removal of barriers in political, security, economic, and cultural relations would also boost chances for the development of the region beyond security concerns and, in doing so, would contribute to the establishment of a regional free trade bloc similar to the European Union. Since key member states rely heavily on energy resources for the bulk of their exports, a collective effort to protect production and export of energy in the region and to stabilize the international energy market would be essential.

For security in the Persian Gulf, steps would be required for regional countries to conduct joint military cooperation and mitigate the risk of misunderstandings by opening channels of communication between their respective military establishments. With tensions high in the region, prior notification and transparency of large-scale military exercises would ensure regional countries do not interpret them as offensive actions but, rather, as part of defensive readiness.[48] To enhance transparency in such activities, the country conducting the military exercise could include multilateral observation by regional countries, clarify the scope, and share nonsensitive military information prior to the exercises. To decrease the chances of miscommunication, a regional military "hot line" could be established for crisis management and also to increase transparency on military exercises that could include missile tests in close proximity to a neighboring countries' maritime and land borders.[49] In the longer-term, subregional joint military exercises could expand to include neighboring forces in areas with strategic importance to multiple stakeholders, specifically the naval exercises in the Persian Gulf.[50]

Maritime security is another area in which countries of the region can cooperate within the framework of the PGCSA. The Persian Gulf's waterways are vital to international maritime trade and to key economies of the region. The narrow Strait of Hormuz links the Persian Gulf to the Indian Ocean, providing the only gateway for the oil tankers that transport a quarter of the world's international energy exports.[51] A binding regional agreement is required to ensure the safe and secure maritime passage of energy and other commodities through these maritime points. Furthermore, with piracy causing considerable disturbances on major maritime routes through the Red Sea and the Sea of Oman, an arrangement for joint antipiracy patrols could be included in the framework.

Such steps would contribute to decreasing the presence of foreign military forces in the region and could establish a system in which regional countries would provide the bulk of security in the Persian Gulf region.[52] By the same token, regional crises, such as conflicts in Syria, Iraq, and Yemen; instability stemming from the Arab uprisings (the popular protests that originated in Tunisia and swept across the Middle East and North Africa in 2011, resulting in the collapse of decades-old dictatorships in Tunisia, Egypt, and Libya); and the rise of terrorism and extremism could be tackled through regional and multilateral diplomacy in cooperation with influential international powers.[53] Realizing this security cooperation system in the Persian Gulf will require a de-escalation of tensions between Iran and the United States. It also will require engaging other external players, like the EU, Russia, China, Japan, and India, to acknowledge their respective national security and economic interests in the region to incentivize mutual cooperation.[54]

The PGCSA, however, needs to be fused with the larger drive toward the WMDFZ in the Middle East. The security arrangement would, undoubtedly, contribute to confidence-building and increased trust among Persian Gulf countries and, in doing so, facilitate nonproliferation efforts.

Once progress has been made in establishing the PGCSA, the next step would be to incorporate the subregional WMDFZ, which can go into more technical detail and further provide institutional steps to achieving nonproliferation of all WMD in the region. Fortunately, the ground work toward realizing the subregional zone is already complete, since the presumed member states have signed and ratified all major WMD conventions, which negates a significant obstacle that has, to date, hindered the possibility of a wider regional WMDFZ. Since the suggested subregional zone does not include the sole regional nuclear-weapons state—Israel—it is likely to be a smoother process. Furthermore, Iran's improved security, political, and economic ties with the GCC and Iraq through the PGCSA would reduce mistrust over the country's nuclear ambitions. Furthermore, as a confidence-building measure, Iran would be more open to the concept of a joint consortium on nuclear cooperation with member states of the subregional zone in all facets of peaceful nuclear sector development.

The establishment of a new security system in the Persian Gulf region representing all regional players should be the priority for the regional states and for foreign powers, especially the United States. Meanwhile, to further this goal, major regional countries such as Iran and Saudi Arabia should provide smaller states with necessary security guarantees enshrined within a larger nonaggression pact involving states in the subregional zone. The United States, for its part, should recognize Iran's national security interests and concerns in Iraq, Syria, Afghanistan, and Lebanon. In return, Iran should acknowledge that mitigating the perceived security concerns of some GCC countries over its nuclear program could provide a basis for reduced U.S. military presence in the region.

The establishment of a regional cooperation system to promote security, socioeconomic, cultural, and WMD nonproliferation cooperation among regional states is of vital importance for confidence-building; noninterference by foreign powers in the region; the establishment of sustainable peace, stability, and security; strengthened relations among nations; and the promotion of sustainable development in the region.

Owing to its strategic importance to the energy needs of the globe, the Persian Gulf region and its security will continue to influence Russian, U.S., and Western foreign policy objectives and ensure an outside presence in the region for the foreseeable future. The nature of this presence is in need of reform to define a long-term strategy for stability and security that reflects the realities in the region, ranging from the latest developments following the Arab uprising to the protracted U.S. wars fought in Afghanistan and Iraq.

Iran's pursuit of its rightful place as a regional power can be achieved through cooperation and participation in a joint regional security pact. Similarly, this would enable Iraq to take an independent role in regional developments—without extraterritorial influences from Iran, the United States, and, to a lesser extent, Saudi Arabia—to achieve economic stability and security and revive its status in the region.

On bilateral relations, a regional security pact would transform the hostile rivalry between regional powerhouses Saudi Arabia and Iran, which has only weakened both sides. Instead, it would contribute to mutual cooperation toward growth and development. There are many historical instances for such reorientation in relations, as seen with the creation of the EU, which transformed past foes to present allies, as in the case of Germany and France. The reverberations of such an agreement would be felt beyond the region and ensure the interest of international players such as Russia, China, and the EU for economic stability, security, and cooperation.

While UNSC Resolution 598 has not been implemented under the mandate of the UNSG, efforts to revive it are urgently needed. Cooperation among regional powerhouses (Iran and Saudi Arabia), in addition to regulating their rising power within the framework of a security and regional cooperation treaty, will be the best way to stabilize Iraq, reassure Arab allies of the United States, promote peace in the Middle East, and bring an end to ongoing proxy wars in Syria and Yemen. This formula will be the most enduring and least expensive strategy for effective cooperation among regional and international powers.

Notes

1 "Iran Plans to Build 9 Nuclear Power Plants by 2025," *Tehran Times*, April 9, 2016, www.tehrantimes.com/news/300440/Iran-plans-to-build-9-nuclear-power-plants-by-2025.
2 David E. Sanger, "Saudi Arabia Promises to Match Iran in Nuclear Capability," *New York Times*, May 13, 2015, www.nytimes.com/2015/05/14/world/middleeast/saudi-arabia-promises-to-match-iran-in-nuclear-capability.html.
3 Ali Ahmad and Ryan Snyder, "Iran and Multinational Enrichment in the Middle East," *Bulletin of the Atomic Scientists* 72, no. 1 (2016): 52–57.
4 Alexander Glaser, Zia Mian, and Frank N. von Hippel, "After the Iran Deal: Multinational Enrichment. World Powers Should Buy a Stake in Iran's Enrichment Capacity and Accept the Same Rules," *Science* 348, no. 6241 (June 19, 2015): 1320–22.
5 "Agreement Between the United Kingdom of Great Britain and Northern Ireland the Federal Republic of Germany and the Kingdom of the Netherlands on Collaboration in the Development and Exploitation of the Gas Centrifuge Process for Producing Enriched Uranium," October 1971, accessed August 31, 2016, http://fissilematerials.org/library/urenco70.pdf.
6 Tim Korbmacher, "URENCO: A Multinational Contribution to Non-Proliferation," URENCO, 2015, www.iaea.org/safeguards/symposium/2014/home/eproceedings/sg2014-papers/000108.pdf.
7 Ahmad and Snyder, "Iran and Multinational Enrichment in the Middle East."
8 "URENCO's Customers," URENCO, accessed August 31, 2016, www.urenco.com/about-us/business-activity/urencos-customers/.
9 The centrifuges used in URENCO's plants, including the URENCO-USA plant, and in Areva's plant in France are made on a "black-box" basis by the Enrichment Technology Corporation, which is jointly owned by URENCO and Areva.
10 "European Atomic Energy Community," *Encyclopaedia Britannica*, accessed June 8, 2019, https://britannica.com/topic/European-Atomic-Energy-Community.

11 "Iran Has Nuclear Plans for Neighbors," *Press TV*, April 11, 2016, www.presstv.ir/Detail/2016/04/11/460194/Iran-nuclear-cooperation-neighbors-Persian-Gulf-states-Kamalvandi/.
12 Seyed Hossein Mousavian, "After the Iran Nuclear Deal," *Cairo Review of Global Affairs*, July 16, 2014, www.thecairoreview.com/essays/after-the-iran-nuclear-deal/.
13 Warren Hoge, "Iran Has Been Blocked Many Times from Buying Nuclear Materials," *New York Times*, November 16, 2007, sec. Africa, www.nytimes.com/2007/11/16/world/africa/16iht-iran.4.8367219.html.
14 Ahmad and Snyder, "Iran and Multinational Enrichment in the Middle East."
15 "Proposed Nuclear Fuel Bank Reaches Go-Ahead Funding Level, UN Agency Says," *UN News*, March 6, 2009, https://news.un.org/en/story/2009/03/293262-proposed-nuclear-fuel-bank-reaches-go-ahead-funding-level-un-agency-says.
16 "IAEA and Kazakhstan Agree to Create Nuclear Fuel Bank," *World Nuclear News*, August 27, 2015, www.world-nuclear-news.org/UF-IAEA-and-Kazakhstan-agree-to-create-nuclear-fuel-bank-27081501.html.
17 "IAEA LEU Bank Reaches Milestone with Storage Facility Inauguration in Kazakhstan," IAEA, August 29, 2017, www.iaea.org/newscenter/pressreleases/iaea-leu-bank-reaches-milestone-with-storage-facility-inauguration-in-kazakhstan.
18 "IAEA Low Enriched Uranium Bank," IAEA, April 13, 2016, www.iaea.org/topics/iaea-low-enriched-uranium-bank.
19 "Middle East Region, Asia, Africa, and Europe," Encyclopedia Britannica, accessed August 31, 2016, www.britannica.com/place/Middle-East.
20 "Middle East-North Africa," Pew Research Center's Religion & Public Life Project, April 2, 2015, www.pewforum.org/2015/04/02/middle-east-north-africa/.
21 Excerpt originally published in Seyed Hossein Mousavian, "Globalizing Iran's Fatwa Against Nuclear Weapons," *Survival: Global Politics and Strategy* 55, no. 2 (2013): 147–62.
22 Rolf Mowatt-Larssen, "Islam and the Bomb: Religious Justification for and Against Nuclear Weapons," Belfer Center for Science and International Affairs at Harvard Kennedy School, January 2011, 160, www.belfercenter.org/sites/default/files/legacy/files/uploads/Islam_and_the_Bomb-Final.pdf.
23 J. Cole, "Khamenei Takes Control, Forbids Nuclear Bomb," Informed Comment, March 4, 2012, www.juancole.com/2012/03/khamenei-takes-control-forbids-nuclear-bomb.html.
24 "Part I: Khamenei on Nuclear Weapons," The Iran Primer, accessed August 31, 2016, http://iranprimer.usip.org/blog/2012/aug/31/part-i-khamenei-nuclear-weapons.
25 "Surah Al-Baqarah [2:190]," Quran, accessed August 31, 2016, https://quran.com.
26 Ibid.
27 "The Quranic Arabic Corpus" (English translation), University of Leeds, accessed March 27, 2018, http://corpus.quran.com/translation.jsp?chapter=5&verse=32.
28 Mowatt-Larssen, "Islam and the Bomb: Religious Justification for and Against Nuclear Weapons."
29 Ibid.
30 Mousavian, "Globalizing Iran's Fatwa Against Nuclear Weapons."
31 "Communication Dated 12 September 2012 Received from the Resident Representative of the Islamic Republic of Iran Concerning 'Facts on Iran's Nuclear Policy'," IAEA, September 12, 2012, www.iaea.org/sites/default/files/publications/documents/infcircs/2012/infcirc842.pdf.
32 Shane Harris and Matthew M. Aid, "Exclusive: CIA Files Prove America Helped Saddam as He Gassed Iran," *Foreign Policy*, August 26, 2013, http://foreignpolicy.com/2013/08/26/exclusive-cia-files-prove-america-helped-saddam-as-he-gassed-iran/.
33 Shahriar Khateri, "Iraq's Use of Chemical Weapons Against Iran: UN Documents 1984–1988," Tehran Peace Museum, n.d., www.tehranpeacemuseum.org/files/pdf%20resources/English%20Text-%20chemical%20warfare.pdf.
34 Ibid.

35 "Exclusive VOA Interview with Former Iran Nuclear Negotiator Hossein Mousavian," accessed September 1, 2016, http://voacapitol.blogspot.com/2012/12/normal-0-false-false-false-en-us-x-none_18.html.
36 "Iran's Statement at IAEA Emergency Meeting," Federation of American Scientists, accessed September 1, 2016, http://fas.org/nuke/guide/iran/nuke/mehr080905.html.
37 Patrick Goodenough, "Iranian Nuclear 'Fatwa' Cited by Obama May Not Exist," *CNS News*, October 1, 2013, http://cnsnews.com/news/article/patrick-goodenough/iranian-nuclear-fatwa-cited-obama-may-not-exist.
38 "Charter of the Organisation of the Islamic Conference," Organisation of the Islamic Conference, n.d., www.oic-oci.org/is11/english/charter-en.pdf.
39 "Remarks by President Obama at the Brandenburg Gate—Berlin, Germany," White House, June 19, 2013, www.whitehouse.gov/the-press-office/2013/06/19/remarks-president-obama-brandenburg-gate-berlin-germany.
40 "Toward a Conference on a Nuclear Weapon or WMD Free Zone in the Middle East," Pugwash Conferences on Science and World Affairs, September 26, 2011, https://pugwashconferences.files.wordpress.com/2014/03/20110926_mewmdfz_points.pdf.
41 "Rohani to Improve Relations with World Countries," *Iran Review*, accessed February 7, 2017, www.iranreview.org/content/Documents/Rohani-to-Improve-Relations-with-World-Countries.htm.
42 Seyed Hossein Mousavian, "Opinion: It Is Time for Security Cooperation Between the Gulf States and Iran," *Asharq Al-Awsat*, June 28, 2013, https://hosseinmousavian.com/wp-content/uploads/2013/06/ASHARQ-AL-AWSAT-%C2%BB-Opinion_-It-is-time-for-security-cooperation-between-the-Gulf-states-and-Iran-%C2%BB-Print.pdf.
43 "About SCO," SCO, accessed September 1, 2016, http://rus.sectsco.org/about_sco/.
44 Bates Gill, "Shanghai Five: An Attempt to Counter U.S. Influence in Asia?" Brookings Institution, May 4, 2001, www.brookings.edu/opinions/shanghai-five-an-attempt-to-counter-u-s-influence-in-asia/.
45 Mujtaba Haider Zaidi, "The Shanghai Co-Operation Organisation and US Supremacy," *African Herald Express*, August 20, 2013, http://africanheraldexpress.com/blog8/2013/08/20/the-shanghai-co-operation-organisation-and-us-supremacy/.
46 "The Situation Between Iran and Iraq," United Nations Security Council, July 20, 1987, https://documents-dds-ny.un.org/doc/RESOLUTION/GEN/NR0/524/70/IMG/NR052470.pdf?OpenElement.
47 The joint security committee could be based on the Organization for Security and Cooperation in Europe. To learn more, refer to the following: "What We Do," OSCE, accessed February 7, 2017, www.osce.org/what-we-do.
48 Gamal M. Selim, *Global and Regional Approaches to Arms Control in the Middle East: A Critical Assessment from the Arab World* (New York: Springer, 2013), 8–10.
49 Patricia M. Lewis, "Tiptoe, Stride and Leap: Steps Towards a WMD Middle East," EU Non-Proliferation Consortium, November 6, 2012, http://www.nonproliferation.eu/web/documents/backgroundpapers/lewis.pdf.
50 Ibid.
51 "Strait of Hormuz," Encyclopedia Britannica, accessed September 1, 2016, www.britannica.com/place/Strait-of-Hormuz.
52 Frederic Wehrey Sokolsky Richard, "Imagining a New Security Order in the Persian Gulf," Carnegie Endowment for International Peace, accessed August 31, 2016, http://carnegieendowment.org/2015/10/14/imagining-new-security-order-in-persian-gulf-pub-61618.
53 Robert E. Hunter, "Building Security in the Persian Gulf," Rand Corporation, 2010, www.rand.org/pubs/monographs/MG944.html.
54 Ibid.

3 A phased approach for the zone

Achieving a Middle East free of WMD will require sustained efforts by all stakeholders. The end state of the zone will require commitment by all regional countries to a set of guidelines, principles, and agreements to remain WMD-free and refrain from clandestine weapons programs. Many proposals on how to move forward on the initiative have previously been tabled; these efforts have faced key challenges in this most volatile region.[1]

One of the primary obstacles to realizing the zone is a lack of regional security. The United States and Europe, while advocating for the zone's creation, have mainly refrained from actively pursuing the issue, as it would inevitably impact the Israeli nuclear arsenal and, potentially, that country's security. Other fundamental obstacles include Iran's post-JCPOA potential nuclear capability; threats of military action between Israel and Iran; the tensions—contemporary and historical—between Iran and Saudi Arabia and the smaller Persian Gulf Arab countries; the instability resulting from the Arab uprisings; and the ongoing conflicts in Syria, Libya, Iraq, and Yemen. In a practical sense, to manage these differing issues, a WMDFZ in the Middle East could be achieved in a phased approach for stability and to improve the potential zone's longevity.

The first phase would lay the foundations for the zone and define its characteristics through consensus on definitions, parameters, and guiding principles. The second phase would entail the formation of a nonaggression pact to allay the security concerns of the countries in the region. This phase would also include guidelines on placing limitations on conventional arms. Finally, the third phase would delve into the sequence of steps necessary to achieve the zone by having all prospective member states join and ratify treaties and conventions pertaining to the eradication of WMD, including the CTBT, Biological Weapons Convention (BWC), Chemical Weapons Convention (CWC), treaties countering WMD trafficking and terrorism, and, finally, NPT. No doubt, this will be a long process, require extensive negotiations on an array of issues, and need flexibility in adapting arrangements in other regions to fit the unique characteristics of the Middle East.

Phase I: laying the foundations for the zone

The initial phase of developing a WMDFZ in the Middle East would have to be agreed upon by all regional states, with active or tacit backing by world powers.

This phase would include finalizing the demarcation of the zone's boundaries; consensus on the definition and goals of the zone; a regional conference on identifying the next steps; and a framework for realizing the zone with agreed-upon guiding principles. These steps would ensure that the process commences with transparency, deliberation, and consensus. While this process would be regionally driven, the role of international powers will be crucial, as all countries have a vested interest in a secure WMDFZ in the Middle East and could, using their political and economic weight in the region, place necessary pressure on some regional states to support the initiative.

Definition of the zone

The initial documents of the 1995 Review and Extension Conference on the NPT called for all parties to commit to "not to possess, acquire, test, manufacture or use any nuclear, chemical and biological weapons as well as their delivery systems." The initiative also sought "the adoption of practical measures towards the creation of a Nuclear Weapons and Weapons of Mass Destruction Free Zone."[2] Regional countries and major global powers should reach an agreement on the definition and intended goals of the zone; their backing and support for its realization is an essential step to ensure security and promote peace in the region.

The boundary of the zone would encompass all the countries that are part of the League of Arab States plus Iran and Israel, as suggested in a 1991 study commissioned by the UNSG (shown in Figure 3.1).[3] As of late 2015, all but two of these countries, Israel and Syria, had sent letters to the UNSG confirming their support for declaring the Middle East a region free from nuclear, chemical, and biological weapons.[4] The invitation to expand the zone would be extended to neighboring countries, with the option to join at any point in the process. Thus, the focus would remain within the core countries of the Middle East with the hope of future expansion.

WMDFZ conference

At the 2010 NPT Review Conference, participants agreed to convene a conference composed of official representatives of the countries of the region, the NPT signatory nuclear weapons states, and a group of experts nominated by the UN, as suggested by the states of the region to assess next steps to realize the WMDFZ in the Middle East. Finland's ambassador, Jaakko Laajava, was appointed to serve as facilitator in the initial period. The conference was intended to spawn workshops and analyses to provide recommendations on creating the zone and monitoring its progress.[5] As discussed earlier, the scheduled conference of 2012 was called off by the United States and, once again, in 2015 (this time the United Kingdom and Canada also added their objections), even though all the regional countries, with the exception of Israel, had indicated their readiness to participate in the conference.[6]

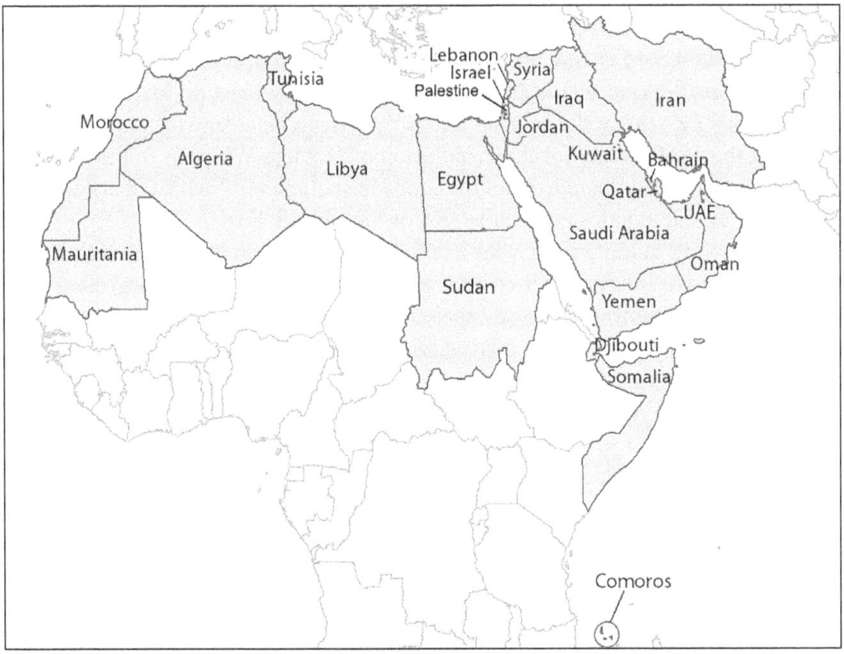

Figure 3.1 The eventual WMD Free Zone in the Middle East will include all twenty-two member states of the Arab League, Iran and Israel.

Source: Tsering Wangyal Shawa, Princeton University.

A concerted effort is required from regional and international powers to convene such a conference in the near future, with full participation by all regional countries. The importance of such a meeting should not be underestimated, as it is intricately connected to the long-term stability and security of the region. The decision to hold the conference should not be held hostage to the current upheaval taking place in the region; rather, it should be seen as a vehicle for regional cooperation and confidence-building.

The conference would enable initial consultation to take place on the overall framework for realizing the zone. Other areas of discussion, with an emphasis on aspects of common interest, would include the appropriate next steps; the application of confidence-building measures; and assessing major challenges and opportunities. Though the geopolitical climate in the region is tense, with raging conflicts, there needs to be an effort to tackle separate issues on an individual basis to reduce the chances of the initiative failing. This process aims to complement, rather than compete or be entangled with, other parallel efforts to bring about resolutions to outstanding matters, ranging from the Middle East peace process, intrastate conflicts, extremism, and transitional governments.

Guiding principles

Facilitating the process requires that all regional states commit to a set of guiding principles that would ensure all parties are well versed in their commitments and rights. A starting point would be to draw from already existing texts formulated for other NWFZs (as in the case of the 2009 African Nuclear Weapon Free Zone Treaty or the 1969 Treaty for the Prohibition of Nuclear Weapons in Latin America and the Caribbean) and expand the scope to include all WMD and account for the unique characteristics and challenges of the Middle East.

The following guiding principles would make a good start: (1) Throughout the phased process, all parties will commit to a set of confidence-building measures; (2) All regional countries will participate in each phase of the process. It is important to note that while there are marred bilateral relations between some countries in the region (such as nonrecognition of Israel by most Arab states and Iran, and hostile Saudi–Iran relations due to conflicts in Syria, Yemen, and Bahrain), these issues should not be lumped into one basket and should be, instead, separated from the principles to achieve the zone; (3) Maintain transparency in the process and sustained communication between regional countries and respective regional and international organizations; (4) Avoid linking the WMDFZ in the Middle East to current and future disputes, such as the Israeli–Palestinian relations or specific positions on intrastate conflicts, as in the case of Syria and Yemen; (5) Maintain the rights of nations committed to all or some WMD conventions to continue their activities in the peaceful use of nuclear, biological, and chemical fields; (6) Facilitate bilateral and multilateral cooperation in advancing nonproliferation activities and efforts; (7) Encourage the establishment of a subcommittee to monitor and evaluate progress toward the zone with annual recommendations and deliberations; (8) Commit to establish robust regional verification and monitoring tools of current and pending nuclear, biological, and chemical facilities. This can be in addition to current WMD conventions and their verification instruments; (9) Incorporate a conflict-resolution mechanism to offset disagreements throughout the process and facilitate dialogue; (10) Obtain commitments from outside actors, specifically the five permanent members of the UNSC, to halt transfer of WMD or nonconventional arms to the region. Furthermore, provide active support for the WMDFZ process in the Middle East; (11) Require that all the countries in the region agree to abide by the resolution adopted by the IAEA General Conference on September 21, 1990, concerning the "Prohibition of all armed attacks against nuclear installations devoted to peaceful purposes whether under construction or in operation."[7]

Phase II: confidence-building measures

The WMDFZ in the Middle East cannot come to fruition in the absence of confidence-building measures (CBMs) designed to address the history of deep-rooted suspicion and mutual distrust among regional states. The current turmoil in the region as a result of the Arab uprising has brought into sharp focus conflicting ideologies battling to shape the future of the region.

In such a climate, therefore, there is an urgent need to introduce practical, gradual, consensual, modest, and nonthreatening means to create reassurance and confidence among states to reduce tensions, distrust, and animosity. The process of adopting CBMs would instill needed confidence in the initiative and address the key objective of the resolution passed at the 1995 Review and Extension Conference on the NPT calling for "the adoption of practical measures towards the creation of a Nuclear Weapons and Weapons of Mass Destruction Free Zone."[8]

The unique security challenges facing the Middle East, the level of mistrust among regional countries, and the scope of the WMDFZ necessitate wide-ranging, innovative, and tailored CBMs. These measures will be divided into general security and WMD nonproliferation-specific CBMs. The former would focus on security and arms control measures, while the latter would provide confidence-building measures to end the production, procurement, stockpile, and use of nuclear, chemical, and biological weapons. The CBMs would be a combination of technical measures to ensure verification and transparency, while others would emphasize legally binding steps to strengthen regional commitment toward the zone. Ultimately, the hope is that CBMs would encourage regional states to engage in a meaningful process that accounts for the realities on the ground, addresses the core security concerns of individual states, and, through a negotiated framework, adopts a step-by-step process to realize the zone.[9]

Nonaggression pacts

The basis for a regional nonaggression pact can be found in the opening article of the Charter of the UN, requiring all states to "take effective collective measures for the prevention and removal of threats to the peace, and for the suppression of acts of aggression or other breaches of the peace, and to bring about by peaceful means, and in conformity with the principles of justice and international law." The importance of nonaggression is cemented in the second article, whereby "all Members shall refrain in their international relations from the threat or use of force against the territorial integrity or political independence of any state, or in any other manner inconsistent with the purposes of the United Nations."[10] A key component of a regional security arrangement would be to introduce a nonaggression pact in accordance with UN principles. Regional countries, by committing to such a pact, would enhance mutual trust and reduce tensions that may erupt in an all-out war.[11]

A regional nonaggression pact would encompass any form of violent act on a fellow state, including civilian, commercial, and governmental sites. Furthermore, a provision within the nonaggression pact could stipulate that no regional country would attack the nuclear, biological, chemical, and military sites of another state. This could expand to include cyberattacks, assassinations, bombings, and sabotage. The nonaggression pact would be signed as a step within a more comprehensive process to realize the WMDFZ.[12] Prohibiting attacks on nuclear facilities is in line with the 1990 IAEA General Conference Resolution 533, which calls for "banning all armed attacks against nuclear installations devoted to peaceful purposes whether under construction or in operation."[13] In August 2009, Iran proposed a UN resolution banning such attacks globally.[14]

In addition, the United States or the five permanent members of the UNSC could give security assurances to Israel in exchange for Israel giving up its nuclear deterrent. This would ensure that no country in the region has a nuclear arsenal.[15]

Conventional arms limitations

The issues and use of conventional and nonconventional arms are intricately linked, as the means of delivery associated with nonconventional weapons requires the country to possess advanced missiles, aircrafts, or submarines. With instability in the Middle East, there is a growing concern over the conventional arms race in the region and the development of means of delivery for nuclear, biological, or chemical warheads. An important step to achieve the WMDFZ would be a "conventional arms treaty" to put an end to the region's arms race. The current conventional arms race is widening the gap between those with access to the latest conventional arms (primarily regional countries allied with the United States and Western countries such as Saudi Arabia, the UAE, and Israel) and those that are barred from this market (the prime example being Iran). This gap in conventional military capability among potential WMDFZ member states could become an obstacle for realizing the zone, as some countries may see the acquisition or development of WMD as a means of leveling the playing field. Therefore, a conventional arms treaty and the WMDFZ would be a strong two-pronged approach to ending the arms race in the Middle East.

The most comprehensive arms control convention to be recognized and adhered to in an eventual WMDFZ is the UN Arms Trade Treaty (ATT), which was passed by the UNGA in 2013. The treaty aims to regulate "the enormous global trade in conventional weapons, for the first time linking sales to the human rights records of the buyers."[16] There is no enforcement mechanism for the treaty, and ratification is voluntary; yet it does set a foundation to build on, and it can be customized to fit the geopolitical realities facing the Middle East. Furthermore, since 1991, the UN Register of Conventional Arms (UNRCA) requires all UN member states submit information on weapons transfers, both imports and exports. While not legally binding, regional countries' commitments to the convention would be supportive of transparency and confidence-building.[17]

In 1991, within the context of the Middle East peace negotiations, the Arms Control and Regional Security in the Middle East (ACRS) working group represented a historic effort to contribute to confidence-building in the Middle East. While these talks failed to reach any comprehensive agreement and were terminated in 1995, lessons learned from the ACRS talks could be included in the framework of WMDFZ negotiations and contribute positively to disarmament.[18]

The 2002 Hague Code of Conduct (HCoC), with signatures from 134 member states, encourages limiting the production and stockpiling of ballistic missiles, requires members to declare on an annual basis the state of their missile program, and requires members provide advance notification of missile tests.[19]

Unfortunately, most member countries within the zone have yet to sign the HCoC, with the exception of Comoros, Jordan, Libya, Mauritania, Morocco, Sudan, and Tunisia.[20]

Transparency initiatives could also build on the Transparency in Armaments (TIA) resolution passed by the UNGA in 1991, which requests nations annually provide data on their arms imports and exports.[21] Arrangements in other regions, such as the Treaty on Conventional Armed Forces in Europe (CFE), which places limits on major conventional military equipment, and weapons in Europe, also would be invaluable.[22]

Cooperation on peaceful nuclear, biological, and chemical fields

All major WMD nonproliferation conventions—the NPT, the BWC, and the CWC—have two primary components. First, they strengthen WMD nonproliferation efforts through commitments made by signatories. Second, in return for upholding their commitments to the conventions, signatory states are permitted to pursue the peaceful use of nuclear, biological, and chemical materials. Commitments and rights are the foundations of the WMD conventions.

The most practical way to incentivize nations to join WMD nonproliferation conventions is through offering the prospect of a WMDFZ and guaranteeing nations the right to the peaceful use of nuclear, biological, and chemical materials. In the nuclear field, Article 4 of the NPT stipulates that, "Nothing in this Treaty shall be interpreted as affecting the inalienable right of all the Parties to the Treaty to develop research, production and use of nuclear energy for peaceful purposes without discrimination."[23] The treaty goes further, to encourage member states to "co-operate in contributing alone or together with other States or international organizations to the further development of the applications of nuclear energy for peaceful purposes, especially in the territories of non-nuclear-weapon States."[24]

Regional cooperation on the peaceful uses of nuclear energy could also help build mutual understanding and trust among countries in the zone. With growing regional interest and a need for peaceful nuclear energy, the risk of enrichment and reprocessing is certain to dominate the debate. These issues are not insurmountable, as the JCPOA has proved. The lessons learned over a decade of nuclear negotiations with Iran can serve as a basis to resolve future proliferation issues. The settlement of Iran's nuclear issue has brought about new mechanisms for verification and monitoring of fissile material and nuclear facilities. As noted, a constructive step would be to establish a regional or multinational enrichment facility with an oversight agency that ensures the peaceful nature of the fissile material under close cooperation of regional and international players. Another possible avenue for cooperation could include joint ventures to build nuclear power plants and regional infrastructure to transport electricity generated from such joint nuclear facilities.

The CBMs will go beyond the nuclear dimension; participants in the zone would also need to sign and ratify the BWC and the CWC, paving the way for cooperation on the peaceful use of biological and chemical materials for multiple sectors, ranging from agriculture to pharmaceuticals. Article 10 of the BWC states the following:

> The States Parties to this Convention undertake to facilitate, and have the right to participate in, the fullest possible exchange of equipment, materials and scientific and technological information for the use of bacteriological (biological) agents and toxins for peaceful purposes. Parties to the Convention in a position to do so shall also cooperate in contributing individually or together with other States or international organizations to the further development and application of scientific discoveries in the field of bacteriology (biology) for prevention of disease, or for other peaceful purposes.[25]

Similarly, Article 11 of the CWC calls for "international cooperation in the field of chemical activities for purposes not prohibited under this Convention including the international exchange of scientific and technical information and chemicals and equipment for the production, processing or use of chemicals for purposes not prohibited under this Convention."[26]

Measures encouraging peaceful cooperation of chemical industries in the region and in the field of environmental standards and protection would be another constructive step.[27] In the biological field, it would be desirable to establish a regional biological center designed to advance the peaceful use of modern biotechnology in the interest of bettering humanity and public welfare. This could include cooperation on research and development, manufacturing, and distribution of vaccines to sharing information on the latest advances in detecting, diagnosing, and treatment of relevant pathogens.[28]

This regional biological center could host meetings of experts to assess regional preparedness and countermeasures in the event of a disease outbreak. Furthermore, it could host regular workshops relating to border security cooperation to curb movement of sensitive materials between states. Topics for discussion could vary from drafting domestic laws to safeguarding sensitive biological material as well as building regional capacity in biosecurity and biosafety to conducting joint operations to ensure rapid and effective preparedness in the wake of biological attacks.[29]

In the biological realm, data exchanges among nations on such materials were agreed upon at the Second Review Conference of the BWC in 1986 "in order to prevent or reduce the occurrence of ambiguities, doubts and suspicions."[30] An expert group to assist with verification techniques and experiences from previous cases could be established in cooperation with regional and international organizations. A prime example would be to learn from the experience of the UN Special Commission (UNSCOM), created by UNSC Resolution 687 in April 1991. UNSCOM was primarily responsible for overseeing the destruction of Iraq's WMD and limiting the missile program in the aftermath of the Gulf War.[31] This experience would be invaluable toward establishing the WMDFZ in the Middle East.

More broadly, there could also be joint academic research initiatives or expansion of current programs in all fields pertaining to chemical, biological, and nuclear technology. One existing initiative is the Synchrotron-Light for Experimental Science and Applications in the Middle East (SESAME) initiative, hosted by Jordan with members from Bahrain, Cyprus, Egypt, Iran, Israel, Jordan, Pakistan, the Palestinian Authority, and Turkey. The program is under the auspices of the IAEA and the UN Educational, Scientific and Cultural Organization (UNESCO).[32]

Finally, one mechanism for trust-building among regional countries could be for them to share information on an array of issues and topics related to nonproliferation. This form of dialogue could be built in two stages. The first would be information sharing of available material that is required to be submitted to the UN and its affiliated agencies, ranging from reports on national laws to counter non-state actor proliferation (as required by UNSC Resolution 1540) and public research reports on scientific fields, including nuclear, biological, and chemical. In the second phase, cooperation could expand to more sensitive topics, such as sharing terrorism and nuclear-proliferation intelligence, and to mitigating misunderstandings by sharing national reports on current and future planned nuclear, biological, and chemical facilities.

Going beyond these steps, meetings of regional experts could assess existing measures to counter proliferation and improve on them. Such information-sharing mechanisms would enhance communication among states with a history of troubled relations. Facilitating off-the-record meetings would also be crucial in building trust among regional states. As the political situation in the region is rife with disagreements and public discussions among rival states can be presented from a maximalist position, the utility of having off-the-record meetings allows for candid discussions without the media or public scrutiny. These efforts can pave the way for building relationships among key stakeholders and policymakers who would otherwise not even speak with each other (mainly due to political disagreements and a lack of diplomatic relations among some regional countries—two examples are Iran and Saudi Arabia, and Israel and Lebanon).[33]

Providing incentives, institution-building, oversight mechanisms, and regional collaboration can ensure cooperation in these areas and is geared toward scientific and technological advancement. Adherence to the conventions will only succeed if the rights extended to signatories, in combination with transparency and confidence-building measures, are respected and promoted. The benefits of joining such nonproliferation conventions by promoting technology transfer and international cooperation would also strengthen commitments by states to uphold all articles.

Phase III: regional universalization of WMD conventions

The third phase of this approach is the most daunting and most likely to reveal major obstacles that require a long-term plan to initiate specific confidence-building measures, to build trust in combination with stringent verification measures and political pressures.

Bringing regional countries into the WMD conventions requires key supplementary steps to enhance trust and confidence in the process. This includes mitigating regional friction through a subregional WMDFZ and conventional arms arrangements. Special attention would be needed to deal with Israel's nuclear weapons program. Efforts would also need to be made to ensure no state has the capability to launch WMD warheads. This is particularly difficult, as there is a wide range of conventional arms and equipment that can serve as a potential delivery system for WMD.

Table 3.1 shows which of the states in the proposed WMDFZ in the Middle East have signed and ratified the CWC, the BWC, and the NPT. Many also have signed and ratified the CTBT. Some are members of the African NWFZ, created by the Treaty of Pelindaba, which came into force in 2009.

Sequence of steps to achieve the WMDFZ

The WMDFZ will require all regional countries to sign and ratify WMD-related nonproliferation conventions, which includes CTBT, BWC, CWC, NPT, and numerous conventions to counter WMD trafficking and terrorism. Each of these conventions carries varying degrees of political and technical challenges for regional countries to sign and ratify. The sequence of steps proposed subsequently, therefore, envision regional countries committing first to those conventions that have the least barrier to entry, such as the CTBT. Progress on achieving universalization of any convention will build crucial momentum needed for more challenging conventions. Specifically, the NPT will prove to be the most difficult, as it requires arduous negotiations and political expediency to dismantle Israel's nuclear weapons and have it join the treaty as a nonnuclear weapon state.

Comprehensive Nuclear Test Ban Treaty

A major step toward building trust among regional countries is for all parties to sign and ratify the CTBT, which "bans nuclear explosions by everyone, everywhere: on the Earth's surface, in the atmosphere, underwater and underground." The CTBT creates a barrier to nations trying to develop and modify their nuclear weapons, whether for the first time or to further advance them. It also aims to protect the environment and humans from radioactivity from nuclear explosions.[34] The overwhelming majority of the eventual member states of the proposed Middle East WMDFZ have signed the CTBT, while Egypt, Iran, and Israel have yet to ratify it. Those that remain outside of the treaty include Saudi Arabia, Somalia, and Syria. All countries that have yet to sign and ratify the CTBT, except Israel, are, nevertheless, part of the NPT as nonnuclear weapon states and are likely to join the CTBT if it were part of a comprehensive deal to reach the zone. There is also some expectation that Israel, too, would ratify the CTBT, as it is one of the few WMD nonproliferation conventions that Israel has signed onto.

Ratifying the CTBT could serve as a confidence-building measure. However, it is important to note that there are some reservations held by countries in the region toward the ratification of the CTBT and, therefore, attempts to address such concerns would be needed. For example, while Iran has signed the CTBT,

	NPT	*BWC*	*CWC*	*CTBT*
Algeria	January 12, 1995	July 22, 2001	August 14, 1995	July 11, 2003
Bahrain	November 3, 1988	October 28, 1988	April 28, 1997	April 12, 2004
Comoros	October 4, 1995	September 17, 2006	August 18, 2006	(S) December 12, 1996
Djibouti	October 16, 1996	–	January 25, 2006	July 15, 2005
Egypt	February 26, 1981	(S) April 10, 1972	–	(S) October 14, 1996
Iran	February 2, 1970	August 22, 1973	November 3, 1997	(S) September 24, 1996
Iraq	October 29, 1969	June 19, 1991	January 13, 2009	September 26, 2013
Israel	–	–	(S) January 13, 1993	(S) September 25, 1996
Jordan	February 11, 1970	May 30, 1975	October 29, 1997	August 25, 1998
Kuwait	November 17, 1989	July 18, 1972	May 28, 1997	May 6, 2003
Lebanon	July 15, 1970	March 26, 1975	November 20, 2008	November 21, 2008
Libya	May 26, 1975	January 19, 1982	January 6, 2004	January 6, 2004
Mauritania	October 26, 1993	January 28, 2015	February 9, 1998	April 30, 2003
Morocco	November 27, 1970	March 21, 2002	December 28, 1995	April 17, 20001
Oman	January 23, 1997	March 31, 1992	February 8, 1995	June 13, 2003
Palestine	February 10, 2015	January 9, 2018	June 16, 2018	–
Qatar	April 3, 1989	April 17, 1975	September 3, 1997	March 3, 1997
Saudi Arabia	October 3, 1988	May 24, 1972	August 9, 1996	–
Somalia	March 5, 1970	(S) July 3, 1972	May 29, 2013	–
Sudan	October 31, 1973	October 17, 2003	May 24, 1999	June 10, 2004
Syria	September 24, 1969	(S) April 14, 1972	September 12, 2013	–
Tunisia	February 26, 1970	May 18, 1973	April 15, 1997	September 23, 2004
UAE	September 26, 1995	June 19, 2008	November 28, 2000	September 18, 2000
Yemen	June 1, 1979	June 1, 1979	October 2, 2000	(S) September 30, 1996

Table 1. Dates of ratification/accession [or signature (S) for states that are not yet parties] to the 1968 Nuclear Nonproliferation Treaty (NPT), 1972 Biological Weapons Convention (BWC), 1993 Chemical Weapons Convention (CWC), and 1996 Comprehensive Test Ban Treaty (CTBT) for states that might be included in a Middle East Nuclear Weapons Free Zone.

it is reluctant to ratify it due to security concerns; chief among them is the CTBT monitoring mechanism that can be extended to conventional arms tests, which may not be related to nuclear weapons testing.

In a discussion with the authors of this book, an Iranian CTBT expert, who requested anonymity, aired other concerns of Tehran regarding ratification. First, if all countries in the Middle East sign and ratify the CTBT without the stipulation that Israel first join the NPT, then they have, in effect, conceded to the Israeli nuclear weapons monopoly and supremacy in the Middle East. Second, Iran views Israeli or any other country's nuclear weapons in the Middle East not as a source of stability but rather instability.

Next, although Iran has accepted stringent inspections, transparency measures, and verification under the JCPOA, similar measures under the CTBT would have implications for conventional arms testing. This is of particular concern for the Iranian military leadership, as it sees such procedures as a means for Israel and the United States to gain insight into Iran's military capabilities. Particularly concerning is the requirement for an International Monitoring System (IMS), which is part of the overall CTBT verification regime. The primary purpose of the IMS is to detect possible nuclear testing worldwide. The system uses four different but complementary verification methods (seismic, hydro-acoustic, infrasound, and radionuclide) to monitor the planet for nuclear explosions from 321 monitoring stations and sixteen laboratories worldwide. The data gathered at the IMS are then transmitted via the Global Communications Infrastructure (GCI) to the International Data Centre (IDC) located at the headquarters of the CTBT in Vienna, Austria, for processing and analysis.[36]

The crux of the Iranian concern is that such verification methods could also gather information and data on conventional arms testing and, by doing so, expose national security information to Iran's adversaries, mainly the United States and Israel. Another concern is that member states have access to the raw data gathered by IMS stations and analysis reports.[37] As part of the IMS, Israel has two auxiliary seismic stations (AS048 in Eilat and AS049 in Mount Meron) and the Middle East's sole radionuclide laboratory at the Soreq Nuclear Research Center.[38] The auxiliary seismic stations "measure the three spatial components of seismic waves—up-down, East-West and North-South. This set-up provides information on the depth and strength of an event."[39] These stations do not send data in real-time (unlike the primary seismic network that sends data continuously in real time to Vienna), but upon request only.

The fourth concern is that Iran is suspicious of the fact that Israel, having not signed or ratified most WMD conventions (BWC and NPT), was quick to sign the CTBT. Tehran is convinced that the proactive support of the United States for Middle East countries to join the CTBT was predicated on satisfying Israeli security interests. Iran suspects that the Israeli strategy on WMD treaties is that if it impacts the production side of developing and maintaining WMD then it refrains from joining, but if the treaty is on the monitoring side of testing WMD, then Israel finds it useful, as it provides intelligence on regional conventional and unconventional arms activities.

While the concerns just outlined are by no means universal, it is necessary for the CTBT organization to address them in to accelerate the ratification of the treaty.

Biological Weapons Convention

The most likely follow-up to the CTBT would be the BWC, with almost universal ratification; only Israel, Mauritania, and Djibouti remain non-parties in the region, and Syria has signed up but is yet to ratify the convention.[40] The 1972 BWC requires states to forego the production, stockpile, acquisition, and use of biological weapons. Meanwhile, the 1925 Geneva Protocol (GP) prohibits the use of chemical and biological weapons during war. The fact that almost all states of the region are parties to the 1925 GP or the 1972 BWC is a positive sign that the eradication of biological weapons will not face as stringent obstacles as other WMD and can, therefore, play a positive role toward realizing the zone.[41]

Countries that are likely to constitute the eventual WMDFZ but are yet to become members of the GP are Oman, the UAE, Djibouti, Mauritania, and Somalia. Yet most of these states are likely to join the GP, since they are part of the BWC (with the exception of Djibouti and Mauritania) and within the wider WMDFZ context. While Israel is a key country in the region that is not a signatory to the BWC, development of the WMDFZ would require increased pressure on Israel to make a decision on the issue. During the BWC's 2001 Fifth Review Conference, member countries proposed improving and broadening confidence-building measures; while they did not reach consensus, many of their recommendations could play a major role for the advancement of the BWC and eventual WMDFZ. Some of their key recommendations include sharing information on national biological defense research and development programs; sharing information on outbreaks of infectious diseases; publications of studies in the field for broad dissemination; strengthening local legislation, regulations, and other measures; fostering close regional cooperation among experts and maintaining such relations; and declaring vaccine production facilities.[42]

As the use of biological weapons can be counterproductive in military operations, with possible harm to the nation's own soldiers and local population, it is likely that the military establishment of member states can be persuaded to support measures to adhere to the convention.[43]

Chemical Weapons Convention

Chemical weapons are defined as "toxic chemicals and their precursors" fitted into "munitions or devices" to cause "death or other harm."[44] With the aim of establishing the WMDFZ in the Middle East, all states would also be required to sign and ratify the CWC. Most states in the Middle East have signed and ratified the 1993 CWC. Only Comoros, Egypt, and Somalia have yet to join and ratify the convention. Israel is a signatory but is yet to ratify the treaty. With the overwhelming majority of states already a signatory to the CWC, the topic of eradicating chemical weapons creates a lot of common ground between parties.[45]

The history and use of chemical weapons in the region includes Egypt's use of chemical weapons in the North Yemen Civil War (1962–1967), Libya's use of toxic gas and napalm against Chad in 1987,[46] and the Iraqis inflicting hundreds of thousands of casualties with their use of chemical agents against Iran during the Iran–Iraq war (1980–1988) as well as against the Iraqi Kurds. With the horrific effects of chemical weapons still fresh in recent memory, there should be a major impetus to advance and strengthen the CWC.[47]

The destruction of Syria's chemical weapons following a deal brokered by Russia and Iran and the country's subsequent accession to the CWC have provided an opportunity to strengthen the role of the CWC in the Middle East. To achieve an all-out commitment by all countries in the region to the CWC would require specific confidence-building measures in chemical weapons nonproliferation. As a first step, countries in the Middle East could announce their commitment to the eradication of such weapons from their military arsenal. This would be an important move, as concerns over their use are prevalent within Arab, Iranian, and Israeli communities.

The ongoing Syrian conflict has heightened the need to address chemical weapons. As the destruction of Syria's chemical and biological weapons has not been verified, there are growing concerns over the Syrian stockpile reaching the hands of terrorist groups such as ISIS. To prevent such weapons falling into the hands of terrorists, there are a number of measures states can take. They should verify current holdings and sign memoranda of understanding committing to eliminating stockpiles of chemical weapons, in conjunction with commitments from others to refrain from acquiring or procuring such weapons. Prospective adherents must go through the Verification Division or Inspectorate Division of the Organization for the Prohibition of Chemical Weapons (OPCW), and states in the Middle East could sign an agreement banning chemical weapons in the region as a step to building trust and moving toward establishing a WMDFZ.[48]

Countering WMD trafficking and terrorism

With increasing intrastate conflict along sectarian, religious, and ethnic lines, there is a growing need for a regional working group, composed of regional powers, to address tensions and reach a compromise with conflicting parties; this could be applied to the current Syrian conflict and the decades-old Israeli–Palestinian issue.[49] Terrorism, as a major WMD-proliferation threat facing the region and beyond, is discussed in more detail in the following chapter. Here, the focus is on regional efforts to mitigate this challenge.[50] The UN counterterrorism Resolution 1373, which was passed on September 28, 2001, in the aftermath of the 9/11 terrorist attacks, can serve as the basis for a regional mechanism to combat terrorism. Under the terms of this UN resolution, "all States should prevent and suppress the financing of terrorism, as well as criminalize the willful provision or collection of funds for such acts." The resolution also reiterates that all member states should ensure that terrorists do not use their territories to garner funds and other financial assets and should "refrain from providing any form of support to entities or persons involved in terrorist acts; take the necessary steps to prevent the commission of terrorist acts and deny [them] safe haven."[51]

The resolution paved the way for domestic laws and regulations within member states to ensure terrorist acts are treated as serious criminal offenses. In the area of cooperation among states to counteract terrorism, the resolution "calls on all States to intensify and accelerate the exchange of information regarding terrorist actions or movements; forged or falsified documents; traffic in arms and sensitive material; use of communications and technologies by terrorist groups; and the threat posed by the possession of weapons of mass destruction."[52]

Another primary attempt to curb WMD proliferation was UNSC Resolution 1540, adopted in April 2004. The resolution sought to address enforcement gaps in global nonproliferation treaties that did not include the threat of WMD acquisition by non-state actors.[53] The resolution obligates all UN member states to "take appropriate and effective actions against any threat to international peace and security caused by the proliferation of nuclear, chemical and biological weapons and their means of delivery."[54] The resolution goes further to include the risk posed by terrorist groups seeking weapons of mass destruction and demands all member states adopt effective laws prohibiting such activities.

In essence, the resolution aims to limit the proliferation of WMD capabilities worldwide, as existing or expanding WMD capabilities within states constitute an important risk for the proliferation of such weapons to non-state actors.[55] Resolution 1540, passed under Chapter VII of the UN Charter, established the first universal mandatory obligation within the nonproliferation regime, thus permitting the UNSC to take punitive measures, such as imposing sanctions and, in extreme cases, to use force against countries failing to comply with the resolution.[56]

Nuclear terrorism is a daunting security risk for any nation in the region, but its existence may motivate cooperation on strategies to protect fissile and radiological materials. One way to achieve this would be for countries in the region to commit to the Convention on the Physical Protection of Nuclear Material (CPPNM). The convention was adopted in October 1979 and came into force in February 1987; at present, 145 member states are committed to it (refer to Table 3.2 for the status of regional countries regarding the CPPNM). The treaty aims to "avert the potential dangers posed by the unlawful taking and use of nuclear material." An amendment to the convention in 2005 highlighted the need to prevent illicit trafficking by adopting "appropriate and effective measures to ensure the prevention, detection and punishment of such offences."[57] As a further step, countries in the region can abide by the IAEA Code of Conduct on the Safety and Security of Radioactive Sources and its supplementary guidance approved by the IAEA board of governors in September 2003.[58] The code is not legally binding, but its objective is to assist member states to "achieve and maintain a high level of safety and security of radioactive source" and "prevent unauthorized . . . transfer of radioactive sources, so as to reduce the likelihood of accidental harmful exposure to such sources or the malicious use of such sources to cause harm to individuals, society or the environment."[59]

Another convention that could be used to counter WMD trafficking and terrorism is the International Convention for the Suppression of Acts of Nuclear

Terrorism (ICSANT), adopted by the UNGA in April 2005 and entered into force in July 2007, with 115 signatories (refer to Table 3.2 for the status of regional countries regarding the ICSANT). The convention criminalizes the use of "radioactive material or devices or sabotage of nuclear facilities" for malicious intentions. It also encourages member states to cooperate on these matters and prosecute offenders under their national law by applying "appropriate penalties, which take into account the grave nature of these offences."[60]

The risk of biological materials falling into the hands of extremist groups is yet another possibility, which is further exacerbated by the fact that contagions released following the detonation of biological weapons would be difficult to control. This vulnerability necessitates regional mechanisms to safeguard biological materials through stringent control over procurement and distribution channels. Such cooperation at the regional level would, in itself, serve as a confidence-building measure.[61] One avenue for cooperation is to ensure the maintenance and expansion of already established infrastructures aimed at strengthening regional cooperation on biological threats, such as the Middle East Consortium on Infectious Disease Surveillance (MECIDS).[62,63,64]

Table 3.2 Status of Regional Countries Regarding the CPPNM

	CPPNM	*ICSANT*
Algeria	Yes	Yes
Bahrain	Yes	Yes
Comoros	Yes	Yes
Djibouti	Yes	No
Egypt	No	No
Iran	No	No
Iraq	No	No
Israel	Yes	No
Jordan	Yes	No
Kuwait	Yes	No
Lebanon	Yes	Yes
Libya	Yes	Yes
Mauritania	Yes	Yes
Morocco	Yes	Yes
Oman	Yes	No
Qatar	Yes	No
Saudi Arabia	Yes	Yes
Somalia	No	No
Sudan	Yes	No
Syria	No	No
Tunisia	Yes	Yes
UAE	Yes	Yes
Yemen	Yes	No

Note: Dates of contracting parties to the 1987 Convention on the Physical Protection of Nuclear Material[65] and 2007 International Convention for the Suppression of Acts of Nuclear Terrorism for states that might be included in a Middle East nuclear weapons-free zone.[66]

Nuclear nonproliferation treaty

Countries in the Middle East, with the exception of Israel, have signed and ratified the NPT. This paved the way for those countries to begin closer cooperation in the peaceful use of nuclear energy. In addition, the possibility of regionalizing the provisions within the Iran nuclear deal to further strengthen nuclear nonproliferation could act as a gateway to more specific confidence-building measures such as establishing regional standards for the safe and transparent development of peaceful nuclear capabilities; developing mechanisms to handle and store nuclear waste; creating communications links and emergency assistance networks in case of accidents; complementing IAEA inspections and verification with a regional inspections agency for the Middle East; and developing regional expert forums to focus on key topics of concern including disarmament measures and verification methods.[67]

Israel's refusal to sign and ratify the NPT is the remaining obstacle to its regionalization. While the primary reason given for Israel resisting nuclear disarmament is about security, in reality the country boasts the most sophisticated conventional military capability in the Middle East. This is coupled with having the strongest bilateral relations with the United States among regional countries in military, intelligence, and security sectors. Ultimately, the United States will continue to be the key guarantor of Israel's security in the region and, therefore, the only country capable of pressing Tel Aviv to begin nuclear disarmament, to sign and ratify the NPT, and to open up its nuclear facilities to IAEA inspection.

If the United States wishes to support its ally and guarantee Israel's security, the most obvious way to achieve this is by ensuring that no country in the Middle East (including Israel) has WMDs as the possession of such devices risks human error and possible terrorist access. While the United States does not have a formal defense treaty with Israel, there is no doubt that, for decades, under successive administrations, it has pledged to protect and support Israel. The United States has also signed dozens of memorandums of understanding with Israel in a wide range of sectors—health, education, science, and technology—with a particular focus on defense and security matters, ranging from R&D, intelligence, and joint military exercises to counter terrorism.[68] Israel also continues to be the largest recipient of U.S. military aid, over $130 billion to date.[69] With this reality, the U.S. security blanket for Israel can be modeled or incorporated into other defense treaties, such as the North Atlantic Treaty Organization (NATO) or, bilaterally, U.S. security agreements as in the case with Japan, South Korea, and Australia.

Notes

1 For further reading on multiple proposals for the creation of the WMD-free zone in the Middle East, refer to Harald Müller and Daniel Müller (eds.), *WMD Arms Control in the Middle East: Prospects, Obstacles and Options* (London: Ashgate Publishing, February 2015).

2 "WMD-Free Middle East Proposal at a Glance," Arms Control Association, accessed September 1, 2016, www.armscontrol.org/factsheets/mewmdfz#5.

3 "Modalities of Application of Agency Safeguards in the Middle East," IAEA, August 29, 1989, https://www-legacy.iaea.org/About/Policy/GC/GC33/GC33Documents/English/gc33-887_en.pdf.

4 "Middle East Weapons of Mass Destruction Free Zone," UNODA, accessed September 1, 2016, www.un.org/disarmament/menbcletters/.
5 The definition of the activities of the International Committee and the repartition of the costs need to be further specified in detail.
6 "2012 Conference on a Middle East Zone Free of Weapons of Mass Destruction (MEWMDFZ)," U.S. Department of State, November 23, 2012, www.state.gov/r/pa/prs/ps/2012/11/200987.htm.
7 Sinan Ülgen, "A Think Piece on Confidence-Building Measures in the Middle East," Carnegie Europe, November 1, 2012, http://carnegieeurope.eu/2012/11/01/think-piece-on-confidence-building-measures-in-middle-east.
8 Paolo Foradori and Martin Malin, "A WMD-Free Zone in the Middle East," Discussion Paper, December 2012, Belfer Center for Science and International Affairs, Harvard Kennedy School.
9 Emily B. Landau, "Assessing the Relevance of Nuclear CBMs to a WMD Arms Control Process in the Middle East Today," EU Non-Proliferation Consortium, November 6, 2012, www.nonproliferation.eu//wp-content/uploads/2018/10/landau.pdf.
10 United Nations, "Charter of the United Nations," 1 UNTS XVI, October 24, 1945, www.un.org/en/sections/un-charter/chapter-i/index.html.
11 Patricia M. Lewis, "Tiptoe, Stride and Leap: Steps Towards a WMD Middle East," EU Non-Proliferation Consortium, November 6, 2012, www.nonproliferation.eu/web/documents/backgroundpapers/lewis.pdf.
12 Ibid.
13 "Measures to Strengthen International Co-Operation in Matters Relating to Nuclear Safety and Radiological Protection," IAEA, October 1990, www.iaea.org/About/Policy/GC/GC34/GC34Resolutions/English/gc34res-533_en.pdf.
14 "Iran Calls for Ban on Striking Nuclear Facilities," *Fox News*, August 12, 2009, www.foxnews.com/story/2009/08/12/iran-calls-for-ban-on-striking-nuclear-facilities.html.
15 Hans M. Kristensen, "Estimates of the US Nuclear Weapons Stockpile, 2007 and 2012," Federation of American Scientists, accessed September 1, 2016, http://fas.org/blogs/security/2007/05/estimates_of_us_nuclear_weapon/.
16 Neil Macfarquhar, "Arms Trade Treaty Approved at U.N.," *New York Times*, April 2, 2013, www.nytimes.com/2013/04/03/world/arms-trade-treaty-approved-at-un.html.
17 "UN Register of Conventional Arms—UNODA," UNODA, accessed March 26, 2018, www.un.org/disarmament/convarms/register/.
18 Carlo Trezza, "The Issue of 'Delivery Systems' in a Middle East Zone Free of Weapons of Mass Destruction," EU Non-Proliferation Consortium, November 6, 2012, www.nonproliferation.eu/web/documents/backgroundpapers/trezza.pdf.
19 Bruno Gruselle, "Curbing Missile Proliferation in the Middle East: Options for a Comprehensive Policy," EU Non-Proliferation Consortium, November 6, 2012, www.nonproliferation.eu//wp-content/uploads/2018/10/gruselle.pdf.
20 "International Code of Conduct Against Ballistic Missile Proliferation (ICOC)," accessed September 1, 2016, www.armscontrol.org/documents/icoc.
21 "UN Register of Conventional Arms," UNODA, accessed September 1, 2016, www.un.org/disarmament/convarms/Register/.
22 "The Conventional Armed Forces in Europe (CFE) Treaty and the Adapted CFE Treaty at a Glance," Arms Control Association, accessed September 1, 2016, www.armscontrol.org/factsheet/cfe.
23 "NPT Treaty," United Nations, accessed September 1, 2016, www.un.org/en/conf/npt/2005/npttreaty.html.
24 Ibid.
25 John Hart and Ralf Trapp, "Science, Technology, and the Biological Weapons Convention," Arms Control Association, accessed September 1, 2016, www.armscontrol.org/act/2012_10/Science-Technology-and-the-Biological-Weapons-Convention.

26 "Article XI. Economic and Technological Development," OPCW, accessed September 1, 2016, www.opcw.org/chemical-weapons-convention/articles/article-xi-economic-and-technological-development/.
27 Peter Jones, "The Regional Security Architecture and Other Confidence Building Measures," EU Non-Proliferation Consortium, November 6, 2012, www.nonproliferation.eu/web/documents/backgroundpapers/jones2.pdf.
28 David Friedman, "Towards WMDFZ in the Middle East: Biological Confidence-Building Measures," EU Non-Proliferation Consortium, November 6, 2012, 9, www.nonproliferation.eu/web/documents/backgroundpapers/friedman.pdf.
29 Ibid.
30 Ibid.
31 Raymond A. Zilinskas, "UNSCOM and the UNSCOM Experience in Iraq," *Politics and the Life Sciences* 14, no. 2 (1995): 230–35, doi:10.1017/S0730938400019134.
32 "SESAME: Synchrotron-Light for Experimental Science and Applications in the Middle East," SESAME, accessed March 26, 2018, www.sesame.org.jo/sesame/.
33 "Toward a Conference on a Nuclear Weapon or WMD Free Zone in the Middle East," Pugwash Conferences on Science and World Affairs, September 26, 2011, https://pugwashconferences.files.wordpress.com/2014/03/20110926_mewmdfz_points.pdf.
34 "Who We Are: CTBTO Preparatory Commission," CTBTO, accessed February 7, 2017, www.ctbto.org/specials/who-we-are/.
35 "Fact Sheets: Treaty Membership and Signatory Status," Arms Control Association, accessed September 1, 2019, www.armscontrol.org/factsheets/treatymembership.
36 "Overview of the Verification Regime: CTBTO Preparatory Commission," CTBTO, accessed September 1, 2016, www.ctbto.org/verification-regime/background/overview-of-the-verification-regime/.
37 "Radionuclide Data Processing and Analysis: CTBTO Preparatory Commission," CTBTO, accessed September 1, 2016, www.ctbto.org/verification-regime/the-international-data-centre/radionuclide-data-processingand-analysis/.
38 "CTBTO World Map," CTBTO, accessed September 1, 2016, www.ctbto.org/map/.
39 "Seismic Monitoring: CTBTO Preparatory Commission," CTBTO, accessed September 1, 2016, www.ctbto.org/verification-regime/monitoring-technologies-how-they-work/seismic-monitoring/.
40 "Fact Sheets: Treaty Membership and Signatory Status."
41 Friedman, "Towards WMDFZ in the Middle East: Biological Confidence-Building Measures."
42 Ibid.
43 Una Becker-Jakob, "Building Confidence Over Biological Matters in the Middle East," EU Non-Proliferation Consortium, November 6, 2012, www.nonproliferation.eu/web/documents/backgroundpapers/becker.pdf.
44 "Convention on the Prohibition of the Development, Production, Stockpiling and Use of Chemical Weapons and on Their Destruction," OPCW, n.d., www.opcw.org/fileadmin/OPCW/CWC/CWC_en.pdf.
45 Dina Esfandiary, "Building Confidence Towards a MEWMDFZ via a Chemical Weapons Ban," EU Non-Proliferation Consortium, November 6, 2012, www.nonproliferation.eu/web/documents/backgroundpapers/becker.pdf.
46 "Libyan Chemical Weapons," Global Security, accessed September 1, 2016, www.globalsecurity.org/wmd/world/libya/cw.htm.
47 Esfandiary, "Building Confidence Towards a MEWMDFZ via a Chemical Weapons Ban."
48 Ibid.
49 Jones, "The Regional Security Architecture and Other Confidence Building Measures."
50 Harald Müller and Claudia Baumgart-Ochse, "A Weapons of Mass Destruction-Free Zone in the Middle East: An Incremental Approach," EU Non-Proliferation

Consortium, July 7, 2011, www.hsfk.de/fileadmin/HSFK/hsfk_downloads/A_weapon_of_mass_destruction.pdf.

51 "Security Council Unanimously Adopts Wide-Ranging Anti-Terrorism Resolution," United Nations, September 28, 2001, www.un.org/press/en/2001/sc7158.doc.htm.

52 Ibid.

53 "Resolution 1540 (2004)," United Nations Security Council, April 28, 2004, www.un.org/ga/search/view_doc.asp?symbol=S/RES/1540%282004%29.

54 Ibid.

55 Joseph Adams and Ayman Khalil, "Achieving a Balanced Implementation of UN Security Council Resolution 1540, the Middle East as an Example," Arab Institute for Security Studies, n.d., www.stanleyfoundation.org/1540/acsis1540_paper.pdf.

56 "Resolution 1540 (2004)."

57 "The International Legal Framework for Nuclear Security," IAEA, 2011, http://www-pub.iaea.org/MTCD/publications/PDF/Pub1486_web.pdf.

58 "Toward a Conference on a Nuclear Weapon or WMD Free Zone in the Middle East."

59 "Code of Conduct on the Safety and Security of Radioactive Sources and the Supplementary Guidance on the Import and Export of Radioactive Sources," IAEA, December 29, 2005, www.iaea.org/sites/default/files/publications/documents/infcircs/2005/infcirc663.pdf.

60 "The International Convention for the Suppression of Acts of Nuclear Terrorism (ICSANT)," United Nations, 2005, https://treaties.un.org/doc/db/Terrorism/english-18-15.pdf.

61 Becker-Jakob, "Building Confidence Over Biological Matters in the Middle East."

62 "Background," MECIDS, accessed September 1, 2016, http://www.mecidsnetwork.org/content/background.

63 "Convention on the Physical Protection of Nuclear Material (CPPNM), Treaties & Regimes," NTI, accessed September 1, 2016, www.nti.org/learn/treaties-and-regimes/convention-physical-protection-nuclear-material-cppnm/.

64 "International Convention on the Suppression of Acts of Nuclear Terrorism, Treaties & Regimes," NTI, April 3, 2015, www.nti.org/learn/treaties-and-regimes/international-convention-suppression-acts-nuclear-terrorism/.

65 "Convention on the Physical Protection of Nuclear Material (CPPNM), Treaties & Regimes."

66 "International Convention on the Suppression of Acts of Nuclear Terrorism, Treaties & Regimes."

67 Jones, "The Regional Security Architecture and Other Confidence Building Measures."

68 "Formal Agreements Between US & Israel," accessed September 1, 2016, www.jewishvirtuallibrary.org/jsource/US-Israel/MOUs.html#Security.

69 Shirl McArthur, "Congress Watch: A Conservative Estimate of Total U.S. Direct Aid to Israel: More Than $130 Billion," *WRMEA*, accessed September 1, 2016, www.wrmea.org/2013-october-november/congress-watch-a-conservative-estimate-of-total-u.s.-direct-aid-to-israel-more-than-$130-billion.html.

4 WMD challenges

Previous chapters outlined multiple avenues for moving toward a closer realization of a WMDFZ in the Middle East, but to accomplish this goal, daunting WMD proliferation challenges from both within and outside the region must be faced. There are at least seven key concerns.

First, the vast majority of WMD (in particular nuclear weapons) globally are possessed by the five permanent members of the UNSC, which must go beyond rhetoric and take tangible measures to move forward toward their own commitments to disarmament and toward the realization of the WMDFZ. The second issue is the origin of the Israeli nuclear weapons program and maintenance of its nuclear weapons arsenal to date. A third concern is the continuing challenge to rid Syria of its chemical weapons stockpile, even with positive developments arising from international efforts to eradicate such weapons in the country.

Fourth, the long history of Iraq's WMD proliferation and the various mechanisms the international community have used to resolve this—diplomacy, sanctions, and, ultimately, military action—must be addressed. Fifth, destabilization in the region following the U.S. wars with Iraq and Afghanistan and the Arab Awakening have created an opportunity for extremists and terrorist groups to pose a proliferation threat from illicit trade, transfer, and use of such deadly weapons.

Sixth, the major Middle Eastern countries continue to have ambitions to expand their nuclear, biological, and chemical capabilities, with an increasing risk of WMD proliferation. Seventh, it is important to look at the genesis of the Iran nuclear program and the role played by the United States in nuclearizing the country and how, ironically, decades later it would prove to be an international proliferation concern. Finally, the historic 2015 Iran nuclear accord (JCPOA) faces formidable challenges from the U.S. Congress, the Trump administration, and opponents in Tehran. The U.S. government is also concerned with the sunset clause in the agreement that will remove some of the limitations on Iran's nuclear program within a decade.

These intertwining challenges render any effort toward a mutually acceptable framework for a WMDFZ in the Middle East a monumental task. On the other hand, they represent the very reasons for urgency in establishing such a zone.

World power WMD

The conventional wisdom is that the strategic location of the Middle East and its importance to the global energy market and commerce will continue to ensure stability in the region. The WMDFZ is one way to accomplish this, yet for decades world powers have paid only lip service to this goal and have lacked the political will to make progress in that direction. When the political will exists, such goals are achievable, as was demonstrated in the case of the Iran nuclear deal.

The five permanent members of the UNSC—China, Russia, the United Kingdom, France, and the United States (P5)—have an obligation to assist with the realization of the zone. The council's key responsibility is "the maintenance of international peace and security," with authority to impose binding obligations on the 193 member states of the UN. The P5 has multiple tools for achieving this mandate, including the ability to call "upon the parties to a dispute to settle it by peaceful means and recommend methods of adjustment or terms of settlement," or to use its mandate under Chapter VII of the UN Charter to impose "sanctions or even authorize the use of force to maintain or restore international peace and security."[1] Issues determined to be threats to peace and security include civil wars, natural disasters, nuclear proliferation, and terrorism—all circumstances currently impacting the Middle East to varying degrees.

Since 2003, when the Iran nuclear issue came under the global spotlight, the international community has left no stone unturned to resolve the matter, including the use of sanctions and sustained diplomatic efforts. The UNSC has passed seven resolutions on Iran's nuclear program since 2006, invoked Chapter VII of the UN Charter, and placed sanctions on Iran. The sanctions were legally binding on all members of the UN and constituted a coercive component of the dual-track approach to resolve the Iran nuclear dispute, with the other track involving proposals to resolve the issue through negotiated settlement.[2] At the core of the successful negotiation of the Iran deal was the political will of the world powers to press forward with negotiations until an agreement was reached. Yet, to date, the same level of persistence and dedication toward a WMDFZ in the Middle East has been lacking and this has resulted in the inability to realize such a zone.

As nuclear weapons states and signatories of the NPT, the P5 are obligated to advance the influence of the treaty through their actions and not just their statements. The three core goals of the NPT are complete nuclear disarmament by the P5, prevention of the spread of nuclear weapons, and cooperation in the peaceful use of nuclear energy.[3]

Although it is more than forty years since the P5 ratified the NPT, they still possess huge stocks of nuclear weapons. The United States, Russia, France, and the United Kingdom have reduced their stockpiles, but significant inventories still remain, and the likelihood of achieving total nuclear disarmament remains distant. Currently, France has about 300 nuclear weapons, the United Kingdom has 215, and China has 270. The majority of nuclear warheads, though, are possessed by Russia and the United States, with 6,850 and 6,450, respectively, accounting for roughly 93 percent of the global stockpile. Of these, the United States has 1,350 deployed strategic warheads, compared to Russia's 1,444, ready to be fired from warships, planes, submarines, or silos.[4]

In addition to their large stockpiles and their lack of commitment to disarmament, all nuclear weapons states have launched ambitious modernization programs that are projected to cost hundreds of billions of dollars over the next decades. For instance, the U.K. government, on July 18, 2016, got the green light from parliament to upgrade its nuclear program, with an estimated cost of approximately $40 billion over the lifetime of the program (thirty-five years). Other estimates vary wildly, with the independent Trident Commission placing the cost at $125 billion, while the British Conservative Foreign Affairs Committee estimates the cost to be around $257 billion—accounting for decommissioning the outdated weapons system and delivery mechanisms, contingency funds, and the cost of upgraded warheads and submarines.[5]

The United States and Russia have extensive nuclear weapons modernization plans in place despite their 2011 bilateral agreement to reduce their nuclear weapons as part of the "new START," officially called the Treaty on Measures for the Further Reduction and Limitation of Strategic Offensive Arms. As per the obligations of the bilateral agreement, in February 2018, the United States and Russia limited their deployed strategic warheads to 1,550 each.[6] This limitation under the new START, however, represents only deployed strategic warheads (ready to be used) and constitutes part of the total number of nuclear weapons that the two countries possess in their arsenal.[7] The United States, however, also plans to spend a staggering $355 billion over the next decade on the modernization, maintenance, and safety of its nuclear weapons.[8] According to the James Martin Center for Nonproliferation Studies (CNS), the United States will "likely spend over $1 trillion during the next three decades to maintain its current nuclear arsenal and purchase their replacement systems."[9] Unfortunately, this contradicts President Obama's 2009 foreign policy speech in Prague calling for "America's commitment to seek the peace and security of a world without nuclear weapons."[10] The election to president of Donald Trump, who in a 140-character tweet on December 22, 2016, suggested that "The United States must greatly strengthen and expand its nuclear capability," is yet another blow to the prospects for global nuclear weapons disarmament.[11]

Israel's nuclear arsenal

Israel's acquisition of nuclear weapons was driven by its history, the Holocaust, and an existential threat from neighboring countries at the time of its creation. The inception and development of the Israeli nuclear weapons program continues to be shrouded in mystery, but thanks to declassified U.S. documents, leaks, and whistle blowers, it is generally accepted that Israel possesses nuclear weapons.[12] Israel's government continues to stick to its official policy of "nuclear opacity" to neither confirm nor deny possessing nuclear weapons.[13] In 1986, however, former Israeli nuclear technician Mordechai Vanunu provided information, backed by photographs of "equipment for extracting radioactive material for arms production and laboratory models of thermonuclear devices," to the *Sunday Times* newspaper.[14]

Furthermore, a declassified 1987 U.S. Department of Defense report, "Critical Technological Assessment in Israel and NATO Nations," stated, "as far as nuclear technology is concerned, the Israelis are roughly where the United States was in the fission weapon field in about 1955 to 1960. It should be noted that the Israelis are developing the kind of codes which will enable them to make hydrogen bombs."[15]

Israel's nuclear weapons could not have been realized without the assistance of the United States, France, the United Kingdom, and Germany, all of which secretly sold material and equipment, provided expertise, and, at times, turned a blind eye to Israel acquiring fissile material and nuclear weapons designs.[16] The United States, in particular, has been aware of the Israeli program for some time, according to the Federation of American Scientists (FAS) report on Israel's nuclear weapons program: "As early as December 8, 1960, the CIA issued a report outlining Dimona's implications for nuclear proliferation, and the CIA station in Tel Aviv had determined by the mid-1960s that the Israeli nuclear weapons program was an established and irreversible fact."[17]

The international community has made various efforts to encourage and also pressure Israel to accede to the NPT. In one such occasion, at the 53rd IAEA General Conference, member countries voiced their concern over Israel's nuclear capabilities and tabled a resolution. Some of the underlying reasons for their concern were detailed by Arab states: "the Israeli nuclear capabilities and about the threat posed by the proliferation of nuclear weapons to the security and stability of the Middle East . . . [and] States directly concerned by the issue of the Israeli nuclear capabilities, whether on account of their geographical position or their influential role in the international arena."[18]

On September 18, 2009, the assembly adopted Resolution 17, expressing "concern about the Israeli nuclear capabilities," and called upon "Israel to accede to the NPT and place all its nuclear facilities under comprehensive IAEA safeguards."[19] Israel rejected the resolution, calling it "politically motivated" and "incompatible with basic norms and principles of international law."[20]

Israel also rejected UN calls for nuclear transparency as well as an invitation to attend the WMDFZ conference scheduled for December 2012 (cancelled by the United States, which cited disagreement among regional countries over modalities and agenda. The U.S. State Department also stated that they "would not support a conference in which any regional state would be subject to pressure or isolation," a clear reference to Israel).[21] An Iranian diplomat told the UNGA, "The truth is that the Israeli regime is the only party which rejected the conditions for a conference and there needs to be strong pressure on that regime to participate in the conference without any preconditions."[22]

On December 4, 2012, the UNGA voted 174 to 6 for a nonbinding call that Israel join the NPT "without further delay," to create a legally binding nuclear-free Middle East.[23] Israel called the suggestion a "meaningless mechanical vote" of a body that has "lost all its credibility regarding Israel."[24] Israel's reluctance to adopt nuclear nonproliferation measures without repercussions highlights the disparity in the approach by world powers to sanction Iran—a country that does not possess a nuclear bomb, is a signatory to the NPT, and accepts IAEA surveillance of its nuclear facilities. There is a counterargument, particularly from the Israeli government and proponents of Israeli nuclear weapons policy, that since Israel is not a signatory to the NPT it is not obligated to adhere to calls by the international community to enforce transparency, verification, and monitoring of its program.[25] Nevertheless, there is a need for concerted diplomatic efforts, with incentives and repercussions, to alter the Israeli position to advance the prospects for the realization of the zone.

Successive Israeli governments have insisted first on reaching a comprehensive peace agreement with the Palestinians and attaining full recognition by other regional countries before any move toward realizing a NWFZ or the wider WMDFZ in the Middle East. As far back as September 1975, then Israeli Prime Minister Yitzhak Rabin stated, "in case that there would be an overall settlement, that is to say a peace agreement, we will sign every agreement about a non-proliferation treaty."[26] Such preconditions, particularly intertwined with a protracted conflict, have not only hampered any progress toward the zone, they have also formed the basis for Israel to maintain its nuclear arsenal.

While Israel is a member state of the United Nations, it continues to be isolated in the Middle East, only Egypt and Jordan have officially recognized Israel.[27] On the issue of the illegal Israeli settlement expansion, then U.S. Secretary of State John Kerry was prompted on December 28, 2016, to warn that such policies were isolating Israel where "virtually every country in the world other than Israel opposes settlements."[28]

While the issue of Israeli–Palestinian conflict will be covered in more detail in the following chapter, it is worth mentioning here that the Israeli government has been criticized for a lack of effort toward an agreement on a two-state solution with the Palestinians and has failed to halt the expansion of illegal settlements on Palestinian lands, a policy perspective that was opposed by the Obama administration.[29]

In addition to these preconditions, there are three primary concepts used to justify Israel's nuclear weapons arsenal: deterrence, no first use, and the so-called Begin doctrine (maintaining a nuclear weapons monopoly). The first ensures Israel has a nuclear deterrence option to discourage regional aggression, particularly since Israel has been at war with its Arab neighbors on many occasions (for example: the 1948 Arab–Israeli War; the 1967 Six-Day War; the 1967 War of Attrition; the 1973 Yom Kippur War; the 1982 Lebanon War; and multiple outbreaks of violence between Israelis and Palestinians).[30] Israel is also not recognized by the overwhelming majority of Muslim countries (twenty-nine UN member states with Muslim majority populations).[31] This justification was articulated by then Prime Minister Shimon Peres: "We didn't build this [nuclear] option to get to Hiroshima, but rather to get to Oslo. We felt that the reason Israel was attacked several times, without any provocation, was because some of our neighbors thought they could overpower us, and we wanted to create a situation in which this temptation would no longer exist."[32]

The Israeli nuclear deterrence doctrine, however, has proved ineffective in deterring hostilities toward Israel. Although there have been no large-scale attacks, Israel's nuclear arsenal and advanced conventional military have not prevented Hamas's rockets or led to Hezbollah's demise.

To maintain the status quo, Tel Aviv has been successful for decades (since the Eisenhower administration in the 1950s) in maintaining a "special relationship" with Washington that has been the cornerstone of Israel's national security strategy.[33] This special relationship ensures that Israeli conventional and unconventional military capabilities have an advantage over Israel's neighbors, in both quality and technological advancement.[34] Unfettered support from the United States also includes shielding Israel from international calls for nuclear disarmament and joining the NPT. The U.S. National Security Archive, in 2006, published declassified U.S. government documents revealed that President Richard Nixon and his Israeli counterpart Golda Meir reached, in 1969, an understanding on Israel's nuclear weapons.[35] The key findings reveal that "Meir pledged to maintain nuclear restraint—no test, no declaration, no visibility—and after the meeting the Nixon White House decided to 'stand down' on pressure on Israel" to disarm and join the NPT.[36] While this special relationship between Tel Aviv and Washington continues, there were a number of policy disputes between the Israeli government and the Obama administration.

The most visible difference between the Obama and Netanyahu governments was how to resolve the dispute over the Iranian nuclear program; Obama's administration emphasized diplomacy over the repeated calls by Israel to strike militarily at Iran's nuclear infrastructure.[37] The Israeli push for a military solution was seen as credible, with warning signs from Israeli Prime Minister Netanyahu, such as his statement that, "If sanctions don't work, they [Iran] have to know that you'll [United States] be prepared to take military action—that's the only thing that will get their attention."[38] A unilateral military strike by Israel or in collaboration with the United States, however, would further destabilize the region, a concern voiced by former Israeli President Shimon Peres, who professed his most important achievement during his presidency as: "I stopped Netanyahu from attacking Iran. . . . I can tell you that he was ready to launch an attack and I stopped him. I told him the consequences would be catastrophic."[39]

Since the 1990s, one of the underlining reasons for Israel's deterrence policy was to defend itself from an imminent existential threat from a nuclear weapons-armed Iran. In 1992, then Foreign Minister Peres, in an interview with French TV, warned that Iran would be armed with a nuclear bomb by 1999.[40] In July 2001, then Minister of Defense Binyamin Ben-Eliezer confirmed that by the year 2005 Iran would have a nuclear bomb.[41]

Prime Minister Netanyahu has a long history (dating back to 1996) of warning about Iran developing nuclear weapons; while addressing a joint session of the U.S. Congress in 1996, he stated: "If Iran were to acquire nuclear weapons, this could presage catastrophic consequences, not only for my country, and not only for the Middle East, but for all mankind," adding that "the deadline for attaining this goal is getting extremely close."[42] Fast-forward to February 2009, when Netanyahu continued the same mantra to the U.S. congressional delegation that Iran was only one or two years away from nuclear weapons.[43] In September 2012, he claimed Iran could have a nuclear bomb by mid-2013,[44] and in July 2013, he once again warned that Iran was only weeks away from crossing the "red line" on developing a nuclear weapon.[45]

This justification, however, lost some of its credibility after Iran and the EU3 + 3 signed the nuclear accord in 2015, which was implemented in January 2016. While Israel continues to be concerned with Iran's nuclear capabilities, it can no longer claim that Iran has not fulfilled its obligations under the accord. Similarly, the confirmation by the IAEA that Iran has fully complied with the JCPOA has removed yet another underlying reason for Israel's nuclear weapons.[46]

Netanyahu's opposition to the nuclear accord, however, finally had a receptive ear with the election of U.S. President Donald Trump, particularly since Trump made no secret of his distaste for the accord and has carried through with his promise to scrap the deal, ultimately withdrawing in May 2018. In the lead up to that decision, Netanyahu took every opportunity to discredit the JCPOA and proactively seek U.S. withdrawal. In one key instance to shape the discourse surrounding the JCPOA, Netanyahu on April 30, 2018, gave a highly anticipated presentation showing "something that the world has never seen." In a theatrical performance, he revealed a covert operation by the Israeli intelligence agency, Mossad, in which they stole a large archive of Iranian nuclear plans that he insisted were proof that Iran was deceiving the international community regarding its nuclear activities. The majority of the documents, however, dealt with Iran's covert nuclear program from the years 1999 to 2003, which were known facts and were dealt with during the negotiations that lead to the JCPOA.[47] According to Rob Malley, a former senior official in Obama's National Security Council and a member of the negotiating team with Iran, while Netanyahu provided no new evidence that Iran was continuing with its nuclear activities or in violation of the JCPOA, his whole spectacle had "an audience of one: Trump."[48] With President Trump pulling out of the JCPOA a little over a week after Netanyahu's "revelations," it seems the gamble had paid off. However, with continuing confirmation by the IAEA that Iran has fully complied with the JCPOA, Netanyahu will find it hard to convince the rest of the world of Iran's imminent danger of developing nuclear weapons and to justify Israel's own nuclear arsenal.[49]

"No first use" is another Israeli justification to hold on to its nuclear arsenal as long as security threats remain. This position was first voiced by then Israeli Deputy Minister of Defense Peres in a meeting with President John Kennedy on April 2, 1963. In response to President Kennedy's question regarding nuclear weapons development in the Middle East, Peres responded, "I can tell you most clearly that we will not introduce nuclear weapons to the region, and certainly we will not be the first."[50] In a February 2011 report in the *Bulletin of Atomic Scientists*, senior Israeli nuclear experts advanced the policy of nuclear weapon "no first use" for the Middle East, claiming it would encourage "cooperation and trust" among regional states "without confronting head-on the most difficult security issues."[51] The logic of this position, however, conveniently provides a smokescreen for Israel to keep its nuclear weapons as a deterrent in an unlikely event that another regional country threatens the use of similar weapons.

Therefore, no first use legitimizes both the possession and the use of nuclear weapons by Israel in retaliation, leaving open the risk that other countries in the region could adopt this position to justify their own development of nuclear weapons. This logic has also legitimized Israel's second-strike capability in the form of nuclear-tipped missiles installed in submarines provided by Germany.[52] With the acquisition of the submarines, modified fighter jets capable of carrying nuclear warheads, and Jericho ballistic missiles, Israel has developed its own nuclear triad.[53]

Proponents of Israel maintaining its nuclear weapons suggest Israel's purpose is to deter and, if necessary, respond to biological and chemical weapons threats from Syria, Iran, and Egypt, and, if another nuclear-armed state emerges, to nuclear threats and/or attack.[54] This argument, however, fails to address the fact that the Israeli nuclear weapons program dates back to 1960s and the development of other regional nuclear programs, specifically Iran's, came to international attention only in 2002.[55] Similarly, Egyptian, Syrian, and other WMD proliferation attempts followed the Israeli nuclear weapons program.[56] Israel's tendency to strike first (as in previous cases of preemptive military strikes on Iraq's Osirak and Syria's Al Kibar nuclear facilities) and to ask questions later suggests that its nuclear weapons use policy might involve first use of nuclear weapons in the name of preventing a grave threat to the state of Israel.[57]

Israel's official position on biological and chemical weapon programs also remains ambiguous. Jane's Chemical Biological Radiological Nuclear (CBRN) assessment concluded in July 2014 that, "Israel may be able to deploy a biological weapons capability immediately. If no such capability presently exists, an order to proceed would probably take no longer than a few weeks to develop."[58]

While Israel has signed the CWC, it is yet to ratified it based on the premise that all other countries in the region must first sign and ratify the treaty, a position about which former Israeli foreign ministry spokesman Yigal Palmor commented, "some of these states don't recognize Israel's right to exist and blatantly call to annihilate it."[59] This argument has been immensely weakened as Israel's foe, Syria, signed and ratified the CWC in 2013, leaving only Egypt to sign and ratify the convention. Egypt, however, has signed a peace treaty with Israel (since 1979), recognizes it and has forged a political, military, and intelligence relationship with Tel Aviv. It is true that Iran does not recognize Israel, but it is in full compliance with the CWC.

During a closed-door conference held in Europe on eradicating WMD in the Middle East, a member of the Israeli delegation justified Tel Aviv's no first use policy as a natural step for any nuclear-armed state because it is a clear acknowledgment that such weapons should not be used except in the most extreme circumstances and only in response to a nuclear attack initiated by another state. While this scenario is highly unlikely, the key contention with the no first use policy is that it legitimizes possession of nuclear weapons, whereas the WMDFZ leaves no room for any justification or grounds for possession of such weapons, including other WMD.

Another justification used by Israel for maintaining its nuclear weapons monopoly in the region is based on the Begin doctrine, which requires the Israeli government to take any measure, including military action, to prevent other regional countries from acquiring or developing nuclear weapons,[60] such as the bombing of Iraq's Osirak reactor in 1981.[61] Shortly after that event, the Begin doctrine was established, with the Israeli government stating, "On no account shall we permit an enemy to develop weapons of mass destruction against the people of Israel. We shall defend the citizens of Israel in good time and with all the means at our disposal."[62] The same logic was also behind the more recent attack on Syria's Al Kibar nuclear reactor in 2007.[63]

Israel is believed to be behind other forms of sabotage to damage the Iranian nuclear program and is alleged to have collaborated with Iranian dissident group Mujahideen-e Khalq (MEK) to assassinate five Iranian nuclear scientists from 2007 to 2012.[64] In yet another case, Israel, in partnership with the United States, conducted cyber sabotage by infecting the Natanz uranium enrichment facility with the Stuxnet virus in 2010, causing damage to hundreds of centrifuges, in a covert operation code named Olympic Games.[65] After an eighteen-month investigation into the matter, veteran *New York Times* reporter David Sanger wrote, "collaboration with Israel was driven by two imperatives. Israel's Unit 8200, a part of its military, had technical expertise that rivaled the N.S.A.'s, and the Israelis had deep intelligence about operations at Natanz that would be vital to making the cyberattack a success."[66]

Israel's reliance on "preventive" military force to destroy the nuclear facilities of other sovereign states is troublesome, as there are more appropriate channels to address WMD proliferation attempts within the confines of the UNSC and the IAEA. The reality is that as long as Israel maintains its nuclear weapons, there is no future for a Middle East free from weapons of mass destruction. If Israel wants to maintain its nuclear supremacy, then Kenneth Waltz, the prominent international relations scholar, makes a strong point: "Israel's regional nuclear monopoly, which has proved remarkably durable for the past four decades, has long fueled instability in the Middle East. In no other region of the world does a lone, unchecked nuclear state exist. It is Israel's nuclear arsenal, not Iran's desire for one that has contributed most to the current crisis. Power, after all, begs to be balanced."[67]

The ultimate choice is clear for the world powers and Israel: pressing the only nuclear weapons state in the region to disarm will ensure that no other country in the region will be able to introduce nuclear weapons. One can also argue that even if Iran and other states acquire nuclear weapons capabilities such states could be politically forced to reverse course if Israel gave up its nuclear weapons.

Syria's chemical weapons

The Syrian war has been devastating in all aspects: human, material, historical, and environmental. On August 21, 2013, the war in Syria took a turn for the worse following the use of chemical weapons in the Ghouta suburbs near Damascus.

The death toll reached 1,400, with opposition forces and the Syrian government blaming each another for using chemical weapons. Less than a month following the incident, on September 16, 2013, the UN published its report, stating that "the environmental, chemical and medical samples, we have collected, provide clear and convincing evidence that surface-to-surface rockets containing the nerve agent sarin were used."[68]

The subsequent international outcry and the Obama administration's "red line" on Syria's use of chemical weapons escalated the situation to the point where Washington was on the verge of commencing punitive airstrikes on the Syrian government. At the eleventh hour, a rhetorical suggestion by then U.S. Secretary of State John Kerry, on September 9, 2013, that "Syria turns over all of its chemical weapons within a week" received a positive response from the Syrian government.[69] This sparked a series of steps, including high-level discussion between Iran, Russia, and Syrian officials, that ultimately led to the U.S.–Russia joint agreement on September 14, 2013, the "Framework for Elimination of Syrian Chemical Weapons," which demanded Syria's chemical weapons stockpiles be destroyed by June 30, 2014.[70] The framework agreement, specific timeline, and responsibilities of the Syrian government became binding with the unanimous passing of UNSC Resolution 2118 on September 27, 2013.[71] The Syrian government promptly provided information on twenty-three chemical weapons sites to the Organization for the Prohibition of Chemical Weapons (OPCW) and committed to provide unfettered access to all chemical weapons sites.[72]

Despite the compressed timetable and difficult conditions on the ground, the initial dismantling of Syrian chemical weapons stock and capability progressed relatively smoothly with OPCW Director-General Ahmet Uzümcü stating that the Syrian government's cooperation "has been quite constructive."[73] This early optimism faded when the Syrian government repeatedly missed deadlines. On June 24, 2014—ahead of the June 30 deadline—however, the OPCW announced that removal of Syrian chemical weapons material was complete.[74]

While it is undoubtedly a major achievement to rid Syria of its chemical weapons and capabilities, verification and monitoring remain challenging. The ongoing war in Syria makes it increasingly difficult, due to security concerns, for the OPCW inspections to visit all suspected sites. Regrettably, since the completion of the initial operation by OPCW, there have been multiple instances of chemical weapons use (sarin and chlorine gas) in Syria.[75] In one chemical weapons attack on April 4, 2017, sarin gas was used in Idlib province and killed dozens of people. Initial reports alleged the Syrian government perpetrated the attacks based on the type of aircraft witnessed near the scene. The following day, on April 5, 2017, the UNSC held an emergency meeting that ended in no resolution and, instead, the Trump administration, on April 6, took unilateral military action to launch cruise missiles targeting a Syrian government airbase, where the aircraft suspected of conducting the chemical attack had originated.[76]

In the fog of war, while specific blame for chemical attacks has been difficult to place on parties involved in the Syrian conflict, it is, nevertheless, a worrying sign that terrorist groups, in particular ISIS, may have access to undeclared or unreachable sites under their control. In March 2015, the UNSC adopted Resolution 2209, condemning the use of chlorine as a weapon in Syria's civil war and threatening to impose measures under Chapter VII of the UN Charter following a subsequent resolution.[77] Failure to rid Syria of its chemical weapons and material will continue to undermine international nonproliferation efforts and hope for the universalization of the CWC.

Iraq's WMD program

Iraq has a long history of WMD proliferation, dating to the 1970s, even though the country no longer possesses such weapons. However, the genesis of its WMD program and the methods used by the international community to disarm the country provide an invaluable experience and key lessons to address future WMD challenges in the region. Furthermore, as a result of tackling the challenges of Iraq's WMD program, more robust nonproliferation tools, laws, and mechanisms were developed that can be applied in other WMD proliferation cases. The Iraqi WMD case ultimately ended with the unilateral use of military force by the United States (and the United Kingdom) and serves as a contrast to the final multilateral diplomatic resolution to Iran's nuclear program. This important distinction provides two alternatives to dealing with future proliferation attempts by regional countries, and these two approaches set an important precedent for multilateral diplomacy versus military action. The instability that followed the U.S. military invasion of Iraq in 2003 (one justification was based on ridding Iraq of WMD) has contributed to the current regional quagmire. Furthermore, WMD proliferation risks arising from instability in Iraq are no longer centered on the government but on the possibility of non-state actors and extremists taking advantage of Baghdad's fragility to acquire, produce, and use WMD.

With the 1979 ascendance of Saddam Hussein to power, Iraq accelerated its covert nuclear, biological, and chemical programs.[78] Iraq went on to use chemical weapons multiple times, both on its Kurdish population and during the 1980–1988 war with Iran. No UNSC resolutions were passed during the war condemning Iraq's use of chemical weapons. However, once Iraq invaded Kuwait in 1990, then U.S. President George H. W. Bush justified military action due to concerns over the possibility for Saddam to use WMD.[79]

A 2004 report penned by the special adviser to the director of Central Intelligence on Iraq's WMD found that Saddam Hussein viewed the use of such weapons as at the heart of his tactical and strategic aims. The report further noted:

> Events in the 1980s and early 1990s shaped Saddam's belief in the value of WMD. In Saddam's view, WMD helped to save the Regime multiple times. He believed that during the Iran–Iraq war chemical weapons had halted Iranian ground offensives. . . . Similarly, during Desert Storm [the first Gulf War in 1991], Saddam believed WMD had deterred Coalition Forces from pressing their attack beyond the goal of freeing Kuwait. WMD had even played a role in crushing the Shia revolt in the south following the 1991 cease-fire.[80]

In 1991, the U.S.-led international coalition liberated Kuwait in the first Gulf War/Operation Desert Storm. Following Iraq's defeat, the UNSC passed its first resolution addressing WMD in Iraq on April 3, 1991. Resolution 687 required Iraq to "not use, develop, construct or acquire any weapons of mass destruction," and limited its ballistic missiles with ranges beyond 150 kilometers. The resolution also created the United Nations Special Commission to oversee the inspection, destruction, and monitoring of Iraq's chemical and biological weapons, while its nuclear weapons program would be verified by the IAEA.[81] On April 6, 1991, Iraq reluctantly accepted Resolution 687, agreeing to disclose information on its WMD program and take preliminary steps to ensure the safety, rights, and unfettered access for UNSCOM inspectors in the country.

Following a report by UNSCOM chief Richard Butler that stated that Iraq was refusing to cooperate with inspectors, the UN ordered all UNSCOM and IAEA inspectors to leave Iraq on December 16, 1998.[82] Hours later, the United States began air strikes on Iraq. The inspectors faced many challenges throughout their mission in Iraq, including interruptions, accusations that the inspectors were CIA agents, a lack of cooperation, and limited access to suspected WMD sites.[83] Nevertheless, UNSCOM and IAEA inspectors were able to provide invaluable insight into Iraq's WMD program, as detailed subsequently.

Chemical Weapons. Iraq's chemical weapons infrastructure was extensively damaged during the first Gulf War and, according to Iraq's own declaration (mandated by UNSC Resolution 687), it had produced 3,859 tons of chemical weapons agents (including mustard, tabun, sarin, and cyclosarin) from 1982 to 1990.[84] UN inspectors completed the destruction of the declared chemical weapons agents and related production equipment and facilities in 1994. The inspectors also discovered that Iraq was producing chemical nerve agent VX and had developed other advanced chemical weapons capabilities.[85]

Biological Weapons. Iraq's covert biological weapons program began in the 1970s but reached advanced levels during the war with Iran. By 1990, Iraq had accumulated lethal and debilitating agents: 19,000 liters of botulinum toxin, 8,500 liters of anthrax solution, and 2,000 liters of aflatoxin.[86] In preparation for the first Gulf War, Iraqi forces had at their disposal more than 180 biological weapons ready to use in the battlefield.[87] In the aftermath of the war, Iraq initially denied having a biological weapons program but later admitting to a limited "defensive" one.[88] However, the 1995 defection of Iraq's former director of the Military Industrialization Corporation, General Husayn Kamil, forced Iraq to reveal a far more extensive biological weapons program. As a result, two major biological weapons production facilities were destroyed under UNSCOM supervision.[89]

Nuclear Weapons. In 1968, the Soviet Union built Iraq's first nuclear research reactor near Baghdad. Subsequently, in the 1970s, Iraq's nuclear program expanded with the construction of the French-built Osiraq nuclear reactor. Around the same time, then head of the Iraq Atomic Energy Commission (IAEC) Saddam Hussein initiated a covert nuclear weapons program.[90] In 1981, prior to the Osiraq reactor coming online, Israel conducted a preemptive strike, suspecting that Iraq planned to build nuclear weapons at the site.[91] Despite the damage to the reactor,

Iraq continued to enrich uranium at the facility and further entrench Saddam's effort to develop nuclear weapons.

Prior to the first Gulf War, Iraq had managed to amass 36.3 kilograms of weapons-usable HEU in the form of research reactor fuel, expanded its covert operations, and completed a prototype nuclear weapons design (although Iraq did not go beyond the design phase).[92] During the first Gulf War, however, nearly all of Iraq's primary nuclear facilities were destroyed. In the aftermath, the IAEA inspectors led the investigation to unearth and destroy Iraq's remaining nuclear weapons capabilities. As in the case of Iraq's biological weapons, Baghdad initially denied having nuclear weapons or weapons-grade nuclear material. From September 21 through 30, 1991, IAEA inspectors discovered large numbers of documents related to Iraq's nuclear weapons program. Though Iraqi officials failed to confiscate the damning documents and prevented the inspectors from leaving the site for four days,[93] the documents revealed that Iraq's covert nuclear weapons program was far more extensive than previously estimated, with advances in uranium enrichment. In 1995, further incriminating evidence on all covert WMD programs surfaced with the defection of General Husayn Kamil.[94] The IAEA's intrusive inspections throughout the 1990s led to the discovery and dismantling of Iraq's nuclear weapons program, and the ultimate conclusion that by 1997 most of Iraq's nuclear weapons programs had been incapacitated.

On multiple occasions in 1998, Iraq ceased cooperation with UNSCOM, demanding changes to the composition of the inspectors (who were suspected of spying for the United States) and an end to the crippling UN oil embargo. Iraq's refusal to cooperate ultimately triggered several days of U.S. and U.K. military strikes in December 1998, dubbed Operation Desert Fox. Receiving prior notice from the United States, inspectors working for UNSCOM and IAEA were removed from Iraq. Then U.S. President Bill Clinton stated that the aims of the military action were to "attack Iraq's nuclear, chemical and biological weapons programs and its military capacity to threaten its neighbors."[95]

Amid news reports that confirmed Iraq's allegations that the United States was collecting intelligence from members of the UNSCOM, UNSC Resolution 1284 replaced UNSCOM with the UN Monitoring, Verification, and Inspection Commission (UNMOVIC), under the leadership of Swedish national Hans Blix.[96] UNMOVIC and IAEA inspections commenced again in Iraq after a four-year hiatus, in 2002.

Following the September 11, 2001, terrorist attacks in New York City and Washington D.C., then U.S. President George W. Bush, during his January 2002 State of the Union address, accused Iraq of being part of an international "axis of evil." He went on to warn the U.S. Congress that "Iraq continues to flaunt its hostility toward America and to support terror. The Iraqi regime has plotted to develop anthrax and nerve gas and nuclear weapons for over a decade."[97] He would continue his dire warnings in September 2002, during an address to the UNGA, saying: "We know that Saddam Hussein pursued weapons of mass murder even when inspectors were in his country. Are we to assume that he stopped when they left? The history, the logic, and the facts lead to one conclusion: Saddam Hussein's regime is a grave and gathering danger."[98]

President Bush's rhetoric made it clear that his administration would not tolerate Iraq with Saddam Hussein at the helm armed with weapons of mass destruction. To convince the international community of the imminent danger Iraq posed, the Bush administration, along with the United Kingdom, embarked on a campaign that provided briefings and documents detailing their conclusions concerning Iraq's WMD program. On November 8, 2002, the gamble paid off with the passage of UNSC Resolution 1441, which required Iraq to accept a "final opportunity to comply with its disarmament" commitments through intrusive inspections, to be carried out by the IAEA and UNMOVIC, or face "serious consequences." Iraq agreed to the terms, and inspections resumed on November 27, 2002.[99]

On December 7, 2002, Iraq submitted a 12,000-page report in response to the resolution, claiming there were no WMD programs or weapons. The report was scrutinized, with UNMOVIC chief inspector Hans Blix calling its content "largely recycled material."[100] Regardless, both Blix and IAEA's director-general, Mohamed ElBaradei, on January 9, 2003, reported to the UNSC that thus far there had been no sign of WMD in Iraq. Less than a month later, then U.S. Secretary of State Colin Powell's brief to UNSC, instead, presented evidence obtained by U.S. intelligence that Iraq had misled inspectors and had "to come clean and disarm." In the run-up to the U.S.-led invasion of Iraq, ElBaradei reiterated, "we have to date found no evidence or plausible indication of the revival of a nuclear weapon program in Iraq."[101]

Ultimately, the U.S.-led military coalition invaded Iraq, overrunning the capital, Baghdad, on April 9, with President Bush declaring victory on May 1. Shortly after the invasion, the Pentagon announced the formation of the Iraq Survey Group (ISG) to search for Iraq's WMD. On September 30, 2004, the ISG released its final report following sixteen months of investigation, concluding that Iraq possessed no chemical weapons, no biological weapons, and no "nuclear device, nor had it tried to reconstitute a capability to produce nuclear weapons."[102] The chief inspector of the report, Charles Duelfer, testified before the U.S. Congress about his team's findings, effectively invalidating President Bush's primary justification for going to war with Iraq.[103] This final report speaks volumes to the then U.S. government's eagerness to take unilateral military action on Iraq without support from international institutions such as the UNSC. Furthermore, the fact that there was no active WMD program in Iraq and that the United States took such drastic actions without international consent eroded the authority of the UNSC and international conventions. The Iraqi example also shows that diplomatic efforts were not exhausted and that, even directly prior to the U.S. attack, the IAEA and UNMOVIC chiefs did not affirm that Iraq had WMD.

Rise of extremism and risk of WMD acquisition

The socioeconomic and political change sweeping the Middle East as a result of the Arab uprisings has brought new challenges for nonproliferation. The Middle East is shedding decades of dictatorial rule that has been backed primarily by the United States. At the same time, new political forces have come to the fore, with Islamist political parties gaining ground through elections and more radical groups attempting to advance their fundamentalist vision for the region through terrorism. The political and military battles ahead will be fought between moderate and radical Islamists to dominate the power equation in the region. The outcome of this rivalry will have a profound impact on nonproliferation in the region. If moderate Islamist forces gain the upper hand, their priority for security and stability could pave the way for progress on the WMDFZ in the Middle East.

The alternative scenario, with ISIS and Al-Qaeda extremists or likeminded political parties in power, would threaten nonproliferation. These radicals will not be bound by any limitation. They would seek weapons of mass destruction to unleash havoc and terror on population centers, particularly U.S. allies and interests, including Israel. A sobering declaration on the justification of the use of WMD was made by the extremist Saudi Sheik Nasir bin Hamad al-Fahd: "If the unbelievers can be repelled . . . only by using" weapons of mass destruction, then "their use is permissible, even if you kill them without exception."[104]

The possibility that extremists within weak regimes may acquire access to fissile or other WMD materials makes matters worse. An expanding network of illicit trade in nuclear or other radioactive material will exacerbate this situation across international borders. Such illicit trafficking of nuclear or radioactive material has been ongoing for decades, although in relatively small quantities. The IAEA acknowledges this trafficking has taken place since it began collecting information on this issue in 1993.[105] It is plausible to assume that such illicit trade will become a more prominent concern as non-state actors such as Al-Qaeda or ISIS seek weapons of mass destruction. A conference organized by the IAEA in 2007 concluded that "terrorist groups have the intention of attempting to acquire and use nuclear or radioactive material for malicious acts."[106] The former leader of Al-Qaeda, Osama bin Laden, claimed it was an "Islamic duty" to acquire and use WMD in the context of all-out war. The justification he cited was that "all these crimes and sins committed by the Americans are a clear declaration of war on God, his messenger, and Muslims. To kill the Americans and their allies—civilians and military—is an individual duty for every Muslim who can do it in any country."[107]

The geographic reality for Israel is that all its neighbors are reeling from the aftermath of the Arab uprisings. It is not a question of if but when the insecurity engulfing the region reaches Israel. A further concern for Israeli security is the close proximity of Iranian forces and their allied militias in bordering Syria. In addition, Hezbollah (the Lebanese militant group that has fought previous wars with Israel in southern Lebanon) has boosted its military capabilities and battle experience beyond Lebanon's border into Syria. As an address by the former deputy assistant secretary for Near Eastern affairs at the U.S. State Department to the U.S. Congress warned, "it is clear that the changes in the region have shifted the nature of the threats facing Israel—from state-centered and nonconventional threats to non-state, terrorist and insurgent threats."[108] The advanced Israeli nuclear weapons program, as well as its capabilities in chemical and biological spheres, may provide security to Israel, but their very existence poses an existential risk if extremists infiltrate or attack such facilities and obtain fissile material to unleash a WMD attack.

Moreover, Israel's adversaries, which include non-state actors and terrorist groups such as ISIS, expose the Israeli nuclear weapons arsenal and the decades-old Dimona reactor situated within the larger Negev Nuclear Research Center to the risk of conventional weapons attack. Such an attack could result in a deadly release of radioactive material and cause widespread destruction to Israel, with significant human cost and irreversible environmental, economic, and psychological impact. While previous attacks on nuclear facilities in the region have taken place, none has resulted in a radiological consequence, as the plants were under construction and not operational, as in the case of Israel's attacks on Iraq's Osirak reactor and Syria's suspected Al Kibar nuclear facility. Also, previous attacks missed their targets, as in the case of Iraq's attack on Dimona during the first Persian Gulf War in 1991 and Hamas's attempts to strike the same facility during the Israel–Gaza war of 2014. Future attacks, if successful, would be disastrous for Israel and impact the region as a whole.

Needless to say, due to instability in Iraq, Syria, Afghanistan, and the GCC and volatility in Egypt and Pakistan, extremists are becoming one of the greatest threats to WMD nonproliferation, with possible acquisition of chemical weapons in Syria and nuclear weapons in Pakistan. The December 2015 European Parliament report "ISIL/Da'esh and 'Non-Conventional' Weapons of Terror" warned member states of possible chemical or biological attack on their territory by ISIS terrorists. In the same report, Wolfgang Rudischhauser, director of the WMD Non-Proliferation Centre at NATO headquarters in Brussels, said "ISIL actually has already acquired the knowledge, and in some cases the human expertise, that would allow it to use CBRN [chemical, biological, radiological, or nuclear] materials as weapons of terror."[109] There are multiple documented cases between June and July 2015 when ISIS has manufactured, acquired, and used chemical weapons against Kurdish areas in Iraq and Syria.[110] Such cases of chemical weapons use highlight the imminent WMD threat to the region but also beyond, to the shores of Europe.

Regional proliferation risks

Increasing security challenges facing the nations in the region, coupled with Israel's refusal to engage in a meaningful process of advancing the WMDFZ, have made the spread of nuclear weapons capabilities throughout the region a real possibility. Due to rivalries and the potential shift in the balance of power, numerous Arab states have demonstrated their interest in acquiring nuclear technology to enhance prestige, bolster regime security, match Iran's capabilities, and deter Israel or other potential adversaries.

Moreover, Saudi Arabia is reported to have discussed the purchase of nuclear weapons from Pakistan. Prince Turki al-Faisal remarked that if all efforts "fail to convince Israel to shed its weapons of mass destruction and to prevent Iran from obtaining similar weapons, [then] we must, as a duty to our country and people, look into all options we are given, including obtaining these weapons ourselves."[111] It is only a matter of time before countries in the region use national security to justify their drive toward a nuclear weapon, bringing to an end Israel's nuclear weapons monopoly. With Iran having achieved a nuclear breakout option (the ability in a short timeframe to amass the necessary amount of enriched uranium to build a nuclear weapon), some analysts believe it will "begin to chip away at Israel's long-standing nuclear-weapons monopoly. That, in turn, might begin to constrain Israel's currently unconstrained freedom of unilateral military action."[112]

Origins and evolution of Iran's nuclear program

The Iran–EU3 + 3 nuclear accord contrasts with a series of failed encounters between Iran and the world powers, particularly the United States. In fact, the history of Iran's nuclear program started when the United States proposed a nuclear-energy program to Iran in the 1960s as part of President Dwight Eisenhower's Atoms for Peace program. In 1967, the United States built the first Iranian nuclear facility, Tehran Research Reactor (TRR).[113] In the 1970s, the United States proposed that Iran build twenty-three nuclear power reactors over twenty years. In this period, European countries were fiercely competing with the United States to win lucrative projects to nuclearize Iran.

Following the 1979 Iranian Revolution, however, Iran decided to forego the ambitious nuclear and military projects of the United States and the shah. The West's response was to withdraw from all civilian nuclear agreements and contracts with Iran, in violation of the nuclear nonproliferation treaty (which stipulates that signatory states have the right to technology and cooperation in peaceful nuclear sector), costing Iran billions of dollars.[114] This planted the seeds of the current Iranian nuclear dilemma. The United States even opposed Iran having a civilian nuclear plant and pressed Germany to decline its contractual agreement to complete the only Iranian civilian nuclear plant at Bushehr.[115] Moreover, Western countries prevented Iran from having access to the international market for nuclear fuel for its sole research reactor (the TRR) at a time when Iran had no plans to have uranium enrichment activities on its own soil.

Thus, Iran was left with little option other than to press for self-sufficiency to complete unfinished projects, such as the Bushehr reactor, and to ensure its domestic supply of reactor fuel in the future. In 2002, Iran mastered enrichment, and the proliferation issue returned to the top of the international agenda. Western countries again began to challenge Iran's nuclear activities under the NPT.[116] In October 2003, right after the IAEA passed the first resolution on Iran's nuclear program, the EU3 (France, Germany, and the United Kingdom) began nuclear talks with Iran.

During the nuclear negotiations from 2003 to August 2005, Tehran made far-reaching overtures on transparency and confidence-building measures, ensuring Iran's nuclear program did not divert toward nuclear weapons. At the time, Tehran agreed to the maximum transparency arrangements, such as the Safeguard

Agreement, Subsidiary Arrangement Code 3.1, and Additional Protocol, suspended enrichment for almost two years, limited enrichment to 5 percent, well below the 20 percent considered the minimum to be weapons grade, and maintained a meager stockpile of enriched uranium.[117] Such efforts failed, however, due to a U.S. policy that denied the legitimate rights of Iran for enrichment under the NPT for peaceful purposes.[118] During President Ahmadinejad's tenure (2005–2013), nuclear negotiations continued with the EU3+3 countries, but throughout this period, nuclear negotiations failed in the absence of a realistic compromise.

The 2013 election of a moderate president in Iran, Hassan Rouhani, opened a new window for a diplomatic resolution during the second term of President Obama. To succeed, the latest nuclear agreement required all parties compromise on the elements of the final comprehensive deal. According to former U.S. secretaries of state Henry Kissinger and George Shultz, there were three major tasks for U.S. diplomacy prior to the breakthrough: "to define a level of Iranian nuclear capacity limited to plausible civilian uses and to achieve safeguards that ensure that this level is not exceeded; to leave open the possibility of a genuinely constructive relationship with Iran; to design a Middle East policy adjusted to new circumstances."[119] Further statements made by informed U.S. figures suggested that, in a final deal, the United States would ask Iran to accept strict limitations on its nuclear program beyond the NPT.[120] The measures agreed upon included dismantling a significant fraction of the installed centrifuges; the elimination of most of Iran's stockpile of LEU; halting enrichment at Fordow, the second enrichment site near the city of Qum; reconstructing the Arak heavy-water-moderated research reactor; and thorough inspections and monitoring that go beyond the NPT and its Additional Protocol.[121]

To find a permanent solution with Iran that would not trigger proliferation from Arab states required new thinking in Washington. "My view is that if you have both a credible threat of force, combined with a rigorous diplomatic effort, that, in fact you can strike a deal," stated President Obama.[122] Regrettably, every time the Iranians demonstrated cooperation, the United States concluded that this was the result of pressure. Instead, a more nuanced interpretation would acknowledge that increased U.S. pressure to curtail Iran's nuclear program had, instead, in every case resulted in its acceleration. This was particularly true during the height of sanctions, when then Iranian President Ahmadinejad responded to punitive measures by expanding the Iranian nuclear program with an increase in centrifuges from a few hundred to 20,000. Therefore, with less combative diplomacy, the Iranian nuclear dispute may have been resolved earlier (a prime example is the initial 2003–2005 EU3 [Germany, the United Kingdom, and France] negotiations with Iran that resulted in a deal but was rejected by then U.S. President Bush). Furthermore, Israeli Prime Minister Netanyahu continued to reiterate (even in the post-accord era), "Pressure on Iran must be increased and not relaxed, and certainly not eased."[123] His position was that all diplomatic efforts must be accompanied by a "credible military threat." This language is even used when Iran played a constructive role in the Middle East, particularly when Iran and Russia jointly convinced Syrian President Bashar Al-Assad to join the CWC, potentially averting yet another U.S. war in the Middle East.[124] However, President Obama maintained the threat of a credible military strike against Iran and warned the country not to assume that because the United States had not attacked Syria it would not attack Iran.[125]

The West has long been focusing on coercion in its approach: comprehensive international sanctions, sabotage, and the threat of military action. Some observers in the West have made the argument that during President Ahmadinejad's tenure, the West was provoked to resort to ever-more coercive pressures.[126] Until the marathon negotiations that commenced in September 2013 on the sidelines of the UNGA, it seemed that all options had been practically and carefully examined—except to find a realistic, face saving, and comprehensive package for a peaceful settlement. Even at the nascent stages of the nuclear negotiations between EU3 + 3 and Iran, President Obama maintained "no options off the table, including military options."[127] Iran did make some diplomatic efforts to reach an agreement with the West, including recognizing the Holocaust as historical fact, condemning the killing of Jews by Nazis, and offering greetings to Jews at their new year, Rosh Hashanah.[128] Iran's response to the EU3 + 3 threats was to continue forward with its uranium enrichment program, compelling the West to negotiate on an equal footing with the Iranians.

Once the United States and the EU, against all odds, reached an interim Joint Plan of Action (JPOA) with Iran in November 2013, skeptics and opponents started mobilizing again, in Tehran as well as in many other capitals, including Washington.[129] In Iran, the internal opposition to the deal was fueled by concerns related to the U.S. policies followed during U.S. President Barack Obama's first term and by Israel's continued challenge of Iran's right to nuclear enrichment for energy use. In the United States, domestic opposition to the deal and concern about Iran's behavior was reinforced by two of its closest allies, Israel and Saudi Arabia.[130] The deep uneasiness in Jerusalem and Riyadh was tangible and immediate, as both countries see Iran as a mortal enemy bent on Israel's destruction and regional hegemony. A Rand Corporation report focusing on regional response to the interim deal revealed Saudi Arabia's position as having "two common themes: First, that the interim deal was evidence of the United States' declining resolve to play the role of security guarantor in the region. And second, that the Western powers were tacitly accepting an Iranian sphere of influence in return for concessions on its nuclear program."[131]

Israel's denouncement of the interim deal was expected and consistent with past opposition to the negotiations. Israeli Prime Minister Netanyahu decried that "What was achieved last night in Geneva is not an historic agreement; it is an historic mistake," adding that "Israel has the right and the obligation to defend itself."[132] Other senior Israeli officials offered doomsday scenarios, with Foreign Minister Avigdor Lieberman warning that the interim deal "brings us to a nuclear arms race," adding that it amounted to Western "capitulation to a charm offensive and fraud by Iran, whose goal is to win time without substantive damage to its military nuclear program . . . the Iranian regime has been given the legitimacy to continue its military nuclear project and continue its worldwide terror activities, while it is no longer internationally isolated and its economy has been strengthened."[133]

In the United States, long before Trump's May 2018 decision to withdraw from the Iran nuclear accord, there was still a risk that powerful domestic forces could succeed in subverting the November 2013 deal between Iran and the EU3+3, which would then "prove" to them that the only option with Iran was military attack. Lindsey Graham, a leading Republican senator on defense issues, said the United States should consider sinking the Iranian navy, destroying its air force, and delivering a decisive blow to the Revolutionary Guard to "neuter" the regime, destroying its ability to fight back, and hope that Iranians would use the opportunity to rise up against the government.[134] With no exception, all top ranking officials in the Obama administration reiterated that, in dealing with Iran's nuclear program, "all options" remained on the table, including a military strike.[135]

Threatening Iran proved counterproductive, as Tehran refused to compromise under threat. Now that Iran and the international community have reached a deal to ensure the peaceful character of Iran's nuclear activities, the main risk of proliferation no longer comes from Iran but from countries that do not recognize the legitimacy of that deal and could be tempted to follow the Israeli approach to security through nuclear weaponization. The most important action for both sides now is to convince the world—the Arab world in particular—that this deal is credible. Otherwise, the voices of the skeptics and opponents will dominate the conversation.

The lack of trust between the two sides risks derailing any offer for engagement between Iran and its neighbors. If the JCPOA collapses following the U.S. withdrawal and is not followed by a more robust Middle East and global nonproliferation regime that expands beyond the Iranian case, it will ultimately lead to heightened tensions, a possible all-out war, and the weakening of the NPT and other WMD conventions.

Threats to the Iran nuclear accord

The formal Implementation Day of the JCPOA, January 16, 2016 (which meant Iran had satisfied the necessary steps required under the JCPOA to begin sanctions relief by the international community), marked a major step forward in the resolution of the dispute over Iran's nuclear program. The IAEA verified that Iran had met its key initial obligations under the JCPOA, including shipping out its excess stock of enriched uranium, reducing the number of its operating and installed centrifuges, and dismantling the Arak reactor for reconstruction. The UNSC lifted international sanctions, and the United States waived its nuclear related sanctions on Iran.[136]

There will, however, be no shortage of opponents to the Iran nuclear accord, which will threaten its very existence. Trump's decision to leave the nuclear deal in May 2018 (discussed in Chapter 1) is part of a concerted effort by his administration to engage in a confrontational stance toward Iran. In addition, the JCPOA faces opponents from across the other two branches of the U.S. government (judicial and legislative), Iranian conservatives, Netanyahu's government, and Saudi Arabia.

While it took Trump eighteen months to scrap the nuclear deal, the writing was on the wall as he spearheaded punitive actions against Iran within days of coming into office. On January 27, 2017, President Trump signed Executive Order 13769, "Protecting the Nation from Foreign Terrorist Entry into the United States."[137] This order entailed suspending entry of refugees into the country for four months and indefinitely for Syrian refugees "to ensure that those approved for refugee admission do not pose a threat to the security and welfare of the United States." In addition, the executive order placed a three-month ban in the United States for nationals from seven Muslim-majority countries (Iran, Iraq, Libya, Somalia, Sudan, Syria, and Yemen) that were considered a terrorist risk.[138] In the signing ceremony, President Trump said the United States "will never forget the lessons of 9/11, nor the heroes who lost their lives at the Pentagon."

In fact, no ban was placed on the countries where the nineteen hijackers who were implicated in the September 11, 2001, terrorist attacks came from—Egypt, Lebanon, Saudi Arabia, and the UAE.[139] Immediately following the executive order, the Trump administration was faced with public, diplomatic, and legal backlash. Reacting to the new U.S. travel restrictions, the Iranian Ministry of Foreign Affairs issued a statement outlining that Tehran would limit visas to American visitors in line with implementing "the principle of reciprocity until the removal of the insulting restriction against Iranian nationals."[140]

Within the United States, protests broke out throughout major metropolitan areas, and legal action led to a nationwide temporary restraining order issued on February 3, 2017, by Judge James Robart in the case *State of Washington and State of Minnesota v. Trump*.[141] Subsequently, on February 9, 2017, the decision was upheld by the United States Court of Appeals for the Ninth Circuit, which halted enforcement by the Department of Homeland Security (DHS), while the U.S. Department of State re-validated previously revoked visas.[142] In response to the backlash that centered on the suspicion that the executive order was a "Muslim ban," President Trump signed a redrafted version (Executive Order 13780) on March 6, 2017.[143] It was, however, also blocked by a temporary restraining order issued by Judge Derrick Watson of the United States District Court for the District of Hawaii on the grounds that the revised travel ban was, indeed, considered a Muslim ban.[144]

The U.S. Supreme Court on December 4, 2017, permitted the travel ban to go into full effect while the legal challenges to it continued. Ultimately, on June 26, 2018, the Court in a 5–4 decision upheld President Trump's controversial travel ban, contending that the policy was not discriminatory against Muslims and was "squarely within the scope of presidential authority." The final version of the travel ban will prohibit entry to the United States by most people from Iran, Libya, Somalia, Syria, and Yemen in addition to two non-Muslim majority countries, North Korea, and select individuals with close ties to or who are involved in the Venezuelan government.[145]

There is no doubt that President Trump's travel ban and other provocative moves have exacerbated tensions in U.S.–Iran bilateral relations and been made worse with Trump's decision to pull out of the nuclear deal. Regardless, the Iranian government continues to abide by the nuclear accord, backed by the IAEA and continuous support for the agreement from the other five negotiating countries of the EU3+3.

The Republican-majority U.S. Congress continues to limit the benefits of sanctions relief for Iran and stymie any broader engagement between the two countries through multiple proposals for Iran-related sanctions legislation. U.S. obstructive policies received a boost following the U.S. withdrawal from the nuclear deal that will spearhead even tougher sanctions and actions against Iran.[146]

The actions by Republican-led Congress not only threaten the longevity of the Iran nuclear accord, they also complicate the task of conducting trade between Iran and the international community—in direct violation of the nuclear deal. This even prompted the Obama White House to veto some of these resolutions—specifically House Resolution (H.R.) 4992, H.R. 5119, and H.R. 5631—that violate the U.S. commitments set forth in the JCPOA to "refrain from any policy specifically intended to directly and adversely affect the normalization of trade and economic relations with Iran."[147] The Obama administration issued a pointed statement that

> these bills, separately or collectively, would impact the continued viability of the JCPOA, a diplomatic arrangement that peacefully and verifiably prevents Iran from acquiring a nuclear weapon. Dismantling the JCPOA would remove the unprecedented constraints on and monitoring of Iran's nuclear program, lead to the unraveling of the international sanctions regime against Iran, and deal a devastating blow to the credibility of America's leadership and our commitments to our closest allies.[148]

More than a dozen legislative measures against Iran have been introduced in the U.S. Congress since the Iran nuclear accord of 2015.[149] Some of the bills have yet to be confirmed into law, and most go beyond the Iran nuclear issue to target Tehran's ballistic missile program, terrorism, and human rights.[150] The following comments provide more detail on some of the key legislations passed on Iran.

December 15, 2015. Quarantining the Ayatollah's State-Sponsored Aggression and Militancy (QASSAM) Act (H.R. 4258). This requires the United States to seize property that is at least 20 percent owned by Iran's Revolutionary Guard Corps (IRGC) and located in the United States or controlled by a U.S. person, "regardless of whether the entity itself is included on the list of specially designated nationals and blocked persons maintained by the Department of the Treasury Office of Foreign Assets Control."[151]

December 18, 2015. Islamic Revolutionary Guard Corps Sanctions Implementation and Review Act (H.R. 4312). This provides amendments to the Iran Threat Reduction and Syrian Human Rights Act of 2012. The bill requires the use of presidential powers to "block and prohibit all transactions in property and property interests of a foreign person" that knowingly works with the IRGC or other sanctioned persons if that property is in the United States or comes under its control.[152]

April 19, 2016. United States Financial System Protection Act of 2016 (H.R. 4992). This bill prohibits the transfer of funds to or from Iran that result in "direct or indirect" benefits for Iranians or the Iranian government. It also bars Iran from U.S. financial institutions and conducting transactions in U.S. dollars.[153]

April 28, 2016. No 2H2O from Iran Act (H.R. 5119). The bill prohibits the use of U.S. funds from a "federal department or agency for any fiscal year" to finance or purchase Iranian heavy water.[154]

July 6, 2016. Iran Accountability Act of 2016 (H.R. 5631). The bill places sanctions on the IRGC, Iran's president and supreme leader, and "financial institutions that engage in certain transactions on behalf of persons involved in human rights abuses or that export sensitive technology to Iran." It also aims to punish Iran for its "support of terrorism and money laundering and human rights abuses."[155]

November 14, 2016. Iran Sanctions Extension Act (H.R. 6297). This bill renews the 1996 Iran Sanctions Act for another decade, which places sanctions on Iran's banking, defense, and energy sectors. The bill was seen by the Obama administration as unnecessary and with potential to impact the nuclear accord. Nevertheless, it became law without President Obama's signature on December 15, 2016.[156] The proponents of the bill, such as Chairman of the Senate Foreign Relations Committee Bob Corker (R-TN), claimed that "extending the Iran Sanctions Act . . . ensures President-elect Trump and his administration have the tools necessary to push back against the regime's hostile actions." Iranian Foreign Minister Javad Zarif emphasized, "To the world community, the extension of sanctions against Iran shows the unreliability of the American government."[157]

March 23, 2017. Iran Ballistic Missiles and International Sanctions Enforcement Act (H.R. 1698). This bill aims to prevent Iran from developing nuclear-capable ballistic missiles by placing sanctions on Iranian government agencies and individuals involved in ballistic missile development. It further stipulates the sanctioning of foreign entities and individuals assisting Iran in acquiring and developing such ballistic missiles.[158]

March 23, 2017. Countering Iran's Destabilizing Activities Act of 2017 (S. 722). This bill requires key national security and policy institutions, such as the Departments of State, Defense, and Treasury and the Director of National Intelligence, to submit in two-year intervals a report on their strategy to curtail Iran's conventional and asymmetric activities in the Middle East and beyond. It further places sanctions against persons responsible for "extrajudicial killings, torture, or other gross violations of internationally recognized human rights that are committed against certain individuals in Iran."[159]

January 9, 2018. Iran Human Rights and Hostage-Taking Accountability Act (H.R. 4766). The bill primarily seeks to impose additional sanctions with respect to serious human rights abuses of the Iranian government. It also reaffirms the U.S. policy of "not to pay ransom for the purpose of securing the release of United States citizens or legal permanent resident aliens taken hostage abroad." In this vein, the bill requires the U.S. Secretary of State to submit a report detailing the strategy to mitigate the Iranian government's ability to engage in the hostage-taking of U.S. citizens.[160]

A reduction in sanctions has been a major condition for Iran to adhere to the nuclear accord. These new sanctions, in conjunction with Trump's decision to scrap the deal, have created new tensions and obstruct full implementation of the JCPOA. Zarif, who was instrumental in securing the Iran accord, showed frustration with such U.S. actions, stating at an Oslo conference in June 2016 that "the U.S. has effectively removed sanctions only on paper, and the European companies would fear any opening of trade with Iran lest the U.S. would punish them in the name of violating sanctions," adding, "the Iranian people wait to see the impact of removal of sanctions in practice."[161]

In yet another negative development, a ruling by the U.S. Supreme Court on April 20, 2016, paved the way for $2 billion of Iranian frozen assets in the United States to be distributed to "victims of terrorist attacks backed by Iran." This unprecedented move came as a result of Congress passing a law in 2012 allowing the courts to seize and distribute Iran's frozen assets to plaintiffs.[162] This seizure was seen as violating the separation of power between U.S. domestic legislation and its infringement on international treaties. The Iranian response has been direct, with Iranian foreign ministry spokesman Hossein Jaberi Ansari stating that the "ruling has mocked [international] law and amounts to appropriation of the Islamic Republic of Iran's property in the US."[163]

Coercive actions by the U.S. Congress and Supreme Court are some of the underlying reasons for the delay in the return of around $55 billion worth of frozen Iranian assets.[164] The bulk of those assets originated from revenue made by Iran's sale of oil and gas during the sanctions era to a limited number of countries, including South Korea, Japan, China, and India. Those revenues were, in turn, held in those respective countries due to U.S. sanctions prohibiting the transfer of funds.[165]

The Obama administration, while a proponent of the nuclear deal, was also implicit in unproductive acts toward Iran. The administration went ahead with the implementation of changes under the Visa Waiver Program Improvement and Terrorist Travel Prevention Act of 2015 passed by Congress (H.R. 158). The Visa Waiver Program (VWP) provides citizens of select countries (all highly developed economies, such as most members of the European Union, Australia, New Zealand, Japan, and South Korea) to travel to the United States for up to 90 days without having to obtain a visa. Under this law, changes to the VWP "bars nationals of Iran, Iraq, Sudan, and Syria, as well as nationals of VWP countries who have traveled to these countries in the past five years, from visa-free entry to the United States."[166] From the Iranian point of view, this law would discourage economic activity in the country and serve as another obstacle for foreign investment and engagement with Iran. This restriction comes as there are still U.S.-based unilateral sanctions on the Iranian banking system related to other issues (Iran's ballistic missile program and human rights) that, to date, have caused other international banks to hesitate to facilitate financial transactions and activities in the Iranian market.

Challenges to the JCPOA are not limited to the actions or rhetoric of President Donald Trump's administration and Congress. There are also critics of the JCPOA within Iran: the conservative camp in the Iranian government; elements within the Islamic Republic Revolutionary Guard (IRGC); and Supreme Leader Ayatollah Khamenei's deep-rooted suspicion of the United States. The actions of the United States, just outlined, have eroded the high expectations that the JCPOA would improve Iran's economy and integration into the global financial system.

The May 19, 2017, Iranian presidential elections were seen as a public mandate on the performance of incumbent President Rouhani in reviving the ailing economy, improving ties with the world, and sustaining the nuclear accord. His main challenger was Ebrahim Raisi, the former hardline prosecutor who leads one of the wealthiest religious foundations in the country. As a conservative candidate, Raisi campaigned on fighting rampant corruption and advocated for an isolationist policy to tackle economic problems.[167] While he endorsed the nuclear accord, Raisi remains suspicious of the West and insists that the agreement has done little to improve the lives of the impoverished population. His main base of support comes from a coalition of religiously conservative groups that includes the powerful IRGC.

While the vetting process by the powerful Guardian Council ensures all presidential candidates are devoted to the principles of the Islamic Republic, the elections in Iran have historically been difficult to predict, as candidates have a wide range of political leanings. The polls had indicated a tight race, but they also revealed that a substantial number of voters were undecided. Ultimately, a high turnout on election day—more than 70 percent of Iran's 56 million eligible voters cast ballots—gave Rouhani a landslide victory with 57 percent of the votes, defeating his chief opponent, Raisi, who received 38.5 percent.[168] One crucial factor that carried Rouhani to a landslide victory was the endorsement from key figures in the reformist movement, such as former President Khatami and leaders of the Green Movement who are currently under house arrest—former Speaker of Parliament Karrubi and former Prime Minister Mousavi.

President Rouhani's first term focused on two key deliverables: resolving the dispute over Iran's nuclear program and revamping the economy. These issues were largely intertwined as the waning economy not only faced fiscal and monetary challenges but also was under the most comprehensive international sanctions. Rouhani managed to achieve the historic 2015 nuclear accord with world powers through diplomacy that removed key international sanctions. Early signs of a rebound for the Iranian economy were shattered with the U.S. withdrawal from the nuclear accord and imposition of draconian sanctions.

There is no doubt, however, that the Iran nuclear accord delivered on its core objectives: effectively and verifiably ensuring Iran's nuclear program remains peaceful, while reducing sanctions and reviving the Iranian economy. Since the historic Iran nuclear accord went into effect in January 2016 until the U.S.

withdrawal from the deal in May 2018, there had been positive tangible outcomes for the Iranian economy: oil production returned to pre-sanction levels of 3.85 million barrels per day, with oil exports doubling to 2.3 million barrels; $11 billion worth of foreign direct investment was poured into Iran—the highest annual level in over two decades; there was a 42 percent increase in trade with the EU (Iran's largest trading partner in the pre-sanction era); and inflation decreased from 45 percent in 2013 to 9 percent by 2018. According to the International Monetary Fund (IMF), the Iranian economy grew 12.5 percent and 3.7 percent in 2016 and 2017, respectively, compared to −1.6 percent prior to the nuclear accord in 2015.[169] Iran also secured major business deals worth billions of dollars throughout the world and gained access to $55 billion in frozen assets. Iran even managed to sign the largest U.S.–Iran business deal since the 1979 revolution, with Boeing, valued at $16.7 billion, to provide eighty civilian planes (even though this achievement crumbled following U.S. withdrawal from the JCPOA in May 2018).[170]

These gains, however, have been overshadowed by continuing U.S. financial sanctions on Iran and the reinstatement of U.S. nuclear-related sanctions as a result of the United States leaving the nuclear deal. Such actions have made international firms hesitant to do business with the second largest economy in the Middle East. Their concern is not unwarranted; since 2004, the United States has levied more than $15 billion in fines to firms for violating sanctions. The tough stance of the Trump administration and Congress on Iran has also renewed fears that increasing sanctions will hamper international efforts to do business with Iran.[171] The Iranian business environment also suffers from lack of transparency, high levels of corruption, and outdated financial instruments.[172] The economic gains from the nuclear deal have also overwhelmingly benefitted large government enterprises, while little has trickled-down to the average Iranian in terms of jobs, salaries, and the prices of basic goods.

Even prior to the complete U.S. withdrawal from the deal, Ayatollah Khamenei did not hold back his dissatisfaction with the lack of U.S. commitment to adhere to the provisions within the JCPOA. In his March 21, 2016, Nowruz (Persian New Year) speech, Khamenei stated, "The Americans have said that they would lift sanctions on paper, but through other methods, they are ensuring the result of sanctions relief will not materialize." He went on to add:

> Today, in all Western countries and in all those countries that are under their influence, our banking transactions have been blocked. We have a problem bringing our wealth—which has been kept in their banks—back to the country. We have a problem conducting different financial transactions that require the assistance of banks. . . . The US Department of the Treasury acts in a way . . . that big companies, agencies and banks do not dare to approach the Islamic Republic and have business transactions with it.[173]

While the Iranian currency, the rial, has continued to weaken against the U.S. dollar, since the JCPOA, the U.S. withdrawal in May 2018 triggered a rapid depreciation of the currency against the U.S. dollar as Iranians braced themselves for the return of crippling sanctions. The rial's value following Trump's decision plummeted by 40 percent on the unofficial market against the U.S. dollar, threatening to reverse the gains in controlling the inflation rate, increasing the cost of imported goods, damaging the standard of living for millions of Iranians, and limiting the ability of Iranians to travel abroad. Making matters worse was the IMF report on a record capital flight of more than $27 billion from Iran in 2017.[174] The unemployment rate has not faired well either and has been on the rise, reaching 13.1 percent in 2017 and 12.43 percent in 2016, compared to 11.6 percent prior to the agreement in 2015. According to a poll conducted by the Center for International and Security Studies at the University of Maryland, only 46 percent of Iranians believe their economy has improved since the Iran Nuclear Accord.[175] The convergence of factors, among them the sliding value of the rial, soaring prices, and the systematic corruption and mismanagement of the economy fused with the uncertainty of looming U.S. sanctions, contributed to public outcry across the country and even among government loyalists in the Tehran bazaar. While those protests were met with stern reaction from the authorities, it is an indication of things to come as the economic hardship worsens in the foreseeable future.[176] Adding insult to injury and remaining hopeful that Iranian leaders will buckle under mounting economic pressure, President Trump at a press conference following a NATO leaders summit in Brussels on July 12, 2018, stated, "I know they're having a lot of problems and their economy is collapsing. But I will tell you this: at a certain point they're going to call me, they're going to say 'Let's make a deal.' They're feeling a lot of pain right now."[177]

The Trump administration's coercive policy of isolating Iran and strong-arming other countries to fall in line is underpinned by threats of barring companies dealing with Iran from the U.S. economy and financial system. The United States has aggressively sought major Iranian trading partners such as Japan, South Korea, India, and the EU to drastically scale back their business and specifically oil imports by the time U.S. unilateral sanctions are fully implemented in November 2018 or face punitive sanctions. The U.S. Special Representative for Iran and Senior Policy Advisor to Secretary of State Brian Hook stated succinctly that the U.S. position is "to increase pressure on the Iranian regime by reducing to zero its revenue on crude-oil sales," adding that the United States will not "grant waivers or licenses" to countries or companies wishing to continue their business operations in Iran and that they "will be subject to the same sanctions that everybody else is if they engage in those sectors of the economy."[178] To mitigate the impact of less Iranian crude oil in the international market, President Trump, to the dismay of Iran, received assurances from Saudi Arabia's King Salman, who agreed to supplement the shortfall by injecting an additional two million barrels per day.[179]

These factors have emboldened hardliners in Iran, who allege that the Rouhani administration has conceded too much in the negotiations and has little to show in return—some going as far as calling for Rouhani's resignation or impeachment over his handling of the economy and foreign policy. The intensifying political infighting has prompted the Iranian Supreme Leader Ayatollah Khamenei to step in and call for unity "to overcome problems and defeat the U.S. conspiracy [for regime change]," adding "the government's economic team is the axis of all activity in the country, calling all the bodies to coordinate with it." This was a direct call to hardline conservatives to tone down their criticism of the Rouhani administration in anticipation of looming sanctions.[180]

Rouhani's government will continue to face daunting domestic and international challenges. Chief among them will be to mitigate the socioeconomic and political implications of the U.S. withdrawal from the JCPOA, while accelerating efforts to make necessary adjustments to the Iranian economic system and tackle the systematic corruption that plagues it. His administration will also have to find innovative ways to reintegrate the Iranian economy into the global system while facing the wrath of U.S. unilateral sanctions.

In the international arena, Rouhani will also have a lot on his plate: rampant regional instability, the fight against terrorism, heightened rivalry with neighboring Saudi Arabia, and a hawkish government in Washington bent on reversing Obama-era Iran engagement policy along with dismantling the nuclear accord. The foreign policy priorities for the Rouhani administration will not only aim to cement relations with key European and Asian trading partners to counter the U.S. sanctions, but also mend relations with Persian Gulf Arab states. This will require considerable political will and confidence-building measures on both sides of the Persian Gulf as the current zero-sum game will only lead to further regional instability fought through proxy wars in Syria, Iraq, and Yemen with the possibility of spilling over to other fragile states.

Notes

1 "United Nations Security Council," accessed September 1, 2016, www.un.org/en/sc/.

2 "UN Security Council Resolutions on Iran," Arms Control Association, accessed September 1, 2016, www.armscontrol.org/factsheets/Security-Council-Resolutions-on-Iran.

3 "Treaty on the Non-Proliferation of Nuclear Weapons (NPT), Treaties & Regimes," NTI, accessed September 1, 2016, www.nti.org/learn/treaties-and-regimes/treaty-on-the-non-proliferation-of-nuclear-weapons/.

4 "Global Nuclear Weapons: Downsizing but Modernizing," SIPRI, accessed February 7, 2017, www.sipri.org/media/press-release/2016/global-nuclear-weapons-downsizing-modernizing.

5 Richard Norton-Taylor, "Replacing Trident Will Cost at Least £205bn, Campaigners Say," *The Guardian*, May 11, 2016, sec. UK News, www.theguardian.com/uk-news/2016/may/12/replacing-trident-will-cost-at-least-205-billion-campaign-for-nuclear-disarmament.

6 "Nuclear Modernization, Arms Control, and U.S.-Russia Relations," Brookings Institution, October 25, 2016, www.brookings.edu/research/nuclear-modernization-arms-control-and-u-s-russia-relations/.

7 Hans M. Kristensen, "After Seven Years of Implementation, New START Treaty Enters into Effect," Federation of American Scientists, February 8, 2018, https://fas.org/blogs/security/2018/02/newstart-ineffect/.

8 Hans M. Kristensen and Robert S. Norris, "Slowing Nuclear Weapon Reductions and Endless Nuclear Weapon Modernizations: A Challenge to the NPT," *Bulletin of the Atomic Scientists* 70, no. 4 (July 1, 2014): 94–107, doi:10.1177/0096340214540062.

9 Jon Wolfsthal, "The US Trillion Dollar Nuclear Triad," James Martin Center for Nonproliferation Studies, January 7, 2014, www.nonproliferation.org/us-trillion-dollar-nuclear-triad/.
10 "Remarks by President Barack Obama in Prague as Delivered," White House, April 5, 2009, www.whitehouse.gov/the-press-office/remarks-president-barack-obama-prague-delivered.
11 Max Fisher, "Trump's Nuclear Weapons Tweet, Translated and Explained," *New York Times*, December 22, 2016, www.nytimes.com/interactive/2016/12/22/world/americas/trump-nuclear-tweet.html.
12 Avner Cohen, "Israel and the Bomb," *New York Times*, accessed March 26, 2018, https://archive.nytimes.com/www.nytimes.com/books/first/c/cohen-israel.html.
13 "Israel's 'Nuclear Ambiguity' Policy," Reut Institute, June 15, 2009, http://reut-institute.org/en/Publication.aspx?PublicationId=3655.
14 "From the Archive: The Secrets of Israel's Nuclear Arsenal Revealed," *Sunday Times*, October 5, 1986, www.thesundaytimes.co.uk/sto/news/world_news/article237419.ece.
15 Edwin S. Townsley and Clarence A. Robinson, "Critical Technological Assessment in Israel and NATO Nations," Office of the U.S. Under Secretary of Defense, April 1987, http://irmep.org/cfp/DoD/071987_CTAIIANN.pdf.
16 Julian Borger, "The Truth About Israel's Secret Nuclear Arsenal," *The Guardian*, January 15, 2014, sec. World News, www.theguardian.com/world/2014/jan/15/truth-israels-secret-nuclear-arsenal. For further reading, see: Warner D. Farr, "Israel's Nuclear Weapons," USAF Counterproliferation Center, Future Warfare Series, Counterproliferation Paper, no. 2, September 1999, https://fas.org/nuke/guide/israel/nuke/farr.htm.
17 Farr, "Israel's Nuclear Weapons."
18 "Israeli Nuclear Capabilities," IAEA, September 3, 2010, www.iaea.org/About/Policy/GC/GC54/GC54Documents/English/gc54-14_en.pdf.
19 Ibid.
20 Ibid.
21 "Israel Says Won't Attend WMD-Free Middle East Meeting, Analysis," NTI, accessed September 1, 2016, www.nti.org/gsn/article/israel-rules-out-participation-wmd-free-middle-east-meeting/.
22 "Israel Rejects UN Call for Nuclear Transparency," *RT International*, December 5, 2012, www.rt.com/news/israel-rejects-un-nuclear-transparency-298/.
23 Ibid.
24 Ibid.
25 Barak Ravid, "Netanyahu: Israel Is Not Bound by NPT Resolution," *Haaretz*, May 29, 2010, www.haaretz.com/israel-news/netanyahu-israel-is-not-bound-by-npt-resolution-1.292891.
26 Ran Marom, "Israel's Position on Non-Proliferation," Hebrew University of Jerusalem Policy Studies, no. 16, June 1986, www.iaea.org/inis/collection/NCLCollectionStore/_Public/18/058/18058251.pdf.
27 "International Recognition of Israel," accessed March 26, 2018, www.jewishvirtuallibrary.org/international-recognition-of-israel.
28 "Full Transcript: Kerry Blasts Israeli Government, Presents Six Points of Future Peace Deal," *Haaretz*, December 28, 2016, www.haaretz.com/israel-news/criticizing-netanyahu-warning-against-one-state-kerry-s-full-speech-1.5479380.
29 "US Condemns Israel's Plan to Expand West Bank Settlement Bloc," *The Times of Israel*, accessed September 1, 2016, www.timesofisrael.com/us-condemns-israels-plan-to-expand-west-bank-settlement-bloc/.
30 Ray Sanchez, "Israel and Its Neighbors: Decades of War," *CNN*, August 13, 2014, www.cnn.com/interactive/2014/08/world/israel-neighbors/index.html.

31 "Israel's Diplomatic Missions Abroad: Status of Relations," Israel Ministry of Foreign Affairs, accessed September 1, 2016, http://mfa.gov.il/MFA/AboutTheMinistry/Pages/Israel-s%20Diplomatic%20Missions%20Abroad.aspx.
32 Gawdat Bahgat, "Israel and Nuclear Proliferation in the Middle East," *Middle East Policy Council* 13, no. 2 (2006), www.mepc.org/journal/israel-and-nuclear-proliferation-middle-east.
33 For more details on US-Israel special relationship, see: "The Israeli–US Special Relationship," Reut Institute, May 18, 2009, http://reut-institute.org/en/Publication.aspx?PublicationId=3622.
34 For further reading on the influence of the Israel lobby on U.S. foreign policy, see: John J. Mearsheimer and Stephen M. Walt, "The Israel Lobby and U.S. Foreign Policy," *Middle East Policy Council* 85, no. 5 (2006): 175, https://doi.org/10.2307/20032117.
35 Avner Cohen, "Israel Crosses the Threshold," National Security Archive, April 28, 2006, https://nsarchive2.gwu.edu//NSAEBB/NSAEBB189/index.htm.
36 Ibid.
37 Jim Zanotti et al., "Israel: Possible Military Strike Against Iran's Nuclear Facilities," Congressional Research Service, September 28, 2012, 61.
38 "Israeli PM Threatens to Strike Iran," *Al Jazeera*, English, July 17, 2013, www.aljazeera.com/news/middleeast/2013/07/2013714214528446397.html.
39 Steve Linde, "Peres Bombshell: I Stopped an Israeli Strike on Iran," *Jerusalem Post*, September 30, 2016, www.jpost.com/Israel-News/Politics-And-Diplomacy/Peres-bombshell-I-stopped-an-Israeli-strike-on-Iran-469112.
40 Scott Peterson, "Imminent Iran Nuclear Threat? A Timeline of Warnings Since 1979," *Christian Science Monitor*, November 8, 2011, www.csmonitor.com/World/Middle-East/2011/1108/Imminent-Iran-nuclear-threat-A-timeline-of-warnings-since-1979/Israel-paints-Iran-as-Enemy-No.-1-1992.
41 Justin Elliott, "Israel on Iran: So Wrong for so Long," *Salon*, December 5, 2010, www.salon.com/2010/12/05/israeli_predictions_iranian_nukes/.
42 Murtaza Hussain, "Benjamin Netanyahu's Long History of Crying Wolf About Iran's Nuclear Weapons," *The Intercept*, March 2, 2015, https://theintercept.com/2015/03/02/brief-history-netanyahu-crying-wolf-iranian-nuclear-bomb/.
43 Ibid.
44 Paul Richter, "Israel Leader Demands 'Red Line' to Stop Iran Nuclear Program," *Los Angeles Times*, September 27, 2012, http://latimesblogs.latimes.com/world_now/2012/09/israel-leader-demands-red-line-to-stop-iran-nuclear-program.html.
45 "Netanyahu Calls for US Action to Check Iran Nuclear Program," *Big News Network*, July 16, 2013, www.bignewsnetwork.com/news/215845813/netanyahu-calls-for-us-action-to-check-iran-nuclear-program.
46 "UN Closes File on Iran's Past Nuclear Work," The Iran Primer, December 15, 2015, http://iranprimer.usip.org/blog/2015/dec/15/un-closes-file-iran%E2%80%99s-past-nuclear-work.
47 Krishnadev Calamur, "What Netanyahu Did and Didn't Say About Iran's Nuclear Program," *The Atlantic*, April 30, 2018, www.theatlantic.com/international/archive/2018/04/netanyahu-iran-nuclear-program/559295/.
48 David M. Halbfinger, David E. Sanger, and Ronen Bergman, "Israel Says Secret Files Detail Iran's Nuclear Subterfuge," *New York Times*, July 16, 2018, sec. World, www.nytimes.com/2018/04/30/world/middleeast/israel-iran-nuclear-netanyahu.html.
49 "UN Closes File on Iran's Past Nuclear Work."
50 "'Israel and the Bomb': Documents: Miscellaneous Hebrew," accessed September 1, 2016, http://nsarchive.gwu.edu/israel/documents/hebrew/index.html.
51 David Friedman et al., "WMD No-First-Use in the Middle East: A Way to Move Forward in 2012?" *Bulletin of the Atomic Scientists* (February 7, 2011), http://thebulletin.org/wmd-no-first-use-middle-east-way-move-forward-2012.

52 "The World from Berlin: 'Helping Israel Defend Itself Is Germany's Duty'," *Spiegel*, June 5, 2012, www.spiegel.de/international/world/german-press-supports-sale-of-submarines-to-israel-a-837093.html.
53 Robert S. Norris, "Israeli Nuclear Forces, 2002," *Bulletin of the Atomic Scientists* 58, no. 5 (September 2002): 73–75.
54 Louis René Beres, *Surviving Amid Chaos: Israel's Nuclear Strategy* (Lanham, US: Rowman & Littlefield Publishers, April 2016): 294.
55 Borger, "The Truth About Israel's Secret Nuclear Arsenal."
56 Gitty M. Amini, "Weapons of Mass Destruction in the Middle East," NTI, February 1, 2003, accessed March 27, 2018, www.nti.org/analysis/articles/weapons-mass-destruction-middle-east/.
57 David Makovsky, "The Silent Strike," *The New Yorker*, September 17, 2012, www.newyorker.com/magazine/2012/09/17/the-silent-strike.
58 "Israel," NTI, accessed September 1, 2016, www.nti.org/learn/countries/israel/biological/.
59 Mark Fitzpatrick, "High Time for Israel to Adhere to the Chemical Weapons Convention," International Institute for Strategic Studies (IISS), accessed September 1, 2016, www.iiss.org/en/politics%20and%20strategy/blogsections/2013-98d0/september-2013-62a6/high-time-8110.
60 Gerald Steinberg, "The Begin Doctrine at 25," *Jerusalem Post*, June 4, 2006, www.jpost.com/Features/The-Begin-Doctrine-at-25.
61 "1981: Israel Bombs Baghdad Nuclear Reactor," *BBC News*, accessed September 1, 2016, http://news.bbc.co.uk/onthisday/hi/dates/stories/june/7/newsid_3014000/3014623.stm.
62 "Israeli and Iraqi Statements on Raid on Nuclear Plant," *New York Times*, June 9, 1981, www.nytimes.com/1981/06/09/world/israeli-and-iraqi-statements-on-raid-on-nuclear-plant.html.
63 Daveed Gartenstein-Ross, "The Attack on Syria's Al-Kibar Nuclear Facility," Jewish Policy Center, February 28, 2009, www.jewishpolicycenter.org/2009/02/28/the-attack-on-syrias-al-kibar-nuclear-facility/.
64 Robert Windrem and Richard Engel, "Israel Teams with Terror Group to Kill Iran's Nuclear Scientists, U.S. Officials Tell NBC News," *NBC News*, accessed September 1, 2016, http://rockcenter.nbcnews.com/_news/2012/02/09/10354553-israel-teams-with-terror-group-to-kill-irans-nuclear-scientists-us-officials-tell-nbc-news.
65 David E. Sanger, "Obama Ordered Wave of Cyberattacks Against Iran," *New York Times*, June 1, 2012, www.nytimes.com/2012/06/01/world/middleeast/obama-ordered-wave-of-cyberattacks-against-iran.html.
66 Ibid.
67 Kenneth Waltz, "Why Iran Should Get the Bomb," *Foreign Affairs*, January 17, 2016, www.foreignaffairs.com/articles/iran/2012-06-15/why-iran-should-get-bomb.
68 Matthew Weaver and Tom McCarthy, "Syria Crisis: Ban Ki-Moon Says Sarin Gas Chemical Attack a 'War Crime'—As It Happened," *The Guardian*, September 16, 2013, sec. World News, www.theguardian.com/world/2013/sep/16/un-inspectors-submit-syria-chemical-weapons-report-live.
69 "Putin, Obama Discussed Syria Arms Control Idea Last Week-Kremlin," *Reuters*, September 10, 2013, www.reuters.com/article/syria-crisis-russia-usa-idUSL5N0H61XG20130910.
70 "Framework for Elimination of Syrian Chemical Weapons," Press Release | Media Note, U.S. Department of State, September 14, 2013, www.state.gov/r/pa/prs/ps/2013/09/214247.htm.
71 "Security Council Requires Scheduled Destruction of Syria's Chemical Weapons, Unanimously Adopting Resolution 2118 (2013)," United Nations, accessed September 1, 2016, www.un.org/press/en/2013/sc11135.doc.htm.
72 "Chemical Weapons: Frequently Asked Questions," Arms Control Association, accessed September 1, 2016, www.armscontrol.org/factsheets/Chemical-Weapons-Frequently-Asked-Questions.

73 "Chemical Weapons Watchdog Says Syria Cooperating with Mission," *VOA*, accessed September 1, 2016, www.voanews.com/a/syria-cooperation-with-chemical-weapons-mission/1766027.html.
74 "UN News—Removal of Syria's Chemical Weapons Material Complete, Announces OPCW-UN Mission," *UN News*, Service Section, June 23, 2014, www.un.org/apps/news/story.asp?NewsID=48103#.V8fdZJMrKRt.
75 "Timeline of Syrian Chemical Weapons Activity, 2012–2017," Arms Control Association, April 2017, www.armscontrol.org/factsheets/Timeline-of-Syrian-Chemical-Weapons-Activity.
76 Ibid.
77 "United Nations Security Council Resolution 2209," United Nations Security Council, March 6, 2015, www.un.org/ga/search/view_doc.asp?symbol=S/RES/2209%20(2015).
78 "Iraq," NTI, accessed March 27, 2018, www.nti.org/learn/countries/iraq/.
79 Jeffrey Richelson, "Iraq and Weapons of Mass Destruction," The National Security Archive, February 11, 2004, https://nsarchive2.gwu.edu/NSAEBB/NSAEBB80/#1.
80 "Regime Strategic Intent," Central Intelligence Agency, April 22, 2007, www.cia.gov/library/reports/general-reports-1/iraq_wmd_2004/chap1.html.
81 "Saddam Hussein's Defiance of United Nations Resolutions," White House, accessed March 27, 2018, https://georgewbush-whitehouse.archives.gov/infocus/iraq/decade/sect2.html.
82 "Timeline: Iraq Weapons Inspections," *BBC News*, November 18, 2002, http://news.bbc.co.uk/2/hi/middle_east/2167933.stm.
83 "Iraq: A Chronology of UN Inspections," Arms Control Association, October 1, 2002, www.armscontrol.org/act/2002_10/iraqspecialoct02.
84 Amini, "Weapons of Mass Destruction in the Middle East."
85 "UNSCOM Main Achievements," UNSCOM, March 1998, www.un.org/Depts/unscom/Achievements/achievements.html.
86 Amini, "Weapons of Mass Destruction in the Middle East."
87 "Iraq."
88 "Regime Strategy and WMD Timeline Events," Central Intelligence Agency, April 22, 2007, www.cia.gov/library/reports/general-reports-1/iraq_wmd_2004/WMD_Timeline_Events.html.
89 "Iraq: Chronology of Main Events," United Nations, December 1999, www.un.org/Depts/unscom/Chronology/chronologyframe.htm.
90 "Iraq."
91 "Osiraq," Federation of American Scientists, October 9, 2000, https://fas.org.
92 Amini, "Weapons of Mass Destruction in the Middle East."
93 "Iraq."
94 "Key Findings of Iraq Survey Group (ISG)," Central Intelligence Agency, April 22, 2007, www.cia.gov/library/reports/general-reports-1/iraq_wmd_2004/chap4.html.
95 "Transcript: President Clinton Explains Iraq Strike," *CNN*, December 16, 1998, http://edition.cnn.com/ALLPOLITICS/stories/1998/12/16/transcripts/clinton.html.
96 "Iraq: A Chronology of UN Inspections."
97 "President Delivers State of the Union Address," White House, January 29, 2002, https://georgewbush-whitehouse.archives.gov/news/releases/2002/01/20020129-11.html.
98 Wright Bryan, "Iraq WMD Timeline: How the Mystery Unraveled," *NPR*, November 15, 2005, www.npr.org/templates/story/story.php?storyId=4996218.
99 United Nations, November 8, 2002, www.un.org/press/en/2002/SC7564.doc.htm.
100 Bryan, "Iraq WMD Timeline: How the Mystery Unraveled."
101 "Transcript of ElBaradei's U.N. Presentation," *CNN*, March 7, 2003, http://edition.cnn.com/2003/US/03/07/sprj.irq.un.transcript.elbaradei/.

102 "Key Findings of Iraq Survey Group (ISG)."
103 Bryan, "Iraq WMD Timeline: How the Mystery Unraveled."
104 Noah Feldman, "Islam, Terror and the Second Nuclear Age," *New York Times*, October 29, 2006, www.nytimes.com/2006/10/29/magazine/29islam.html.
105 "Illicit Trafficking of Nuclear and Other Radioactive Material: The Legislative Response: Arms Control and Disarmament/National Implementation Measures Programs," VERTIC, April 2012, www.vertic.org/media/assets/Publications/ITR_WEB.pdf.
106 "President's Findings, International Conference on Illicit Nuclear Trafficking: Collective Experience and the Way Forward," IAEA, November 22, 2007, http://www-pub.iaea.org/MTCD/publications/PDF/Pub1316_web.pdf.
107 Rolf Mowatt-Larssen, "Al Qaeda's Religious Justification of Nuclear Terrorism," Belfer Center for Science and International Affairs at Harvard Kennedy School, n.d., 11/2010.
108 Brian Reeves, "The Shifting Nature of Threats to Israel in Its Neighborhood," Brookings Institution, May 2, 2016, www.brookings.edu/blog/markaz/2016/05/02/the-shifting-nature-of-threats-to-israel-in-its-neighborhood/.
109 "ISIL/Da'esh and 'Non-Conventional' Weapons of Terror," European Parliament, December 2015, www.europarl.europa.eu/RegData/etudes/BRIE/2015/572806/EPRS_BRI(2015)572806_EN.pdf.
110 Associated Press, "Islamic State Used Chemical Weapons Against Peshmerga, Kurds Say," *The Guardian*, March 14, 2015, sec. World News, www.theguardian.com/world/2015/mar/14/islamic-state-isis-used-chemical-weapons-peshmerga-kurds.
111 "Saudi Arabia May Need Nuclear Weapons to Fend Off Threat from Iran and Israel, Says Former Intelligence Chief," *Daily Mail* Online, December 6, 2011, www.dailymail.co.uk/news/article-2070704/Saudi-Arabia-need-nuclear-weapons-fend-threat-Iran-Israel-says-prince.html.
112 Hillary Mann Leverett and Flynt Leverett, "Iran Is No Existential Threat," *Foreign Policy*, December 4, 2009, https://foreignpolicy.com/2009/12/04/iran-is-no-existential-threat/.
113 Semira N. Nikou, "Timeline of Iran's Nuclear Activities," The Iran Primer, accessed September 1, 2016, http://iranprimer.usip.org/resource/timeline-irans-nuclear-activities.
114 Seyed Hossein Mousavian, *The Iranian Nuclear Crisis: A Memoir* (Washington, DC Carnegie Endowment, June 2012), 48. "In 1976, the German contractor Kraftwerk Union agreed both to commission the Bushehr power plants and to supply them with fuel for thirty years. Following the Islamic Revolution, the contractor suspended the project and the original payment of 5.7 billion Deutsche Marks was never returned."
115 "Bushehr Nuclear Power Plant (BNPP)," NTI, accessed September 1, 2016, www.nti.org/learn/facilities/184/.
116 Nikou, "Timeline of Iran's Nuclear Activities."
117 "Communication Dated 26 November 2004 Received from the Permanent Representatives of France, Germany, the Islamic Republic of Iran and the United Kingdom Concerning the Agreement Signed in Paris on 15 November 2004," IAEA, November 15, 2004.
118 "NPT Treaty," United Nations, accessed September 1, 2016, www.un.org/en/conf/npt/2005/npttreaty.html.
119 George P. Shultz and Henry A. Kissinger, "Kissinger and Shultz: What a Final Iran Deal Must Do," *Wall Street Journal*, December 2, 2013, sec. Opinion, www.wsj.com/news/articles/SB10001424052702304747004579228110944819396.
120 Suzanne Maloney, "President Obama Urges Saban Forum: Don't Underestimate Political Shift in Iran," Brookings Institution, November 30, 2001, www.brookings.

edu/blog/markaz/2013/12/08/president-obama-urges-saban-forum-dont-underestimate-political-shift-in-iran/.

121 "Middle East Security and Non-Proliferation," IISS, accessed September 1, 2016, www.iiss.org/en/events/manama%20dialogue/archive/manama-dialogue-2013-4e92/plenary-5-fbc6/samore-3140.

122 Steve Holland, "Obama Says Syria Deal Could Offer Lesson for Iran Talks," *Reuters*, September 15, 2013, www.reuters.com/article/us-syria-crisis-usa-idUSBRE98D09C20130915.

123 Seyed Hossein Mousavian, "Solution to Iranian Nuclear Dossier & Its Role on the Middle East Zone Free of Weapons of Mass Destruction (MEWMDFZ)," European University Institute, Robert Schuman Centre for Advanced Studies 2013/22, October 2013.

124 David Stout, "Russia, Iran Hail Syria's Move to Sign Weapons Pact," *Time*, accessed September 1, 2016, http://world.time.com/2013/09/13/russia-iran-hail-syrias-move-to-sign-weapons-pact/.

125 Holland, "Obama Says Syria Deal Could Offer Lesson for Iran Talks."

126 "Transcript of Remarks Made by Obama and Netanyahu After Bilateral Meeting," *Haaretz*, September 30, 2013, www.haaretz.com/what-they-said-transcripts-of-obama-bibi-remarks-1.5342452.

127 Elad Benari, "Netanyahu to Obama: Iran Must Take Meaningful Actions," *Arutz Sheva*, January 10, 2013, www.israelnationalnews.com/News/News.aspx/172367.

128 Scott Neuman, "Iran's President Wished Jews 'A Blessed Rosh Hashanah' Or Did He?" *NPR*, September 5, 2013, www.npr.org/sections/thetwo-way/2013/09/05/219309978/iran-s-president-tweeted-jews-a-happy-rosh-hashanah-or-did-he.

129 Daniel Kurtzer, Seyed Hossein Mousavian, and Thomas Pickering, "Iran and the Nuclear Agreement: Trust but Verify," *Al-Monitor*, December 7, 2013, www.al-monitor.com/pulse/originals/2013/12/trust-verify-iran-agreement.html.

130 Ben Caspit, "Israel, Egypt, Gulf Fear US Betrayal," *Al-Monitor*, November 20, 2013, www.al-monitor.com/pulse/originals/2013/11/american-betrayal-israel-saudi-arabia-egypt-obama.html.

131 Dalia Dassa Kaye and Jeffrey Martini, "The Days After a Deal with Iran: Regional Responses to a Final Nuclear Agreement," Rand Corporation, n.d., 26, www.rand.org/content/dam/rand/pubs/perspectives/PE100/PE122/RAND_PE122.pdf.

132 Barbara Opall-Rome, "Netanyahu: Iran-P5+1 Deal 'Historic Mistake'," *Defense News*, November 24, 2013.

133 Barak Ravid, "Netanyahu: Iran Nuclear Deal Endangers Israel, We Will Defend Ourselves," *Haaretz*, November 24, 2013.

134 "'Neuter' Iran: Lindsey Graham Makes the Case for U.S. Strike," *Huffington Post*, 25:07 400AD, www.huffingtonpost.com/2010/11/06/lindsey-graham-calls-for-strike-on-iran_n_779997.html.

135 Robert E. Hunter, "Rethinking Iran," *Survival* 52, no. 5 (October 1, 2010): 135–56, doi:10.1080/00396338.2010.522101.

136 Merrit Kennedy, "Implementation Day Arrives: Sanctions on Iran Are Lifted," NPR, January 16, 2016, www.npr.org/sections/thetwo-way/2016/01/16/463168647/u-n-nuclear-watchdog-confirms-iran-nuclear-deal-set-to-be-implemented.

137 "Executive Order Protecting the Nation from Foreign Terrorist Entry into the United States," White House, January 27, 2017, www.whitehouse.gov/presidential-actions/executive-order-protecting-nation-foreign-terrorist-entry-united-states/.

138 Michael D. Shear and Helene Cooper, "Trump Bars Refugees and Citizens of 7 Muslim Countries," *New York Times*, January 27, 2017, www.nytimes.com/2017/01/27/us/politics/trump-syrian-refugees.html.

139 Thomas Erdbrink and Jeffrey Gettleman, "In Iran, Shock and Bewilderment Over Trump Visa Crackdown," *New York Times*, January 27, 2017, www.nytimes.com/2017/01/27/world/middleeast/trump-visa-muslim-ban.html.

140 Ralph Ellis and Sara Mazloumsaki, "Iran to Take 'Reciprocal Measures' After Trump's Immigration Order," *CNN*, accessed February 7, 2017, www.cnn.com/2017/01/28/middleeast/iran-will-ban-us-citizens/index.html.
141 Bob Ferguson, "AG Ferguson Seeks Halt to Trump's Immigration Executive Order," Washington State Office of the Attorney General, January 30, 2017, www.atg.wa.gov/news/news-releases/ag-ferguson-seeks-halt-trump-s-immigration-executive-order.
142 "President Trump's Muslim Ban Lite," *New York Times*, March 6, 2017, sec. Opinion, www.nytimes.com/2017/03/06/opinion/president-trumps-muslim-ban-lite.html.
143 "Executive Order Protecting the Nation from Foreign Terrorist Entry into the United States," White House, March 6, 2017, www.whitehouse.gov/presidential-actions/executive-order-protecting-nation-foreign-terrorist-entry-united-states-2/.
144 Dan Levine and Mica Rosenberg, "Hawaii Judge Halts Trump's New Travel Ban Before It Can Go into Effect," *Reuters*, March 15, 2017, www.reuters.com/article/us-usa-immigration-court/hawaii-judge-halts-trumps-new-travel-ban-before-it-can-go-into-effect-idUSKBN16M17N.
145 "Top US Court Backs Trump Travel Ban on Muslim-Majority Countries," *Al Jazeera*, English, June 26, 2018, www.aljazeera.com/news/2018/06/supreme-court-upholds-trump-travel-ban-180626142504629.html.
146 "US Congress Plans Anti-Iran Legislation," *Financial Tribune*, January 4, 2017, https://financialtribune.com/articles/national/56912/us-congress-plans-anti-iran-legislation.
147 "Congressional Record," Legislation, Congress, July 15, 2016, www.congress.gov/congressional-record/2016/7/15/extensions-of-remarks-section/article/e1148-1.
148 "Statement of Administration Policy on H.R. 5631—Iran Accountability Act of 2016; H.R. 4992—United States Financial System Protection Act of 2016; and H.R. 5119—No 2H2O from Iran Act," White House, July 11, 2016, www.whitehouse.gov/sites/default/files/omb/legislative/sap/114/saphr5119r_20160711.pdf.
149 "Anti-Iran Moves in Congress," The Iran Primer, April 26, 2016, http://iranprimer.usip.org/blog/2016/feb/08/anti-iran-moves-congress.
150 Kenneth Katzman, "Iran Sanctions," Congressional Research Service, January 31, 2017, https://fas.org/sgp/crs/mideast/RS20871.pdf.
151 Peter Roskam, "H.R.4258-114th Congress (2015–2016): Quarantining the Ayatollah's State-Sponsored Aggression and Militancy (QASSAM) Act," Legislation, Congress, December 15, 2015, www.congress.gov/bill/114th-congress/house-bill/4258.
152 Brad Sherman, "H.R.4312-114th Congress (2015–2016): Iran's Revolutionary Guard Corps Sanctions Implementation and Review Act," Legislation, December 18, 2015, www.congress.gov/bill/114th-congress/house-bill/4312.
153 Edward Royce, "H.R.4992-114th Congress (2015–2016): United States Financial System Protection Act of 2016," Legislation, July 14, 2016, www.congress.gov/bill/114th-congress/house-bill/4992.
154 Mike Pompeo, "H.R.5119-114th Congress (2015–2016): No 2H2O from Iran Act," Legislation, Congress, July 14, 2016, www.congress.gov/bill/114th-congress/house-bill/5119.
155 Kevin McCarthy, "H.R.5631-114th Congress (2015–2016): Iran Accountability Act of 2016," Legislation, July 14, 2016, www.congress.gov/bill/114th-congress/house-bill/5631.
156 "Part II: White House on Iran Sanctions Act," The Iran Primer, accessed February 7, 2017, http://iranprimer.usip.org/blog/2016/dec/15/part-ii-white-house-iran-sanctions-act.
157 Ibid.
158 Edward Royce, "H.R.1698-115th Congress (2017–2018): Iran Ballistic Missiles and International Sanctions Enforcement Act," Congress, October 30, 2017, www.congress.gov/bill/115th-congress/house-bill/1698.

159 Bob Corker, "S.722-115th Congress (2017–2018): Countering Iran's Destabilizing Activities Act of 2017," Congress, June 29, 2017, www.congress.gov/bill/115th-congress/senate-bill/722.
160 Michael McCaul, "Actions—H.R.4744-115th Congress (2017–2018): Iran Human Rights and Hostage-Taking Accountability Act," Congress, May 7, 2018, www.congress.gov/bill/115th-congress/house-bill/4744/actions.
161 Robin Wright, "Will the Iran Nuclear Deal Survive?" *The New Yorker*, July 14, 2016, www.newyorker.com/news/news-desk/will-the-iran-nuclear-deal-survive.
162 Allen Cone, "Terror Victims Can Seize Iranian Money, Supreme Court Rules," *UPI*, accessed September 1, 2016, www.upi.com/Top_News/US/2016/04/20/Terror-victims-can-seize-Iranian-money-Supreme-Court-rules/9151461178230/.
163 "US Ruling Amounts to Money Theft: Iran," *Press TV*, accessed September 1, 2016, www.presstv.com/Detail/2016/04/21/461887/Iran-US-Supreme-Court-Beirut-bombing-Jaberi-Ansari/.
164 Ali Hashem, "How the Nuclear Deal's Failings Ignited Anti-Western Sentiment in Iran," *Al-Monitor*, April 29, 2016, www.al-monitor.com/pulse/originals/2016/04/iran-jcpoa-implementation-zarif-kerry-westtoxification.html.
165 Matt Pearce, "Where Are Iran's Billions in Frozen Assets, and How Soon Will It Get Them Back?" *Los Angeles Times*, accessed September 1, 2016, www.latimes.com/world/middleeast/la-fg-iran-frozen-assets-20160120-story.html.
166 "Visa Waiver Program Improvement and Terrorist Travel Prevention Act of 2015," Congress, December 9, 2015, www.congress.gov/bill/114th-congress/house-bill/158/text.
167 Thomas Erdbrink, "Rouhani Wins Re-Election in Iran by a Wide Margin," *New York Times*, May 20, 2017, www.nytimes.com/2017/05/20/world/middleeast/iran-election-hassan-rouhani.html?_r=0.
168 "Iran's Rouhani Wins Decisive Re-Election," *BBC News*, May 20, 2017, sec. Middle East, www.bbc.com/news/world-middle-east-39984066.
169 "World Economic Outlook," International Monetary Fund, 2018, www.imf.org/external/datamapper/NGDP_RPCH@WEO.
170 "Implementing the Iran Nuclear Deal: A Status Report," International Crisis Group, January 16, 2017, www.crisisgroup.org/middle-east-north-africa/gulf-and-arabian-peninsula/iran/173-implementing-iran-nuclear-deal-status-report.
171 Cameron Glenn, "A Year on, Iran's Nuclear Deal Is Helping Its Economy, but Not as Much as Some Hoped," *Quartz*, July 13, 2016, https://qz.com/729036/a-year-on-irans-nuclear-deal-is-helping-its-economy-but-not-as-much-as-some-hoped/.
172 Frud Bezhan, "Iranian President Scrambles to Sell Nuclear Deal as a Win for Tehran," *RadioFreeEurope/RadioLiberty*, accessed February 7, 2017, www.rferl.org/a/iran-rohani-khamenei-jcpoa-nuclear-deal-benefits-anniversary/28234265.html.
173 Mohammad A. Shabani, "Banking Sanctions Take Center Stage as Iranian Rhetoric Toughens," *Al-Monitor*, accessed September 1, 2016, www.al-monitor.com/pulse/originals/2016/03/iran-sanctions-jcpoa-banking-khamenei-nowruz-speech.html#ixzz47ZopwIt8.
174 "Iran Rial Plunges to New Lows as U.S. Sanctions Loom," *Reuters*, June 24, 2018, www.reuters.com/article/us-iran-economy-rial/iran-rial-plunges-to-new-lows-as-u-s-sanctions-loom-idUSKBN1JK0HZ.
175 Ebrahim Mohseni, Nancy Gallagher, and Clay Ramsay, "Iranian Public Attitudes Before & After Parliamentary Elections," The Center for International and Security Studies at Maryland (CISSM), March 2016, https://bit.ly/2mp7aQb.
176 Ted Regencia, "Can Iran Stop the Downward Spiral of Its Currency?" *Al Jazeera*, English, June 29, 2018, www.aljazeera.com/news/2018/06/iran-stop-downward-spiral-currency-180628063235075.html.
177 "Trump Says Iran Will Seek Fresh Deal as Looming Sanctions Weigh on Economy," *Reuters*, July 12, 2018, www.reuters.com/article/us-nato-summit-iran/trump-says-iran-treating-u-s-with-more-respect-idUSKBN1K21LY.

178 Eric Cortellessa, "Trump Administration Seeks to Drop Iran's Oil Revenue to Nothing," *The Times of Israel*, July 3, 2018, www.timesofisrael.com/trump-administration-seeks-to-drop-irans-oil-revenue-to-nothing/.

179 Ibid.

180 "Iran's Supreme Leader Calls for Government to Be Backed in Face of U.S. Sanctions," *Reuters*, July 15, 2018, www.reuters.com/article/us-iran-nuclear-usa-khamenei/irans-supreme-leader-calls-for-backing-government-in-face-of-u-s-sanctions-website-idUSKBN1K50K8.

5 Broader challenges

While the previous chapter outlined WMD proliferation challenges facing the region, this chapter focuses on some of the factors contributing to instability and insecurity there. Ultimately, the hope is that by working jointly on the zone a rare opportunity can be provided for all regional countries to take steps toward the mutually beneficial goals of stability, security, and prosperity.

Key structural points will be analyzed in this chapter. First under consideration is the presence of foreign forces and the increasing conventional weapons sales by world powers (specifically the United States and Russia) to the Middle East that perpetuate the growing militarization of the region. This growth comes at a cost to socioeconomic development and fuels the means to war. The second point to be reviewed are the tensions between Iran and other Persian Gulf countries on a multitude of issues, both historical and contemporary. These tensions have come into sharp focus as the two regional powerhouses—Saudi Arabia and Iran—compete to reshape the geopolitical landscape to their advantage. Saudi Arabia's direct interventions in Bahrain and Yemen, while Iran increases its involvement in Syria and Iraq, have further destabilized an already fragile region.

The third point to be analyzed are the attempts to bring an end to the Palestinian–Israeli, and wider Arab–Israeli, conflicts, which continue to contribute to distrust and provide fodder for radicalization in the Middle East. The final issue to be examined in this chapter are the Arab uprisings that swept the region from Tunisia to Syria—with various impacts on the security, stability, and geopolitical configuration of the region. These issues continue to cause daunting challenges to weak transitional governments in Libya, Tunisia, and Egypt, and the destabilizing culmination of the Arab uprisings have brought about the destruction of government institutions, failure to apply the rule of law, and, in some cases, a complete breakdown of nation states. In Syria, the popular and peaceful nature of protests in the beginning of March 2011 have mutated into a nightmarish civil war that also has divided the Middle East into two camps—supporters and opponents of the Assad government—spilling over into regional countries and increasingly involving international powers. Syria and other zones of conflict in Iraq, Libya, and Yemen have resulted in de facto failed states due to the breakdown of governance, stability, and institutional structures.

Foreign powers and regional militarization

The decades-long presence of transregional powers in the Middle East and the Persian Gulf has greatly altered the region. The Cold War between the former Soviet Union and the United States manifested their ideological competition (capitalism versus communism) throughout the world, and the Middle East was no exception. Most countries in the region pegged their security to either the United States (for example, Saudi Arabia and Israel) or the former Soviet Union (for example, Syria and Yemen). While the two superpowers settled their differences through proxy wars, including in the Middle East (for example, the former Soviet Union supported the Egyptian and Syrian attack on the nascent Israeli state in 1967, while the United States backed Tel Aviv), they counterbalanced each other in the region. The fall of the Soviet Union in 1991, however, opened the gates for the United States to dominate the region uncontested, with growing instability caused by U.S. invasions of Iraq and Afghanistan; the use of force to promote a new order in the region; and the escalation of militarism culminating in more divergence than convergence in this sensitive part of the world.[1] The consequences of the U.S. drawdowns in Iraq and Afghanistan; the uprisings in the Arab world; potential internal unrest in the countries of the Gulf Cooperation Council (Bahrain, Kuwait, Oman, Qatar, Saudi Arabia, and the UAE); the increasing role of Russia in the region; and the unpredictability of Trump's Middle East policy, all coupled with the ongoing rise in extremism and terrorism, are factors that have exacerbated the ongoing crises in the region. Such developments are going to have a major impact on the political-security situation of the region and prospects for establishing the WMDFZ.

Following Iraq's invasion of Iran in 1980, Washington formulated an "Iran containment" policy, which focused on strengthening the military power of other Persian Gulf states and establishing military bases in those countries to confront Iran. It encouraged trilateral cooperation among the United States, Arab nations, and Israel to reduce the regional clout of Tehran and to pave the way for an agreement over a Palestine–Israel peace accord.[2] Regional and American security concerns with perceived Iranian hegemonic ambitions have since dominated the debate while overshadowing the many decades of disputes between the Arab nations and Israel.

After the 1991 Persian Gulf War, in which Saudi Arabia was forced to allow some 500,000 U.S. troops into the kingdom to protect it from Ba'athist Iraq, followers of the ultraconservative Salafist branch of Sunni Islam led the uproar over the religious legitimacy of allowing non-Muslim soldiers to be present on Islamic holy grounds in Saudi Arabia.[3] Today, extremism derived from Salafist ideology has spread across the Arab world and beyond. The military presence of foreign powers in the region and the resultant militarization has, in fact, been a contributing factor to the rise in extremism while also disrupting socioeconomic development in many regional countries. A large part of the investments made by regional countries is in security-related matters (most notably weaponry), while underdevelopment of national infrastructures has made those countries prone to political and economic crises.[4] Although the presence of foreign powers can be effective in technology transfer and development, the focus in the Middle East has been mainly to build up their military presence.

Since the United States invaded Afghanistan and Iraq, instability in the region has soared, and the subsequent unrest has prevented the establishment of stable governments in these countries. Furthermore, following the 2011 Arab uprisings, what had been only a threat of civil war and sectarian strife is now a fact. Millions of people have lost their lives or livelihood in recent years, with a multitude of negative consequences for regional security, stability, and society.

Efforts to promote guided democracy in Persian Gulf and Middle East countries have changed the situation in the region from cooperation-based actions to defensive reactions; as a result, many regional countries have begun to seek integration into security systems headquartered outside the region. Instead of establishing a broad-based regional security system in the Persian Gulf and formulating needed mechanisms for cooperation and collective security, regional countries are seeking security guarantees from major powers outside the region, and this has led to massive military build-up by foreign forces in the region.

Despite the collapse of two warmongering systems in the region (Saddam Hussein's Iraq and the Taliban's Afghanistan), increased instability from the absence of stable political systems and the presence of foreign forces in those countries have taken up the lion's share of regional countries' capabilities.

In the midst of chaos, terrorism has flourished, becoming a central issue and a major threat to the world order. In the Persian Gulf and Middle East, terrorism has not only destabilized regional countries, it has provided an excuse for interference in the domestic affairs of other countries or for military action against them.[5] Moreover, the extremist interpretations of Islam by Al-Qaeda or ISIS have provided grounds for violent measures in the region. They have helped the Taliban rise to power in the past and are now manifested in domestic unrest in Muslim countries such as Afghanistan, Yemen, Iraq, Syria, Libya, and even Saudi Arabia.[6]

It is no wonder, then, that the Middle East is extremely militarized in both weaponry and personnel. In comparison to other regions of the world, the Persian Gulf region has close to the highest ratio of military personnel to total population and also one of the highest growth rates in the number of military personnel.[7]

While decades of U.S. diplomacy and weapons sales have established strategic defense relations with GCC nations and Israel, it also has resulted in a vast concentration of conventional weapons in the region. According to the Stockholm International Peace Research Institute, from 2012 to 2016, the global arms trade was dominated by the United States (33 percent) and Russia (23 percent).[8] During the same period, three Middle Eastern countries made it to the list of top five global importers of arms, with the second largest buyer of weapons globally being Saudi Arabia (which is also the largest recipient of U.S. arms sales), followed by the UAE (coming in second as recipient of U.S. arms sales). Fifth place goes to Algeria (Russia accounted for 60 percent of Algerian arms imports).

The Middle East received the lion's share of U.S. arms exports, amounting to 47 percent of the total. Iran's arms imports are a fraction of the Persian Gulf Arab states, due to a partial UN arms embargo and economic pressures, as well as having a robust domestic military industry. During the same period (2012–2016), Iran's arms imports accounted for only 1.2 percent of total arms imports to the Middle East.[9] In addition, Israel and Egypt continue to be the largest recipients of U.S. military aid, with an annual average of $3.8 billion and $1.5 billion, respectively. This amounts to over 75 percent of all U.S. military aid globally.[10] This has allowed countries in the region that are not closely allied with the United States, including Iran, to have closer defense relations with Russia, adding yet another dimension to the complex web of relations in the region.

The high-tech conventional arms provided to allies of the West in the Middle East are also detrimental to WMD nonproliferation efforts. Some nations in the region, as a means to level the playing field with their Western-backed and militarily advanced neighbors, increasingly find WMD an attractive alternative—one that costs less, is easily accessible, will result in deterrence, and will establish a power balance in the region. With a meager defense budget, a state can equip itself with chemical and biological weapons and, with a bit more, may even acquire a crude nuclear warhead.

Needless to say, countries in the region will find it challenging to maneuver through this uncertain period. Making matters even less clear is the role the Trump administration will take vis-à-vis the region. Traditional U.S. allies of the region (specifically Israel, Saudi Arabia, and other members of the GCC) have eagerly supported and advocated for President Trump's decision to reverse the Obama-era policies of engagement with Iran and U.S. hesitance to use a military option to topple the Assad government in Syria. They are also hoping to receive security reassurances from Washington.[11] There are early indications that President Trump will provide increased security assurances, compared to his predecessor, to Middle East allies. This is exemplified by the April 7, 2017, cruise missile attack on a Syrian airbase in retaliation for the alleged use of chemical weapons by the Assad government.[12] President Trump has also continued his threats to dishonor or, at best, remain ambiguous on the Iran nuclear deal.[13] President Trump's scrapping of the Iran nuclear deal was yet another example of his administration's willingness to showcase their determination to curtail Iran's perceived nuclear ambitions and influence in the region.[14]

Finally, on May 19, 2017, President Trump devoted his first foreign trip as president to Saudi Arabia and Israel—as a show of support to U.S. closest allies in the region.[15] During his trip to Riyadh, President Trump inked one of the largest U.S. weapons sales in history with Saudi Arabia, valued at over $110 billion, with an additional $350 billion spanning a decade.[16]

If Trump's rhetoric and actions are anything to go by, however, there is a likelihood that bloated government bureaucracy will be trimmed, laissez-faire economic policy will be implemented, immigration reform will hit a wall, further scandals will entangle the administration (particularly allegations of Russian intervention in the 2016 U.S. presidential elections and ties to the Trump presidential campaign team), and all this will impact the Trump administration's ability to conduct a robust foreign policy.

With an increasing focus on economic growth and security issues closer to home, inevitably the U.S. footprint in global security matters will diminish.[17] In the absence of a region-wide security cooperation system and with a possible reduction in U.S. engagement in the region, it is likely that the Trump "America First" doctrine will outsource the job of the global policeman to regional powers to sort out their own security issues in their neighborhood. If this comes to pass, faith in the United States as an ally will evaporate, and this vacuum will be filled by countries in the region through either pragmatic diplomacy, finding new external partners (most likely Russia), or by maintaining the current zero-sum policies.

The United States will likely continue to supply the means for war and security but refrain from getting entangled in far-flung conflicts that cost U.S. lives and monetary resources. This seems to be in line with Trump's suggestions that the United States would not come to the defense of NATO allies if they have not "fulfilled their obligation to us," adding "the US must be prepared to let these countries defend themselves."[18] Regrettably, such a scenario will increase the desirability of regional powerhouses to maintain, expand, develop, and acquire WMD and their delivery systems as deterrents to real or perceived external threats to their sovereignty.[19]

Regional rivalry

The primary justification for the increasing militarization of the region is centered on the perceived threat from Iran toward its neighbors, in particular member states of the GCC, headed by Saudi Arabia. The marred relations between Iran and the GCC have historical and contemporary roots. Historically, relations between Iran and its Arab neighbors in the Persian Gulf have been strained under both the rule of the Pahlavi monarchy and the Islamic Republic.

In the aftermath of the Iranian revolution in 1979, the Arab countries in the Persian Gulf formed the GCC in 1981 out of concern about the potential "export of the Iranian revolution."[20] A year later, the GCC formed a joint military force called Peninsula Shield Force (PSF) to counter possible threats from Iran.[21] During the 34th GCC Summit in 2013, the decision was made to establish a joint defense force of around 100,000, with half of the troop contribution coming from Saudi Arabia.[22] Security, defense, and intelligence adviser Dr. Sami Alfaraj stated that the decision was made to counter a growing threat from Iran "and its subversive terrorist elements across the GCC."[23]

Multiple strategic considerations shape the GCC's geopolitical concerns about Iran. Among them is Iran's demographic weight, which has no equivalent among any of the GCC nations. Iran's population, nearly 80 million, is more than three times that of the six GCC member-states combined.[24] Iran's expertise in sensitive nuclear, chemical, and biological technologies, coupled with its self-sufficiency in defense and the missile industry, are also of concern. The religious and revolutionary nature of Iran's system of governance and political dynamics is seen as a direct threat to the legitimacy of GCC monarchies.

Iran's deep-rooted societal ties with millions of Arabs on the other side of the Persian Gulf continue to be an important bridge but, at times of tension, they are seen as a destabilizing factor for domestic relations in GCC countries. Owing to Iran's well-established higher education and training institutions, its human resources are in demand throughout the region, with around 500,000 Iranians working in the UAE alone.[25] Another consideration is Iran's influence and reach in the Muslim world and Arab nations such as Iraq, Syria, Yemen, Sudan, Lebanon, and Palestine. This regional influence is at the heart of the GCC concern, as highlighted in a *New York Times* op-ed by the Saudi foreign minister Adel Bin Ahmed Al-Jubeir: "Iran is the single-most-belligerent-actor in the region, and its actions display both a commitment to regional hegemony and a deeply held view that conciliatory gestures signal weakness either on Iran's part or on the part of its adversaries."[26]

Proximity is also a factor, with Iran's shoreline spanning almost the entire length of the Persian Gulf, leaving the GCC countries feeling vulnerable and highly exposed geographically with no physical barriers separating them from their ambitious Iranian neighbor. There are also real fears regarding the Persian Gulf's intraregional balance of power, especially in the aftermath of the 2003 U.S. invasion of Iraq, which eliminated a major national security problem for Iran. The fall of Saddam Hussein's regime, and the new Shia-dominated Iraqi government (with close ties to Tehran), saw the regional balance tilt favorably toward Iran at a significant cost to the GCC.

Iran, too, has a long list of grievances toward its Arab neighbors, going back to the Arab Muslim invasion of Iran approximately 1,400 years ago; Iranians welcomed Islam but did not forget the invasion of their land.[27] In the more contemporary era, a lingering dispute exists regarding borders and sovereignty, where Iran considered Bahrain as its fourteenth province in the early 1900s. In late 1960s and early 1970s, the Shah of Iran agreed to the independence of Bahrain in return for the British recognizing the three islands located in the Persian Gulf—the Greater and the Lesser Tunb Islands and Abu Musa—as long-standing parts of Iranian territory. The UAE, however, continues to have a territorial dispute with Iran over those islands, and this has been a source of ongoing tension between Iran and the GCC. There are other border issues, as well, since Iran shares more than a dozen oil and gas fields with Arab states, including Iraq, Kuwait, Oman, Qatar, Saudi Arabia, and the UAE. One recurring dispute concerns their respective share in siphoning from these joint gas and oil fields. Specifically, Iran accuses Qatar of extracting far more than its share in the joint gas field of South Pars, which is the biggest in the world. Iran's ability to extract the gas has been hampered by years of economic sanctions, leaving the country's oil and gas infrastructure in dire need of an overhaul. Eckart Woertz, a visiting fellow at Princeton University, described it plainly by saying that Qatar and Iran have "straws in the same gas field, but only Qatar is sucking."[28]

In the post-Islamic Revolution era, Iran viewed the mere formation of the GCC in 1981 with suspicion and as a threat to the nascent revolutionary government in

Tehran. Iran's relations with the GCC, particularly, deteriorated following their support for Iraq during the eight-year war with Iran (1980–1988). The Iraqi invasion of Iran cost hundreds of billions of dollars; about 1 million people perished and many more were injured.[29] The GCC fully supported the invasion by generously funding Saddam Hussein's war effort, including contributions from Saudi Arabia ($30.9 billion), Kuwait ($8.2 billion), and the UAE ($8 billion). When the war ended in 1988, the GCC did not acknowledge responsibility or take steps toward compensating Iran for war damages.[30]

Iran viewed GCC's accusation of interference in their domestic affairs as hypocritical. In March 1991, the six GCC countries, together with the foreign ministers of Egypt and Syria, signed the Damascus declaration, committing themselves to the principle of noninterference in one another's domestic affairs.[31] Iran was not invited; it, instead, signed a separate agreement with Syria for strategic alliance. Since the Syrian crisis in 2011, the GCC has clearly violated its agreement with Damascus by supporting opposition forces in the country to bring about regime change and remove Bashar Al-Assad.[32] Iran, instead, has maintained its agreement with Damascus, supporting the Syrian government and resisting regime change in Syria. Therefore, Syria has become the center of new conflict, mistrust, and challenge between Iran and the GCC.

A major divergence between Iran and the GCC is centered on how to attain security and stability in the Persian Gulf. Iran contends that this issue has been dominated by Western powers for the past four centuries with no major part played by regional countries, and stresses the need for the region to take a more prominent role in its own security and stability. The GCC argues that the only way to preserve its security is through political and security alliance with superpowers, specifically the United States. Western military presence, particularly the large number of U.S. forces in the region at the behest of GCC, is viewed by Tehran as a direct provocation. Iran also asserts that Western powers have supported, over much of the past half century, traditional systems of governance in the region, most notably military dictatorships and monarchies, and this has impeded political development toward representative democracy in the Persian Gulf. The GCC monarchies, however, perceive this notion as an Iranian attempt to sow popular dissent and interference in their domestic affairs.

The Iranian nuclear program is another contributing factor in strained Iran–GCC relations. Throughout the Iranian nuclear saga, Tehran accused most GCC countries of supporting comprehensive international pressure and sanctions on Iran. Saudi Arabia also played a proactive role, calling for more pressure on and isolation of Iran to decimate its economy, going as far as supporting U.S. coercive efforts to contain Iran.[33] WikiLeaks revealed that, in 2008 U.S.–Saudi diplomatic discussions, then Saudi Foreign Minister Saud Al Faisal called for "more severe US and international sanctions on Iran, including a travel ban and further restrictions on bank lending . . . [and] the use of military pressure against Iran should not be ruled out." In the same leaked diplomatic cable, then Saudi King Abdullah gave his backing to a possible U.S. military action on Iran to "cut off the head of the snake."[34]

The 2015 nuclear accord was a turning point in Middle Eastern politics. While world powers and most of the international community welcomed the agreement, Israel and some members of the GCC voiced concern and warned of negative consequences. Saudi Arabia led the charge that Iran's hegemonic ambitions and its newfound strength could cause regional destabilization.[35]

Most GCC countries, in particular Saudi Arabia, viewed the nuclear accord as strengthening Iran's position in the region and concluded that Tehran would be more assertive in its relations with regional countries. Also, the easing of economic sanctions and renewed efforts by the international community to engage with Iran on wider issues facing the region came as a setback for Saudi Arabia's efforts to counter Iran's influence. Economic benefits arising from the nuclear accord have also been perceived as giving Tehran much-needed resources to support its proxies in the region, namely Assad's Syrian government, Lebanese Hezbollah, and the Houtis in Yemen.[36]

Additionally, the marathon negotiations on the nuclear issue resulted in Iran having direct discussions with the United States at the highest level since the 1979 revolution. The possibility of warming relations between Iran and United States was a major concern for the GCC countries, who saw it coming at their expense.[37] These views were also aired during a closed-door meeting held in Berlin (April 2015), when policy experts from the GCC stated that U.S. President Barack Obama was a "dreamer who continued to hold onto the illusion that Washington could place its relations with Tehran on a new footing while maintaining its strategic partnership with traditional allies in the region."[38]

These factors have, instead, put further strain on relations between Iran and its GCC neighbors, with Saudi Arabia taking ever more assertive and unilateral measures to counter Iran's re-emergence as a regional power. Another outcome from the nuclear accord is that the GCC states underlined that since Iran has managed to continue with its nuclear program (albeit curtailed by limitations under the JCPOA), they, too, would like to commence or expand their domestic nuclear programs. With this rationale, some GCC countries conclude that the nuclear agreement is, instead, counterproductive and will ultimately lead to further nuclear proliferation in the region.[39]

In the context of the ascension of King Salman, Iranian–Saudi competition has escalated since the nuclear accord. As Brookings Institution's Suzanne Maloney has said: "Saudi leaders have adopted a more aggressive diplomatic, economic and military campaign aimed both at marginalizing Iran and reasserting its own ambitions for regional dominance. Determined to extract Syria from the Iranian orbit and doubtful of the relevance of Iranian moderates, the Saudis have watched the world's tentative rehabilitation of Tehran over the past year with suspicion and mounting indignation."[40]

Saudi–Iran bilateral relations spiraled downward at the beginning of 2016, with Riyadh's decision to execute the outspoken Saudi Shia cleric Nimr al-Nimr, triggering a Shia outcry in Iran and the region. In Tehran, protestors set the Saudi embassy ablaze, a provocative move that led Saudi Arabia to cut off diplomatic relations with Iran. Some members of the GCC—Somalia, Djibouti, and Sudan—followed suit by severing or downgrading their ties with Tehran. This escalation was yet another example of a growing conflict between the two regional powerhouses.[41]

Ultimately, the strained relations between Iran and GCC, in particular Saudi Arabia, are a destabilizing factor in the region and contribute to their multiple battles fought through proxies. This does not bode well for the security cooperation that is badly needed to bring about a reduction in tensions and open the possibility of achieving a WMDFZ in the Middle East.

Israel–Palestine peace process

Over the years, there have been many attempts to bring about a resolution to the Israeli–Palestinian conflict, but peace remains elusive. There have been some limited breakthroughs in talks, such as the 1993 Oslo agreement between Israeli Prime Minister Yitzhak Rabin and Palestinian leader Yasser Arafat, which included mutual recognition and the establishment of the Palestinian authority in West Bank and Gaza Strip.[42] Yet that agreement failed to address major Palestinian concerns, namely the status of Jerusalem; the right of refugees to return; border issues; and an end to Israeli occupation of Palestinian lands, including a halt to settlement building.[43] By not addressing these key factors, the Oslo agreement was doomed to fail from the start, and future attempts to revive the agreement have not materialized, including the Wye River Memorandum signed in October 1998 between Arafat and Israeli Prime Minister Benjamin Netanyahu under the auspices of then U.S. President Bill Clinton.[44] Regrettably, that agreement actually undercut the Oslo agreement and, once again, did not address the main issues facing the Palestinians.

A slew of other attempts led by the United States in recent years also have not succeeded. There was a glimmer of hope in 2000, after months of secret negotiations between Israelis and Palestinians with U.S. and Norwegian negotiators, where both parties had made progress on critical areas such as return of refugees, borders, and holy sites.[45] Those negotiations culminated in the Camp David talks that began on July 11, 2000, yet attempts by President Clinton to secure a deal failed, primarily due to inflexibility on both sides about the future of Jerusalem.[46] During President Bush's tenure, the "Road Map" was introduced by the Quartet—the United States, Russia, the EU, and the UN—but once again failed to provide any realistic proposal to address key issues and was sidelined.[47]

The Obama administration also tried its hand at the Middle East peace process by advocating for direct talks between the Palestinians and Israelis.[48] Those attempts resulted in failure, as well. The lack of cooperation regarding the peace process prompted President Obama to state, "Look at the past eight years [referring to the George W. Bush administration's relationship with Israel], there was no space between us and Israel, and what did we get from that? When there is no daylight, Israel just sits on the sidelines, and that erodes our credibility with the Arab states."[49]

Israel's government, instead, accelerated its illegal settlement building activities in the West Bank, prompting the Obama administration to make a rare statement: "We are deeply disappointed by [the] announcement about accelerated housing construction in Jerusalem and the West Bank. . . . Unilateral actions work against efforts to resume direct negotiations and they do not advance the goal of a reasonable and necessary agreement between the parties."[50] On December 23, 2016, the UNSC voted 14 to 0 and passed Resolution 2334 demanding the halt of settlement activity by Israel on "Palestinian territories occupied since 1967, including East Jerusalem." It is significant that the outgoing Obama administration broke away from U.S. precedence to use its veto power to block UNSC resolutions against Israel by abstaining in the vote.[51]

President Trump, prior to taking office, joined Israeli Prime Minister Netanyahu in voicing discontent with Obama administration's use of veto power to prevent the UN vote against Israeli settlements. Trump also warned that once he took office there would be changes to U.S. relations with the international body, tweeting "as to the U.N., things will be different after Jan. 20th."[52] He also made clear that his administration would bolster U.S.–Israel relations and promised to move the U.S. embassy from Tel Aviv to Jerusalem, a provocative move as the city is at the heart of contention between the Palestinians and Israelis; both groups claim it as their rightful capital. On May 14, 2018, coinciding with the seventieth anniversary of Israeli independence (an occasion marked by Palestinians as the "nakba," or "catastrophe," in which thousands of Palestinians were expelled from their homeland), the United States inaugurated its new embassy in Jerusalem.[53] The United States embassy relocation not only breaks from decades of international norm, but could also be interpreted as Washington's support for a one-state solution rather than a two-state solution to the Israel–Palestine conflict.[54] The Palestinian Authority continued to denounce the move and has expressed hopelessness in the prospects for any peace process to commence where the Trump administration could be seen as an honest broker.

The Israeli government, emboldened with President Trump's inauguration and favorable position on settlements, approved the largest settlement expansion to date, with an additional 2,500 new homes to be built in the occupied Palestinian West Bank. Jerusalem's deputy mayor Meir Turgeman summed up the new reality: "the rules of the game have changed with Donald Trump's arrival as president . . . we no longer have our hands tied as in the time of Barack Obama. Now we can finally build."[55]

If Trump's pick for U.S. ambassador to Israel David Friedman (who supports illegal Israeli settlements and once compared liberal American Jews who support the two-state solution to Nazi collaborators)[56] is any indication, the new U.S. administration will most likely side with the right-wing Israeli government of Netanyahu on key issues such as settlement expansion, the U.S. embassy move, and protection from international isolation, thus weakening Iran and diminishing the hopes of Palestinians for a viable independent state.[57] Ambassador Friedman also claimed in an interview with Israeli newspaper *Haaretz* that Trump doesn't support a two-state solution and would even support an Israeli annexation of all or parts of the West Bank.[58]

The Trump administration's provocative policies could result in (1) sidelining any renewed attempts at the peace process and derailing the "two-state solution" for Israelis and Palestinians that has been the basis for successive Republican and Democratic administrations' policy on the issue; (2) outrage by the Palestinians that could erupt into renewed violence; (3) divergence between the United States and key European and other international actors pressing for a resolution to the Palestinian–Israeli conflict; (4) an outcry from Arab and Muslim countries that will cause tension in their bilateral relations with the United States on this and other regional challenges, most urgent of which is the fight against terrorism; (5) intensify the boycott, divestments, and sanctions movement (BDS) against Israel; and (6) serve as yet another simmering discontent in the region that will be used as a rallying cry for extremist groups such as ISIS to further recruitment activities, to the security detriment of all regional countries.[59]

Arab Awakening

In early 2011, popular uprisings in Egypt and Tunisia unleashed the Arab Awakening, which brought about changes to the political and social fabric of the region—from Tunisia and Libya to Egypt and onward to Bahrain, Yemen, and Syria. Such sweeping changes to decades-old autocratic rule have brought about a great deal of insecurity and instability to an already volatile region.

The downfall of Western-backed dictators—such as Egypt's Hosni Mubarak, Tunisia's Zine El Abidine Ben Ali, and Yemen's Ali Abdullah Saleh—ushered in fast-moving changes in regional geopolitical reality. The instability in the Middle East was no longer bound to the region and increasingly spilled over to other parts of the world, including the current refugee crisis gripping Europe, with millions taking all avenues to reach those shores. In addition, the increase in terrorist attacks in Brussels, Paris, Ankara, and Istanbul are early indications of the real threat from not addressing the interconnected conflicts in the Middle East on an international level. If the current trend continues, there is a high risk of WMD proliferation and possible weapons possession by terrorist groups that could cause havoc not just in the Middle East but also beyond.

The coming pages examine the genesis, evolution, and outcome of the individual uprisings throughout the region. Inevitably, the issue of a WMDFZ will be placed on the margins while governments cope with pressing domestic pressures exacerbated by increasing regional insecurity. It is, however, precisely for the same reason that regional and international communities must back a serious and concerted effort to realize a WMDFZ.

Tunisia

The Tunisian popular uprising began in December 2010 and triggered the Arab Awakening. There were common underpinning reasons for the protests throughout the Middle East and North Africa. Protestors sought greater freedom of expression, political participation, and economic opportunities. Within a few short weeks, the unrest ousted Western-backed president Zine El Abidine Ben Ali and ushered in a new era for the country, with Islamist and secular parties competing for political influence.[60] While there were tensions among competing political factions, the key political parties decided to avoid disintegration of the nation and opted for compromise. This led to popular elections on October 23, 2011, for the Tunisian constituent assembly, with Islamist party Ennahda receiving 37 percent of the vote and forming the government.[61]

Ultimately, in January 2014, Tunisia adopted a new constitution that took into consideration the initial impetus for the uprisings. The text is seen as one of the most progressive in the region. It guaranteed equal rights for men and women; demanded that corruption be addressed; increased human rights; decentralized the government; and recognized Islam as the official state religion while also protecting freedom of belief.[62] Other promising developments included the second elections of October 2014 and the successful transition of power to the secularist Nidaa Tounes party.

Post-Ben Ali, Tunisia faces daunting challenges, among them political infighting that threatens the cohesiveness of the ruling Nidaa Tounes party; terrorist attacks, the most notable of which was committed at a beach resort in Sousse; and subsequent government crackdowns on suspected terrorists, which have weakened constitutional rights and freedoms of expression and protest.[63]

The most disturbing trend in post-revolution Tunisia, however, is the fact that the small North African country has become the largest source of recruits for terrorist groups such as ISIS, accounting for between 6,000 and 7,000 who went to fight in Syria and Iraq. This is much greater than the number of ISIS fighters originating from far more populated Arab states, such as Egypt and Algeria.[64] The Tunisian ISIS fighters are a key component of the resurgence of the terrorist groups in neighboring Libya, as well. Instability and insecurity divert government resources to these pressing issues, and the prospects are dim for Tunisia playing a proactive role in the realization of the WMDFZ.

Egypt

It did not take long for the Tunisian uprising to reach Egypt. The protests that erupted on January 28, 2011, in Cairo led to the ouster of yet another Western-backed dictator, Hosni Mubarak, on February 10, 2011. Following a brief period of military rule, parliamentary elections were held in December 2011, with the Muslim Brotherhood and other Islamist parties gaining 69 percent of the parliamentary seats. A few months later, in June 2012, presidential elections resulted in Mohamed Morsi, a prominent member of the Muslim Brotherhood, winning

51.7 percent of the vote and creating an Islamist government in Cairo.[65] The policies adopted under the new Islamist government were seen by large segments of the population as both divisive and sectarian while at the same time failing to address the socioeconomic and political grievances that prompted the unrest in the first place. The frustration in the populace erupted in domestic opposition to and widespread protests against the new Islamist government.

In July 2013, the Morsi government, after only one year in office, was ousted in a successful coup d'état staged by the Egyptian military. In a fast-moving series of events, the military suspended the constitution, banned the Muslim Brotherhood, appointed an interim leader, and called for early elections.[66] A systematic crackdown on opposition and members of the Muslim Brotherhood commenced, with approximately 1,000 to 2,500 killed, 17,000 wounded, and between 16,000 and 19,000 arrests.[67] The following year, the chief of the armed forces, Abdel Fatah al-Sissi, was elected president, winning 96.91 percent of the votes.[68] He immediately initiated an even harsher crackdown on dissent, with thousands of Islamists and scores of secular activists jailed. His government was also implicated in unlawful killings and torture, arbitrary arrests, and impunity for the security forces.[69] These harsh tactics and the suppression of civil liberties has achieved some semblance of security in the country, while public discontent continues to simmer.

In the aftermath of the 2011 uprising, Egypt continues to struggle to bring about security, stability, and prosperity to its citizens. This has naturally occupied the bulk of the Egyptian government's resources. That said, it is unlikely that, in the near future, Cairo can be robust in its efforts to press for the realization of the WMDFZ. This is regrettable, as Egypt has been the most vocal Arab nation on the matter and was, with Iran, an originator of the proposal to establish the zone in the region.

Libya

Riding the wave of unrest in the region, Libyans, in February 2011, took to the streets of the eastern city of Benghazi in protest of the four-decades-long authoritarian rule of Colonel Muammar Gaddafi. Libyan security forces showed no restraint and opened fire on protestors, triggering nationwide protest and unrest. The protests quickly morphed into an armed uprising against the central government in Tripoli, with opposition armed groups, bolstered by defecting troops, taking control of key cities in the eastern region of the country.[70] The Libyan security forces mobilized to crush the opposition at their stronghold in Benghazi. To stop the anticipated assault on civilians in Benghazi, the UNSC passed Resolution 1973 in March 2011 authorizing "all necessary measures" to impose "an immediate ceasefire in Libya, including an end to the current attacks against civilians, [which] might constitute crimes against humanity . . . imposing a ban on all flights in the country's airspace—a no-fly zone—and tightened sanctions on the Gaddafi regime and its supporters."[71]

The UNSC resolution paved the way for NATO powers to launch air strikes on March 19, 2011, targeting the Libyan government infrastructure and providing air support to anti-Gaddafi rebel groups.[72] With military support from NATO and some Arab states (Qatar, the UAE, and Jordan), Gaddafi was ousted on August 20, 2011, as Tripoli fell to the Libyan opposition groups.[73] Forces loyal to the former regime continued their resistance against the newly formed Libyan National Transitional Council (NTC) until the death of Gaddafi in his hometown of Sirte on October 20, 2011, which officially ended the rule of Gaddafi in Libya. The NTC kept true to its promise of organizing popular elections, and in July 2012, Libyans voted for an interim parliament, the General National Congress (GNC). The majority of votes went to liberal, secular, and independent candidates, defeating the Muslim Brotherhood-aligned Justice and Construction Party.[74]

Since the election, however, Libya's interim authorities have failed to form a stable government, and growing instability, insecurity, and civil war and the rise of extremist groups plague the country. There are two opposing groups who claim to be the legitimate representatives of the Libyan people. The Tobruk government, which won the 2014 elections, is internationally recognized as the Libyan government and is based in the eastern region of the country, while the Islamist National Salvation government is based in the capital, Tripoli. With no viable government, continuing instability and insecurity throughout the country have resulted in state functions crumbling, effectively rendering Libya a failed state.

The absence of rule of law and the presence of chaos and high levels of violence in Libya are perfect ingredients for terrorist groups, such as Al-Qaeda affiliates and ISIS, to thrive and fill the power vacuum with an increasingly strong foothold in Libya. Libya is the only country other than Iraq and Syria where ISIS has occupied territory, with its power centers in the Libyan coastal city of Sirte as well as in territories in Barqah (east), Tarablus (west), and Fezzan (southwest).[75] The expanding network of ISIS and other terrorist groups in Libya also makes the country a focal point for arming, training, and recruiting terrorists bound for the Middle East and beyond. The thriving black market and the smuggling of migrants, weapons, drugs, and oil are lucrative sources of income for both criminals and terrorists alike.[76] As Libya becomes a terrorist safe haven—with control over land, people, weapons, and resources—there is a high likelihood of terrorists using the country as a launching pad for attacks with more lethal means if they gain access to WMD. This is the ultimate risk from failed states.

Bahrain

The GCC countries also have not escaped the consequences of the Arab Awakening; particularly the popular uprising in February 2011 that shook the small Persian Gulf state of Bahrain. While the root reasons for the Bahraini popular unrest are found in socioeconomic and political factors, the awakening, nevertheless, heightened sectarian tensions, since it pitted the majority Shia population against Sunni minority rule. This factor dominated discourse on the popular uprising in Bahrain and was associated with the broader sectarian strife between the two regional powers—Shia-majority Iran and Sunni-majority Saudi Arabia. With fears of Iranian interference in the internal affairs of a GCC country, the Bahraini government, on March 14, 2011, provided passage to thousands of security forces from Saudi Arabia and the UAE to quell the protestors.[77] While the crackdown succeeded—protestors were rounded up, detained, and sometimes tortured—tensions remain high and, to date, public grievances have not been addressed.

As the tensions erupted, the Obama administration repeatedly appealed to the Bahraini government for restraint. President Obama reaffirmed that "we have insisted both publicly and privately that mass arrests and brute force are at odds with the universal rights of Bahrain's citizens, and . . . such steps will not make legitimate calls for reform go away."[78] In addition, instability in Bahrain is of great concern to Washington, as the nation is of strategic military interest, particularly since the U.S. Navy's Fifth Fleet is housed there, with more than 8,500 U.S. servicemen responsible for the naval forces stretching from the Persian Gulf to the East Coast of Kenya.[79] It is worth noting that while the U.S. government did voice its concern, and Congress objected to arms sales to Bahrain in 2012 due to the repression of the protestors, the Obama administration, nevertheless, bypassed this reservation and continued with the arms sale.[80] Such inconsistencies signaled to the Bahraini authorities that the United States was not serious about addressing Bahrain's repressive policies or the human rights conditions in the country.[81]

The military intervention and crackdown of protestors by the GCC also has damaged its reputation and legitimacy in the region, particularly since the GCC was founded to protect the member states against external threats. Yet, the protest movement in the country was led by Bahrainis and constituted as an internal affair.[82] The crackdown on primarily Shia communities in Bahrain has resulted in minority Shia populations within the GCC countries beginning to stand up and demand change. This has caused sectarian tensions to rise in the Shia-dominated eastern region of Saudi Arabia, where the country's major oil deposits lie. In Bahrain, since the population is approximately 75 percent Shia, it is plausible that, sooner or later, Bahraini authorities will have to either address their legitimate grievances or face renewed backlash, placing a key U.S. ally in danger of collapse and generating public opposition toward U.S. military installations and civilian infrastructure.[83]

Yemen

In February 2012, the Arab Awakening-inspired protests in Yemen led to the ousting of Ali Abdullah Saleh, who had ruled the country for thirty-three years. In the aftermath, Saleh agreed to transfer power to his vice president Abed Rabbo Mansour Hadi through an agreement brokered by the GCC. However, the breakdown of Saleh's government created the conditions for a power struggle between different factions and rebel groups in the country. Opposition groups that competed to fill the vacuum left by the collapse of the Saleh government were composed of Houthis and Islamists of all stripes, including Al-Qaeda and ISIS affiliates and members of Yemen's Muslim Brotherhood.[84]

The most apt of these groups were the Houthis, who were long-time opponents of the Saleh government and had engaged in armed insurgency against them since

2004, with six wars being fought between the two sides until Saleh's 2012 ousting. The Houthis are members of the Zaydi sect of Islam (an offshoot of Shia Islam), and comprise upward of 40 percent of Yemen's population. The Zaydis are distinct from the mainstream Twelver Shia Islam that most Middle Easterners, including Iranians, adhere to. Zaydi imams (religious leaders) effectively ruled Yemen for over 1,000 years, up to 1962, when military officers led a coup that overthrew the Zaydi-led state and attempted to establish a republican system.[85]

While the Houthis played an integral role in the protests that led to the removal of Saleh from power, they were sidelined from the GCC-led political process that brought Hadi to power.[86] Their continued marginalization from the transitional government and its seeming refusal to recognize the Houthis movement as a legitimate player soon led to mass protests, which morphed into renewed military conflict.[87] In September 2014, the Houthis ultimately managed to take over key government buildings in the Yemeni capital, Sana'a, prompting a UN-brokered deal aimed at forming a unity government between the Houthis and the beleaguered Hadi government.[88] Attempts at sustaining the unity government were short-lived after the Houthis, in January 2015, stormed the presidential palace and gained control of all strategic civilian and military infrastructures. This led to the resignation of Hadi and his cabinet, and the dissolution of parliament. In its place, the Houthis established a Revolutionary Committee as the interim authority on February 6, 2015.[89] Subsequently, Hadi fled to the southern city of Aden, where he rescinded his resignation, proclaimed he remained the president of the country, and has since attempted to reassemble his government.[90]

The Houthis did not stop at Sana'a, and in partnership with security forces loyal to the ousted president Saleh, they cemented their hold on significant parts of the northern highlands, much of the coastal areas, and the important city of Taiz. They even managed to temporarily take the country's second-biggest city, Aden, in March 2015, again forcing Hadi to flee, this time to Riyadh, Saudi Arabia.[91] In response to the swift advances by the Houthis, and to restore Hadi's government, Saudi Arabia launched airstrikes and a naval blockade, dubbed operation Decisive Storm, on March 15, 2015, in alliance with a few GCC (Qatar, Kuwait, the UAE, and Bahrain) and other Sunni Arab countries (Egypt, Morocco, Jordan, Sudan, and Senegal). The Saudi-led coalition also received logistical, weaponry, and intelligence support from the United States, the United Kingdom, and France.[92]

The Saudi-led military intervention was supposed to be rapid, showcasing the kingdom's more assertive posture in the region and providing a decisive victory for the ambitious, albeit inexperienced, Saudi defense minister and crown prince Mohammad bin Salman Al Saud. Instead, at the time of this writing, the Saudi-led operation in Yemen continues unabated and has yielded little for Riyadh in terms of prestige, stability, or returning President Hadi to the country. Richard Haass, president of the Council on Foreign Relations, summed it up in a tweet: "Further evidence #Yemen becoming Saudi Arabia's Vietnam; blowback may well weaken stability of #Saudiarabia itself."[93]

The Saudi-led aerial bombardment and naval blockade since 2015, in combination with internal power struggles between various groups, has resulted in the utter destruction of Yemen, the Arab world's poorest nation even prior to the conflict. According to the latest UN figures, approximately 10,000 people have lost their lives and 40,000 have been injured, the majority from coalition air strikes. The ongoing conflict and coalition naval blockade has also displaced 3 million people and triggered a humanitarian crisis with 21 million of the almost 26 million Yemenis dependent on emergency aid.[94] In December 2016, the UN's children's agency UNICEF reported that more than 462,000 children are at risk of starvation in Yemen (a tragic increase from only 200 in 2014); a Yemeni child dies of malnutrition every ten minutes.[95]

Saudi Arabia's military involvement in Yemen has not only further destabilized its southern neighbor and border, it has also weakened the Houthis, who are one of the only groups in Yemen that has been successful in fighting Al-Qaeda in the Arabian Peninsula.[96] As numerous and similar foreign interventions in Middle Eastern civil wars have demonstrated over the years, it is unlikely that a positive outcome can be achieved in Yemen through primarily military means. In all likelihood, the instability in Yemen will, instead, empower terrorist groups to further entrench themselves in the country and expand their regional reach.

The war in Yemen has also opened a new front in the regional power struggle between Iran and Saudi Arabia. One of the key justifications for Saudi military intervention in Yemen has been to counter Iran's perceived support for the Houthis and the threat this poses to the national security of Saudi Arabia.[97] While Iranian officials have expressed sympathy for the Houthis, they deny sending any direct military support. The U.S. military, however, has said that it has intercepted arms shipments from Iran to Yemen.[98]

Nevertheless, the idea of direct Iranian intervention in Yemen greatly overstates Iran's ability to influence events in Yemen in such a decisive way. For instance, in the aftermath of the fall of Sana'a to Houthi forces in 2015, Saudi Arabia and members of the Hadi government claimed that the Houthis takeover was possible only with Iranian backing. This viewpoint was challenged by then spokeswoman for the U.S. National Security Council Bernadette Meehan, who stated, "It remains our assessment that Iran does not exert command and control over the Houthis in Yemen."[99]

While Iran does have an interest in how the Yemeni conflict evolves, there are geographical and geopolitical considerations for limited Iranian involvement in the Yemeni conflict. Yemen is considered a peripheral state, and it yields meager strategic advantage for Tehran. Also, the close proximity of Yemen with Saudi Arabia (they share a 1,307-kilometer border) inevitably will carry greater strategic importance for Riyadh—a consideration Tehran takes seriously, as it could drastically escalate tensions between the two countries.[100] Finally, Iran views any involvement in Yemen as entangling itself into a quagmire and, likewise, believes Saudi Arabia and other states have made an unwise decision to escalate the conflict in that country.

Ultimately, the only solution to the Yemeni conflict is a political solution based on addressing the concerns of all parties involved. To end hostilities and stabilize Yemen, the five permanent members of the UNSC, Iran, and Saudi Arabia could discuss an inclusive plan aimed at reaching an immediate and complete cease-fire; ending all foreign military incursions; providing widespread humanitarian assistance; resuming broad national dialogue; addressing the concerns of the various factions and stakeholders inside the country in a non-zero-sum manner; agreeing on a power-sharing system; and establishing a national unity government. This needs to be done with a keen understanding of the root issues and concerns that have led to the present situation in the country.

Syria

The ongoing war in Syria has caused an enormous humanitarian catastrophe. Tens of thousands of Syrians have been killed by government and opposition forces, and more than 4.6 million Syrians are refugees, while 6.6 million are internally displaced.[101] In a broader context, the focal point for regional and international rivalry—including but not limited to the United States and Iran—has begun in Syria. Many countries have entered this battle and are unrelenting in their goal to see the other sides defeated. The stakes are high, as the victor will have a strong say on how the region will be shaped in the future. Both sides assume a zero-sum game, where if they win, the other loses. But the reality is that the conflict in Syria could well unleash an uncontrollable conflict in the region—particularly since Afghanistan, Iraq, Jordan, Lebanon, Yemen, and even Saudi Arabia are fragile—resulting in a lose-lose outcome for the United States, Russia, Iran, the region as a whole, and beyond if events continue on their current course.

The regional and international configuration manifesting itself over the Syrian crisis pits an Eastern Alliance (comprising Russia, China, Iran, Iraq, Hezbollah, and the Assad government) against a Western Alliance (including the United States, the EU, Israel, Turkey, and Saudi Arabia). The Western Alliance has relied on the opposition, which morphed from a variation of legitimate Syrian groups to being composed predominantly of extremist fighters (from all over the globe and closely affiliated with Al-Qaeda and ISIS) to conduct attacks on the ground against the Assad government. These fighters have received funds, weaponry, intelligence, and political support from countries like Saudi Arabia and Qatar.[102]

Concurrently, Russia and China have blocked the Western Alliance by vetoing multiple UNSC resolutions aimed at allowing international intervention in Syria. On September 30, 2015, Russia further entrenched itself in the Syrian conflict by commencing a large-scale military operation (principally airstrikes) at the behest of the Syrian government to counter rebel and terrorist groups.[103] Iran continues to provide a vital lifeline for the Syrian government to maintain its grip on power, even though Tehran had initially objected to the violent tactics Assad uses to curb internal opposition.[104]

The latest intensification in military actions against the insurgency seems to indicate the Assad government will continue its crackdown while aiming to maintain the loyalty of the Alawites, other minority groups, and Sunni populations that have become war weary and oppose extremist groups.

The Syrian quagmire has created a breeding ground for extremism to flourish and, most likely in the midst of this chaos, propagate broadly. Thus, the civil war in Syria will not be confined to its borders and will spill over throughout the Levant, Libya, Jordan, Turkey, and Iraq, with the possibility of spreading to the Persian Gulf states and, ultimately, reaching Israel.

The lack of sustained political efforts has contributed to the failure to resolve the conflict in Syria. Two rounds of UN-backed international peace conferences on the future of Syria, between the Syrian government and the opposition in Geneva (January and February 2014), ended with no breakthroughs because of fundamental flaws in how they were conducted. First, the composition of the participants was heavy tilted toward supporters of the opposition, including members of extremist groups, while excluding key figures from the Syrian government and its allies. The content of the negotiations was dictated by Western and regional allies that opposed the Syrian government, making it almost impossible to reach a compromise. Without all stakeholders at the table and with no preconditions to the talks, the cycle of violence and destruction, of course, continues in Syria.

The second round of Geneva II talks, from February 10 to 15, 2014, were marred by controversy even prior to commencing. Fierce diplomatic controversy erupted over UN Secretary-General Ban Ki-moon's initial invitation and subsequent disinvitation of the Iranian government to partake in the talks. This highlighted the contradictory regional and international complexities that are at play in the Syrian conflict—where Washington's reservations about the composition of participants on behalf of its regional allies and backers of the Syrian opposition negated the essential need for a robust international engagement to bring about an end to the Syrian conflict. Excluding Iran, the main backer of the Syrian government, from the negotiations made meaningful progress impossible. Russian Foreign Minister Sergei Lavrov's reaction was that, "If this list [of countries to attend] does not include Iran, then, in my opinion, the conference will resemble a profanation."[105] Following the Geneva II talks, then UN Special Representative for Syria Lakhdar Brahimi, while expressing his disappointment with the outcome, emphasized that the only achievement of the talks was bringing the opposition and the Syrian government to sit down at the negotiating table.[106]

It would take another eighteen months of backdoor negotiations and preparations before another attempt would be made to bring an end to the Syrian conflict through the Vienna Process on October 30 and November 14, 2015.[107] This time, the composition and conditions for the talks would be fundamentally different. First, the Russian airstrikes in Syria that had begun on September 30, 2015, changed the conditions on the ground in favor of the Assad government, putting the opposition forces on the defensive. Second, the Iranian government accepted a Russian invitation to attend the Vienna talks—the first time Iran would officially be part of the negotiations.[108] Previous U.S. objections to Iran's participation did not rematerialize, primarily as the invitation came on the heels of Iran's historical nuclear accord with the world powers in July 2015 and the realization by the Obama administration that without Iran there could be no sustainable resolution to the Syrian crisis.[109]

Ultimately, the Vienna talks included twenty countries and international organizations, among them regional powerhouses that supported opposing parties in the Syrian conflict: Iran, Saudi Arabia, Turkey, Egypt, and Iraq. Neither the Syrian government nor the opposition took part, since the aim of the talks was to find common ground among the international community on the roadmap toward ending the conflict.[110]

The Vienna talks culminated in a signed joint statement by all participants, the "Final Declaration on the Results of the Syria Talks in Vienna," calling on the UN to prepare the ground for the Syrian government and opposition to commence "a political process leading to credible, inclusive, non-sectarian governance, followed by a new constitution and elections [administered by the United Nations]."[111] The one major sticking point—the fate of President Assad—remained unresolved, with varying viewpoints on how to address this issue. The opponents of President Assad, namely the United Sates, Saudi Arabia, and Turkey, insisted that he step down within a specified timeframe; Iran and Russia emphasized that the decision should be made by the Syrian people through the ballot box.[112]

In the aftermath of the Vienna talks, on December 18, 2015, the fifteen members of the UNSC unanimously passed a resolution endorsing the UN-led roadmap for the Syrian peace process. This would entail (1) achieving a cease-fire; (2) initiating talks between the Syrian government and opposition by January 2016; and (3) beginning a two-year timeline to create a unity government and hold elections. Following the vote, then U.S. Secretary of State John Kerry stated, "this council is sending a clear message to all concerned that the time is now to stop the killing in Syria and lay the groundwork for a government that the long-suffering people of that battered land can support."[113]

On February 1, 2016, the Geneva Peace Conference commenced with participation by the Syrian government and the opposition, aiming to reach a broad cease-fire, guarantee humanitarian aid deliveries, and halt the threat posed by ISIS.[114] The talks once again failed to achieve a concrete outcome amid Syrian government's Aleppo offensive, backed by Russian airstrikes. In other attempts, the United States and Russia brokered two short-lived cease-fires with UNSC backing. The first was enforced from February to July 2016, while the second attempt in September of the same year lasted only a week.[115] The failure of the United States and Russia to sustain and converge their efforts to end the conflict in Syria further deteriorated bilateral relations, ultimately leading to Washington suspending talks with Russia on Syria in early October 2016.[116]

The marred U.S.–Russian relations over Syria paved the way for an unprecedented level of Russian and Syrian bombing of the rebel-held stronghold of eastern Aleppo. The city suffered catastrophic damage during the four-year siege and the latest rounds of bombardment, finally falling into government control in December 2016. There was broad international condemnation of the tactics used by the Syrian government and its allies during the Aleppo offensive, including indiscriminate bombing and the use of cluster and barrel bombs. The UN High Commissioner for Human Rights warned that "crimes of historic proportions" were being committed in Aleppo.[117] The battle for east Aleppo leveled thousands of buildings and represented one of the bloodiest battles thus far in the Syrian civil war, killing an estimated 31,000 people.[118]

The fall of Aleppo was a major blow to the opposition forces, while it consolidated the gains of the Syrian government over strategic centers in the country and dramatically changed the course of the conflict and the possibilities of a political solution. In the midst of the operation to take Aleppo, another key development changed the calculus in favor of the Assad government—the Russian–Turkish rapprochement. Ankara, from the beginning of the Syrian conflict, had backed the opposition forces and insisted that Assad must leave as a precondition to political resolution to the Syrian crisis—positions that ran contrary to Moscow's preferences. Tensions between the two countries further escalated as the Syrian war dragged on and in the aftermath of Turkey taking down a Russian warplane on November 24, 2015, under the premise that it had violated Turkish airspace.[119] Bilateral relations took a positive turn on June 26, 2016, when Turkish President Recep Tayyip Erdoğan wrote a letter to Russian President Vladimir Putin to extend his condolences to the family of the deceased Russian pilot.[120] In a drastic turn of events following the Turkish apology, foreign ministers of the two countries agreed to coordinate their policies on Syria.[121]

The improved bilateral relations also facilitated a new cease-fire deal between the Syrian government and the opposition groups on December 29, 2016, through a trilateral agreement involving Russia, Turkey, and Iran. The cease-fire that went into effect the following day included both the Syrian government and the opposition (excluding UN-designated terrorist groups). The agreement was endorsed unanimously by UNSC Resolution 2336, as a constructive step ahead of UN-facilitated talks to follow in Geneva on February 8, 2017.[122] The contours and enforcement mechanism of the cease-fire agreement were hammered out between the participating groups in Astana, Kazakhstan, on January 23, 2017. A key outcome of the talks was the establishment of a trilateral monitoring body to enforce and minimize violations to the cease-fire.[123]

The Trump administration's Syrian policy has been unpredictable at best, oscillating between more assertive actions to President Trump's surprise announcement for U.S. troop withdrawal in December 2018. Since coming into office, President Trump's shift in U.S. policy in Syria has included military strikes, boosting the number of U.S. troops in Syria, arming Kurdish fighters along with other opposition groups. The first decisive action took place on April 16, 2017, when President Trump approved the first U.S. military strike against the Syrian government since the 2011 outbreak of civil war in the country. As noted in an earlier chapter, the U.S. military strike was aimed at the Syrian airbase which was, allegedly, the home base of the warplane responsible for a chemical attack on the civilians of Khan Sheikhoun.[124] While the strike escalated U.S. involvement in the Syrian conflict, then U.S. Secretary of State Rex Tillerson gave assurances that it did not represent a "change in our policy or our posture in Syria," but added a caveat that it did "demonstrate that President Trump is willing to act when governments and actors cross the line . . . and cross the line in the most heinous of ways."[125]

In March 2017, the United States sent an additional 400 troops to Syria, marking a departure from Obama era avoidance of further entanglement in

Syria through ground troops. The troop surge, according to a spokesperson for the U.S. commander in Syria, Colonel John Dorrian, attempts to provide "logistical and fire support to enable a successful assault on Raqqa, the self-proclaimed capital of ISIS."[126] In May 2017, the U.S. government accelerated direct military support for Syrian Kurdish opposition groups, mainly the Kurdish People's Protection Units (YPG), in the battle to take Raqqa and, more broadly, fight against ISIS.[127] The U.S. move, however, has caused major friction with its close regional ally and NATO member, Turkey. The Turkish government has consistently sought in vain to persuade the United States to cease cooperating with the YPG, a group Ankara considers a terrorist organization and Syrian affiliate to the Kurdistan Workers' Party (PKK) that has waged waves of attacks against the Turkish government since 1984.[128] Turkish Foreign Minister Mevlut Cavasoglu, following the announcement in Washington of the intention to supply the YPG with heavy weaponry, made it clear that "Both the PKK and the YPG are terrorist organizations and they are no different, apart from their names . . . every weapon seized by them is a threat to Turkey."[129]

Then in December 19, 2018 President Trump announced on Twitter that U.S. troops would be withdrawn from Syria. This dramatic change in U.S. policy toward the Syrian conflict was apparently made without consultation with senior advisors, military staff and the U.S. Congress. Such fluctuations in U.S. policy toward Syria, taken as a package, has damaged to the credibility of the U.S. to support its allies in the region, particularly Kurdish groups in Syria. So much so that then U.S. Defense Secretary Jim Mattis resigned a day after Trump's withdrawal announcement.[130] (*As of this writing, this process is ongoing, with no set deadline or end in sight for the eight-year-long, disastrous war in Syria.*)

Notes

1 Sami G. Hajjar, "U.S. Military Presence in the Persian Gulf: Challenges and Prospects," Strategic Studies Institute, March 2002, www.strategicstudiesinstitute.army.mil/Pubs/display.cfm?pubid=185.

2 "Israel: The Arab-Israeli Alliance Against Iran," July 23, 2009, www.strategypage.com/qnd/israel/articles/20090723.aspx.

3 Daniel Silander et al., *International Organizations and the Rise of ISIL: Global Responses to Human Security Threats* (London, UK: Routledge, July 15, 2016), 47.

4 "Israel: The Arab-Israeli Alliance Against Iran."

5 Steven Kull et al., "Public Opinion in the Islamic World on Terrorism, Al Qaeda, and US Policies," WorldPublicOpinion, February 2009, www.worldpublicopinion.org/pipa/pdf/feb09/STARTII_Feb09_rpt.pdf.

6 Ibid.

7 Hossein Askari, Amin Mohseni, and Sharzad Daneshvar, *The Militarization of the Persian Gulf: An Economic Analysis* (Cheltenham, UK: Edward Elgar Publishing Limited, 2010).

8 Aude Fleurant et al., "Trends in International Arms Transfer," SIPRI, February 2016, www.sipri.org/sites/default/files/Trends-in-international-arms-transfers-2016.pdf.

9 Ibid.

10 Ben Norton, "U.S. Boosts Military Aid to Israel to $3.8 Billion Per Year in Largest Package in U.S. History," *Salon*, September 14, 2016, www.salon.com/2016/09/14/u-s-boosts-military-aid-to-israel-to-3-8-billion-per-year-in-largest-package-in-u-s-history/.

11 Aharon Klieman and Yoel Guzansky, "Reading Trump's Middle East Policy," *Foreign Affairs*, November 17, 2016, www.foreignaffairs.com/articles/united-states/2016-11-17/reading-trumps-middle-east-policy.
12 Barbara Starr and Jeremy Diamond, "Syria Missile Strike: Trump Authorizes Action," *CNN*, April 7, 2017, https://edition.cnn.com/2017/04/06/politics/donald-trump-syria-military/.
13 "Why Trump Should Not Ditch the Deal with Iran," *The Economist*, April 27, 2017, www.economist.com/news/leaders/21721381-only-weeks-decide-confusion-reigns-why-trump-should-not-ditch-deal-iran.
14 Ibid.
15 Mark Landler and Peter Baker, "Saudi Arabia and Israel Will Be on Itinerary of Trump's First Foreign Trip," *New York Times*, May 4, 2017, www.nytimes.com/2017/05/04/us/politics/trump-to-visit-saudi-arabia-and-israel-in-first-foreign-trip.html.
16 Alexandra Wilts, "Trump Signs $110bn Arms Deal with Saudi Arabia," *The Independent*, May 20, 2017, www.independent.co.uk/news/world/americas/us-politics/donald-trump-latest-saudi-arabia-billions-arms-deal-military-sales-a7746601.html.
17 Emad Kiyaei, "Trump Means Business," The Cipher Brief, September 29, 2016, www.thecipherbrief.com/article/middle-east/trump-means-business-1095.
18 David Wright and Tom Kludt, "Trump Would Break Sharply with US Foreign Policy Tradition," *CNN*, accessed February 7, 2017, www.cnn.com/2016/07/21/politics/trump-foreign-policy-interview/index.html.
19 Grégoire Mallard and Paolo Foradori, "The Middle East at a Crossroads: How to Face the Perils of Nuclear Development in a Volatile Region," European University Institute, no. 2013/06, November 2013.
20 Alireza Nader, "Iran and a Nuclear-Weapon-Free Middle East," Arms Control Association, accessed September 1, 2016, www.armscontrol.org/print/5013.
21 Kareem Shaheen, "Defensive Shield for the Gulf Since 1982," *The National*, March 16, 2011, www.thenational.ae/news/uae-news/defensive-shield-for-the-gulf-since-1982.
22 Brahim Saidy, *The Gulf Cooperation Council's Unified Military Command* (Philadelphia, US: Foreign Policy Research Institute, 2014).
23 Will Fulton, "GCC-Iran Foreign Relations," AEI, July 21, 2011, www.irantracker.org/foreign-relations/gcc-iran-foreign-relations.
24 "GCC: Total Population and Percentage of Nationals and Foreign Nationals," GLMM, April 29, 2016, http://gulfmigration.eu/gcc-total-population-percentage-nationals-foreign-nationals-gcc-countries-national-statistics-2010-2016-numbers/.
25 Frank Gardner, "Gulf States Divided Over Iran," *BBC News*, January 13, 2014, sec. Middle East, www.bbc.com/news/world-middle-east-25713793.
26 Adel Bin Ahmed Al-Jubeir, "Can Iran Change?" *New York Times*, January 19, 2016, www.nytimes.com/2016/01/19/opinion/saudi-arabia-can-iran-change.html.
27 "History of Iran: Islamic Conquest," *Iran Chamber Society*, accessed March 27, 2018, www.iranchamber.com/history/islamic_conquest/islamic_conquest.php.
28 Dania Saadi, "Qatar Has World in Its Sights for Power Projects," *New York Times*, December 4, 2011, www.nytimes.com/2011/12/05/business/global/qatar-has-world-in-its-sights-for-power-projects.html.
29 Ian Black, "Iran and Iraq Remember War That Cost More Than a Million Lives," *The Guardian*, September 23, 2010, sec. World News, www.theguardian.com/world/2010/sep/23/iran-iraq-war-anniversary.
30 "Iraq Debt: Non-Paris Club Creditors 2004," accessed February 7, 2017, www.globalsecurity.org/wmd/library/report/2004/isg-final-report/ch2_anxd_img06.jpg.
31 Ami Ayalon, "Middle East Contemporary Survey, Volume XV: 1991," *Middle East Contemporary Survey* 15 (1993): 163–65, The Moshe Dayan Center.
32 Will Todman, "Gulf States' Policies on Syria," CSIS, October 18, 2016, https://csis-prod.s3.amazonaws.com/s3fs-public/publication/161019_Gulf_States_Policies_on_Syria.pdf.

33 Nader Habibi, "The Impact of Sanctions on Iran-GCC Economic Relations," Middle East Brief, Brandeis University, Crown Center for Middle East Studies, November 2010, www.brandeis.edu/crown/publications/meb/MEB45.pdf.
34 "08RIYADH649," Wikileaks, n.d., https://wikileaks.org/plusd/cables/08RIYADH649_a.html.
35 Hussein Ibish, "For Gulf Countries, Iran's Regional Behavior Overshadows Nuclear Deal," Arab Gulf States Institute in Washington, July 17, 2015, www.agsiw.org/for-gulf-countries-irans-regional-behavior-overshadows-nuclear-deal/.
36 Sean D. Naylor, "Will Curbing Iran's Nuclear Threat Boost Its Proxies?" *Foreign Policy*, July 20, 2015, https://foreignpolicy.com/2015/07/20/will-curbing-irans-nuclear-threat-boost-its-proxies/.
37 Martin S. Indyk, "U.S. Policy in the Middle East After a Nuclear Deal with Iran," Brookings Institution, June 3, 2015, www.brookings.edu/testimonies/u-s-policy-in-the-middle-east-after-a-nuclear-deal-with-iran/.
38 "After the Nuclear Deal: Perspectives for the Middle East," 15th Körber Dialogue Middle East, Körber Foundation, June 2015, http://epub.sub.uni-hamburg.de/epub/volltexte/2015/42376/pdf/WPMP0R4.pdf.
39 Richard Nephew and Robert Einhorn, "The Iran Nuclear Deal: Prelude to Proliferation in the Middle East?" Brookings Institution, May 31, 2016, www.brookings.edu/research/the-iran-nuclear-deal-prelude-to-proliferation-in-the-middle-east/.
40 Suzanne Maloney, "A Cold Shoulder in the Cold War: Iran's Foreign Minister Snubs a Saudi Invite," Brookings Institution, June 5, 2014, www.brookings.edu/blog/markaz/2014/06/05/a-cold-shoulder-in-the-cold-war-irans-foreign-minister-snubs-a-saudi-invite/.
41 Ilan Goldenberg, "Judging the Iran Nuclear Deal, Six Months in," *National Interest*, accessed September 1, 2016, http://nationalinterest.org/feature/judging-the-iran-nuke-deal-six-months-14875.
42 "Text: 1993 Declaration of Principles," *BBC News*, accessed September 1, 2016, http://news.bbc.co.uk/2/hi/in_depth/middle_east/israel_and_the_palestinians/key_documents/1682727.stm.
43 Ibid.
44 Barton Gellman, "Netanyahu, Arafat Sign Accord: Talks Nearly Founder After Israel Demands Convicted Spy's Release," *Washington Post*, October 24, 1998, A1.
45 Hossein Mousavian, *Iran-Europe Relations, Challenges and Opportunities* (London, UK: Routledge, 2008), 229.
46 "History of Failed Peace Talks," *BBC News*, accessed September 1, 2016, http://news.bbc.co.uk/2/hi/middle_east/6666393.stm#campdavid2.
47 Ibid.
48 Robert Burns, "Obama Opens Long-Shot Talks on Mideast Peace," *BET*, September 1, 2010, www.bet.com/news/news/2010/09/01/obamaopenstalks.html?cid=facebook.
49 Scott Wilson, "Obama Searches for Middle East Peace—The Washington Post," *Washington Post*, accessed September 1, 2016, www.washingtonpost.com/politics/obama-searches-for-middle-east-peace/2012/07/14/gJQAQQiKlW_story.html.
50 Matt Spetalnick and Jeff Mason, "U.S.," *Reuters*, November 2, 2011, www.reuters.com/article/us-palestinians-israel-usa-idUSTRE7A142K20111102.
51 "Resolution 2334 (2016)," United Nations Security Council, December 23, 2016, www.un.org/en/ga/search/view_doc.asp?symbol=S/RES/2334(2016).
52 "Trump Vows Changes at the UN After Israel Vote," *Al Jazeera*, accessed February 7, 2017, www.aljazeera.com/news/2016/12/trump-vows-israel-vote-161224040133216.html.
53 Julie Hirschfeld Davis, "Jerusalem Embassy Is a Victory for Trump, and a Complication for Middle East Peace," *New York Times*, May 14, 2018, www.nytimes.com/2018/05/14/us/politics/trump-jerusalem-embassy-middle-east-peace.html.

54 Stephen Collinson, “What the UN Vote Says About How Trump Will Treat Israel,” *CNN*, accessed February 7, 2017, www.cnn.com/2016/12/23/politics/us-israel-un-vote-donald-trump-netanyahu/index.html.
55 “Plan Approved for 2,500 New Settler Homes in West Bank,” *Al Jazeera*, January 24, 2017, www.aljazeera.com/news/2017/01/israel-approves-plan-2500-settler-homes-170124134719735.html.
56 Matthew Rosenberg, “Trump Chooses Hard-Liner as Ambassador to Israel,” *New York Times*, December 15, 2016, www.nytimes.com/2016/12/15/us/politics/donald-trump-david-friedman-israel-ambassador.html.
57 Ishaan Tharoor, “Trump’s Unquestioning Support Means Trouble for Israel,” *Washington Post*, accessed February 7, 2017, www.washingtonpost.com/news/worldviews/wp/2017/01/25/trumps-unquestioning-support-could-lead-israel-to-disaster/.
58 Marshall Breger, “Trump’s Israel Policy Is Dangerous and Irresponsible,” *The Hill*, July 20, 2016, http://thehill.com/blogs/pundits-blog/presidential-campaign/288245-trumps-israel-policy-is-dangerous-and-irresponsible.
59 Collinson, “What the UN Vote Says About How Trump Will Treat Israel.”
60 Eugenio Lilli, “The Arab Awakening and US Counterterrorism in the Greater Middle East: A Missed Opportunity,” *Journal of Terrorism Research* 6, no. 2 (May 25, 2015), doi:10.15664/jtr.1152.
61 Erin Cunningham, “Tunisia Elections Seen as Litmus Test for Arab Spring,” *Public Radio International*, October 22, 2011, www.pri.org/stories/2011-10-22/tunisia-elections-seen-litmus-test-arab-spring.
62 “Tunisia Signs New Constitution into Law,” *Al Jazeera*, January 27, 2014, www.aljazeera.com/news/africa/2014/01/tunisia-assembly-approves-new-constitution-201412622480531861.html.
63 Laryssa Chomiak, “Five Years After the Tunisian Revolution, Political Frustration Doesn’t Diminish Progress,” *Washington Post*, January 14, 2016, www.washingtonpost.com/news/monkey-cage/wp/2016/01/14/five-years-after-the-tunisian-revolution/.
64 Yaroslav Trofimov, “How Tunisia Became a Top Source of ISIS Recruits,” *Wall Street Journal*, February 25, 2016, sec. World, www.wsj.com/articles/how-tunisia-became-a-top-source-of-isis-recruits-1456396203.
65 “Muslim Brotherhood-Backed Candidate Morsi Wins Egyptian Presidential Election,” *Fox News*, June 24, 2012, www.foxnews.com/world/2012/06/24/egypt-braces-for-announcement-president.html.
66 “President Morsi Overthrown in Egypt,” *Al Jazeera*, English, July 4, 2013, www.aljazeera.com/news/middleeast/2013/07/20137319828176718.html.
67 Lilli, “The Arab Awakening and US Counterterrorism in the Greater Middle East: A Missed Opportunity.”
68 “El-Sisi Wins Egypt’s Presidential Race with 96.91%,” *Al-Ahram* Online, June 3, 2014, http://english.ahram.org.eg/NewsContent/1/64/102841/Egypt/Politics-/BREAKING-PEC-officially-announces-AbdelFattah-ElSi.aspx.
69 “Egypt: Year of Abuses Under Al-Sisi,” Human Rights Watch, January 8, 2015, www.hrw.org/news/2015/06/08/egypt-year-abuses-under-al-sisi.
70 Ali Houissa, “Arab Spring: A Research & Study Guide: Libya,” Cornell University Library, February 5, 2018, http://guides.library.cornell.edu/c.php?g=31688&p=200751.
71 “United Nations Security Council Resolution 1973 (2011),” United Nations Security Council, March 17, 2011.
72 “NATO Air Strikes Hit Tripoli in Heaviest Bombing Yet,” *The Guardian*, May 24, 2011, www.theguardian.com/world/2011/may/24/nato-airstrikes-tripoli-heaviest-bombing-libya.
73 “Libya: Power to the People or Militias?” *France 24*, February 28, 2011, www.france24.com/en/20110228-libya-muammar-gaddafi-unrest-arab-africa-tripoli.
74 Lilli, “The Arab Awakening and US Counterterrorism in the Greater Middle East: A Missed Opportunity.”

75 "Libya, Extremism, and the Consequences of Collapse," Soufan Group, January 2016, http://soufangroup.com/wp-content/uploads/2016/01/TSG_Libya-Extremism-and-the-Consequences-of-Collapse-Jan2016.pdf.
76 Ibid.
77 Elliott Abrams, "How Obama Caved on Bahrain," *Foreign Policy*, February 27, 2015, https://foreignpolicy.com/2015/02/27/how-obama-caved-on-bahrain-manama-human-rights/.
78 Ibid.
79 Megan Eckstein, "DoD, Navy: U.S. 5th Fleet Operations Not Affected by Regional Tensions," *USNI News*, January 4, 2016, https://news.usni.org/2016/01/04/dod-navy-u-s-5th-fleet-operations-not-affected-by-regional-tensions.
80 Josh Rogin, "Obama Administration Using Loophole to Quietly Sell Arms Package to Bahrain," *Foreign Policy*, January 27, 2012, https://foreignpolicy.com/2012/01/27/obama-administration-using-loophole-to-quietly-sell-arms-package-to-bahrain/.
81 Michael Birnbaum and Joby Warrick, "As Bahrain Stifles Protest Movement, U.S.'s Muted Objections Draw Criticism," *Washington Post*, April 15, 2011, sec. World, www.washingtonpost.com/world/as-bahrain-stifles-protest-movement-uss-muted-objections-draw-criticism/2011/04/14/AFziTofD_story.html.
82 Amy Austin Homes, "The Military Intervention That the World Forgot," *Al Jazeera*, America, March 29, 2014, http://america.aljazeera.com/opinions/2014/3/bahrain-uprisinginterventionsaudiarabiaemirates.html.
83 Abrams, "How Obama Caved on Bahrain."
84 "Yemen Crisis: Who Is Fighting Whom?" *BBC News*, October 14, 2016, sec. Middle East, www.bbc.com/news/world-middle-east-29319423.
85 "Key Facts About the War in Yemen," *Al Jazeera*, August 1, 2016, www.aljazeera.com/news/2016/06/key-facts-war-yemen-160607112342462.html.
86 Tony Iltis, "Middle East: Saudi Arabia's US-Backed War on Yemen," *Links International Journal of Socialist Renewal*, accessed February 7, 2017, http://links.org.au/node/4384.
87 "Key Facts About the War in Yemen."
88 "The Peace and National Partnership Agreement," *Saba Net—Yemen News Agency*, September 22, 2014, www.sabanews.net/en/news369204.htm.
89 Mona El-Naggar, "Shifting Alliances Play Out Behind Closed Doors in Yemen," *New York Times*, January 25, 2015, www.nytimes.com/2015/01/26/world/middleeast/yemeni-parliament-cancels-meeting-on-presidents-resignation.html.
90 "Yemen's Hadi Flees to Aden and Says He Is Still President," *Reuters*, February 21, 2015, www.reuters.com/article/us-yemen-security-idUSKBN0LP08F20150221.
91 Ranjit Gupta, "West Asia Six Years After 'Arab Spring': Prognosis for 2017," *Eurasia Review*, January 20, 2017, www.eurasiareview.com/20012017-west-asia-six-years-after-arab-spring-prognosis-for-2017/.
92 "Yemen Crisis: Who Is Fighting Whom?"
93 Richard N. Haass (@RichardHaass), "Further Evidence #Yemen Becoming Saudi Arabia's Vietnam; Blowback May Well Weaken Stability of #Saudiarabia Itself," *Twitter*, June 25, 2015, https://twitter.com/RichardHaass/status/613906812799221760.
94 Mohammad Ghobari, "At Least 10,000 Killed in Yemen Civil War," *Huffington Post*, August 30, 2016, sec. WorldPost, www.huffingtonpost.com/entry/at-least-10000-killed-in-yemen-civil-war_us_57c58703e4b0664f13ca63e4.
95 "UNICEF: One Child Dies Every 10 Minutes in Yemen," *Al Jazeera*, accessed February 7, 2017, www.aljazeera.com/news/2016/12/unicef-child-dies-10-minutes-yemen-161212192354606.html.
96 Gregory Viscusi, "Saudi Claims on Iran's Role in Yemen Face Skepticism in West," *Bloomberg*, April 16, 2015, www.bloomberg.com/news/articles/2015-04-16/u-s-europe-back-saudis-in-yemen-while-skeptical-of-iran-role.

97 Gupta, "West Asia Six Years After 'Arab Spring': Prognosis for 2017."
98 "Key Facts About the War in Yemen."
99 Ali Watkins, "Iran Warned Houthis Against Yemen Takeover," *Huffington Post*, South Africa, April 20, 2015, www.huffingtonpost.com/2015/04/20/iran-houthis-yemen_n_7101456.html.
100 Saeid Jafari, "Why Iran Doesn't Want to Stay in Yemen," *Al-Monitor*, October 27, 2015, www.al-monitor.com/pulse/originals/2015/10/iran-yemen-involvement.html.
101 "UNHCR Syria Regional Refugee Response," UNHCR, accessed September 1, 2016, http://data.unhcr.org/syrianrefugees/regional.php.
102 Seyed Hossein Mousavian, "An Opportunity for a U.S.–Iran Paradigm Shift," *Washington Quarterly* 36, no. 1 (December 17, 2012): 129–44.
103 "Russia Carries Out First Air Strikes in Syria," *Al Jazeera*, September 30, 2015, www.aljazeera.com/news/2015/09/russian-carries-air-strikes-syria-150930133155190.html.
104 "Iran's Ahmadinejad Condemns 'Massacre' in Ally Syria," *Agence France Presse*, accessed September 1, 2016, https://now.mmedia.me/lb/en/archive/irans_ahmadinejad_condemns_massacre_in_ally_syria.
105 "Geneva II Without Iran 'Mistake'," *Press TV*, accessed September 1, 2016, http://edition.presstv.ir/detail/346694.html.
106 Hossein Amir-Abdollahian, "Iran's Four-Part Plan for a Political Solution in Syria," *Al-Monitor*, March 5, 2014, www.al-monitor.com/pulse/originals/2014/03/iran-four-part-plan-political-solution-syria.html.
107 Thomas Erdbrink, David E. Sanger, and Sewell Chan, "After a U.S. Shift, Iran Has a Seat at Talks on War in Syria," *New York Times*, October 28, 2015, www.nytimes.com/2015/10/29/world/middleeast/syria-talks-vienna-iran.html.
108 "Kerry Sees New Syria Talks Next Week, Does Not Rule Out Iran Role," *Reuters*, October 23, 2015, www.reuters.com/article/us-mideast-crisis-talks-idUSKCN0SH1LN20151023.
109 Erdbrink et al., "After a U.S. Shift, Iran Has a Seat at Talks on War in Syria."
110 "Syria Conflict: World Powers to Intensify Quest for Peace," *BBC News*, October 30, 2015, sec. Middle East, www.bbc.com/news/world-middle-east-34673535.
111 "Final Declaration on the Results of the Syria Talks in Vienna as Agreed by Participants," European Union, October 30, 2015, http://eeas.europa.eu/statements-eeas/2015/151030_06.htm.
112 "Syria Conflict: World Powers to Intensify Quest for Peace."
113 "U.N. Endorses Syria Peace Plan in Rare Show of Unity Among Big Powers," *Reuters*, December 19, 2015, http://uk.reuters.com/article/us-mideast-crisis-syria-un-idUKKBN0U10J020151219.
114 "Syria Conflict: Opposition Sets Terms for Geneva Peace Talks," *BBC News*, January 31, 2016, sec. Middle East, www.bbc.com/news/world-middle-east-35452640.
115 "Syria's Civil War: US, Russia Clinch Deal," *Al Jazeera*, accessed February 7, 2017, www.aljazeera.com/news/2016/09/syria-civil-war-russia-clinch-syria-deal-160910031517683.html.
116 Michael R. Gordon and Andrew E. Kramer, "Tension with Russia Rises as U.S. Halts Syria Negotiations," *New York Times*, October 3, 2016, www.nytimes.com/2016/10/04/world/middleeast/us-suspends-talks-with-russia-on-syria.html.
117 "'Crimes of Historic Proportions' Being Committed in Aleppo, UN Rights Chief Warns," *UN News*, Service Section, October 21, 2016, www.un.org/apps/news/story.asp?NewsID=55364#.WJoLqrYrKRu.
118 "Center for Documentation of Violations in Syria—Killed List," Violations Documentation Centre in Syria, accessed February 7, 2017, https://goo.gl/G1VRrE.
119 "Syrian Rebels Fired on Parachuting Russian Pilots, Killing at Least One After Turkey Shot Down Warplane: Official," *National Post*, accessed February 7, 2017,

http://news.nationalpost.com/news/world/turkey-blasts-russian-warplane-out-of-the-sky-says-jet-violated-its-airspace-pilots-fate-unclear.

120 Andrew Roth, "Turkish President Apologizes for Downing of Russian Warplane Last Year," *Washington Post*, June 27, 2016, www.washingtonpost.com/world/turkey-apologizes-for-shooting-down-russian-warplane-last-year/2016/06/27/d969e0ea-3c6d-11e6-9e16-4cf01a41decb_story.html.

121 Zia Weise and Roland Oliphant, "Russia and Turkey to 'Coordinate' Syria Policy," *The Telegraph*, July 1, 2016, www.telegraph.co.uk/news/2016/07/01/russia-and-turkey-to-|coordinate-syria-policy/.

122 "Syria Chronology of Events: Security Council Report," February 2, 2017, www.securitycouncilreport.org/chronology/syria.php.

123 Patrick Wintour, "Sponsors of Syria Talks in Astana Strike Deal to Protect Fragile Ceasefire," *The Guardian*, January 24, 2017, sec. World News, www.theguardian.com/world/2017/jan/24/syria-talks-astana-russia-turkey-iran-ceasefire.

124 Barbara Starr and Jeremy Diamond, "Trump Launches Military Strike Against Syria," *CNN*, April 7, 2017, www.cnn.com/2017/04/06/politics/donald-trump-syria-military/index.html.

125 Ibid.

126 "Why the Trump Administration Is Sending More Troops to Syria," *PBS NewsHour*, March 23, 2017, www.pbs.org/newshour/show/trump-administration-sending-troops-syria.

127 Patrick Cockburn, "Donald Trump Quietly Made a Decision That Will Have a Huge Impact on the Middle East," *The Independent*, May 10, 2017, www.independent.co.uk/news/world/middle-east/donald-trump-isis-syria-crisis-kurdish-fighters-turkey-raqqa-ypg-a7728741.html.

128 "Who Are Kurdistan Workers' Party (PKK) Rebels?" *BBC News*, November 4, 2016, www.bbc.com/news/world-europe-20971100.

129 Niamh McIntyre, "Trump Team Stops Disclosing Troop Deployments in Iraq and Syria," *The Independent*, April 1, 2017, www.independent.co.uk/news/world/americas/us-politics/donald-trump-administration-stops-disclosing-troop-deployments-iraq-syria-islamic-state-isis-a7662016.html.

130 Megan Specia, "The Planned U.S. Troop Withdrawal From Syria: Here's the Latest," *The New York Times*, January 16, 2019.

6 Moving forward

As the preceding chapters have detailed, the realization of the WMDFZ in the Middle East will not be an easy undertaking, and the lack of meaningful progress since it was first proposed by Egypt in 1990 serves as a testament to the long road ahead. This chapter will discuss the benefits of the zone for all member states, the region, and beyond. It aims to generate interest among local, national, and international organizations, institutions, governments, and civil society to expand and explore new ways of reviving the call for the establishment of the WMDFZ in the Middle East.

Wide dissemination of the zone's benefits regarding security, stability, and economic vitality is crucial to generate the political will to press ahead with such an endeavor. The prism through which the zone has been seen thus far requires a shift to demonstrate the array of benefits that go beyond nonproliferation. The zone, by diminishing proliferation risks, sets in motion regional efforts to tackle deep-rooted issues such as the Palestinian–Israeli peace process, energy security, and regional stability. Furthermore, the zone will require regional countries build closer lines of communication and take steps to reduce tensions and mistrust, thus cultivating a new beginning in multilateral and bilateral relations. Finally, the zone could unlock the true potential of a region rich in both natural and human resources in one of the most strategic locations on the planet. With hope of improved regional relations, excessive spending on defense would also diminish, freeing vast amounts of financial resources for high-impact economic, political, and social development.

Constructive role of external powers

World powers will continue to have vested interests in the Middle East, owing to its strategic location, vast natural resources, and deep religious and cultural ties throughout the world. Therefore, the security and stability of the Middle East is vital not only for regional states but also the wider international community, in particular the world powers. The political and security realities of the region necessitate more robust and constructive involvement of the international community for any meaningful advancement toward a WMDFZ in the Middle East.

Therefore, participation by external powers will be paramount to the success of the zone.

All WMD nonproliferation conventions and treaties have primarily three core goals: first, to prevent the spread of WMD and technologies related to their weaponization; second, to guarantee complete disarmament of such weapons by member state signatories; and third, to ensure cooperation in the peaceful use of nuclear, biological, and chemical sectors among all member states.[1]

Since the largest arsenals of WMD are possessed by permanent members of the UNSC (China, Russia, the United Kingdom, France, and the United States), such states should demonstrate their serious determination to reduce their reliance on WMD and orchestrate a "multilateral and collective security cooperation" effort to address global security threats. Any traction on global nuclear disarmament must be spearheaded by the United States and Russia, as they are by far the world's largest nuclear powers. In a positive move toward that aim, President Trump has suggested that both countries should "reduce very substantially" their respective nuclear arsenals. He then went on to propose that his administration would review U.S. sanctions placed on Russia for its actions in Ukraine and Crimea, and would consider lifting them as part of negotiations on nuclear arms control. In response, the Russian foreign ministry welcomed the remarks and showed readiness to discuss mutual nuclear arms control. This development could also stem the chances of a nuclear arms race between the two countries.[2]

The permanent members of the UNSC have opted to modernize their nuclear arsenals, delivery systems, and related infrastructure, which undermines the objectives of the NPT in terms of both nonproliferation and disarmament. The final document of the 2010 NPT Review Conference included recommendations to enhance and accelerate nuclear weapons disarmament by NPT members "in a way that promotes international stability and based on the principle of undiminished security for all." The recommendations included (1) unilateral efforts by nuclear-weapon states to reduce their nuclear arsenals; (2) increased transparency by the nuclear-weapon states with regard to nuclear weapons capabilities; (3) implementation of voluntary confidence-building measures to support further progress in nuclear disarmament; (4) further reduction of nonstrategic nuclear weapons through unilateral and multilateral initiatives; (5) concrete measures to reduce operational status of nuclear-weapons systems; and (6) a diminishing role for nuclear weapons in security policies.[3] Such efforts would strengthen the collective will and legitimacy of attempts to realize a WMD-free zone in the Middle East.

Global powers—such as the five permanent members of the UNSC (the United States, the United Kingdom, Russia, France, and China) in addition to Japan, India, and Brazil—can facilitate a more holistic involvement in the region and place importance on institution-building to strengthen nonproliferation efforts. This can be achieved through regional and international cooperation in the transfer of technology and know-how in fields related to the peaceful nuclear, biological, and chemical industries.

While the scope of the zone in the Middle East would be wider (to include all WMD) and face unique geopolitical challenges, there is no doubt that lessons learned from other nuclear weapons-free zones could overarch in many aspects. Such institutional knowledge garnered by these regional zones over the years can contribute to advancing the Middle East WMDFZ.

The precedent set during the Cold War, when the United States and Soviet Union, at odds on an array of issues, came to an understanding on nuclear weapons control, is yet another source where lessons learned can be applied by regional countries in regard to Israel's nuclear weapons. The basic premise for the U.S.–Soviet Union arms control agreement was that, while both countries may differ on almost every ideological, political, economic, and geopolitical matters, a nuclear war would obliterate them both and, with them, a good chunk of human civilization. Using the same thinking, it is necessary that Israel and the regional countries, including Iran, realize that, on this specific issue, the stakes are high for all and will require every state to take action to realize a WMDFZ in the Middle East. By joining efforts to realize the zone, there would be reduced concern over the development or possession of WMD. With a regional agreement with multi-layered verification, mutual monitoring, and confidence-building and cooperation mechanisms, key regional security worries would diminish.

Beyond the realm of WMD nonproliferation, reduced expenditures in regional defense budgets would free up billions of dollars to rapidly impact economic development in the region. Investment of those resources into all sectors of the economy would boost bilateral relations and integrate the global economy along diverse sectors in the region, benefitting both governments and their people. The opportunity to expand economic and political ties among regional states and international players would undoubtedly promote shared universal values and the responsibility to uphold them.

Strengthening all WMD treaties

The WMDFZ will require all regional countries sign and ratify all related conventions and treaties on banning such weapons, to be implemented in a sequential manner. The first step would be for regional countries to sign and ratify the Comprehensive Test-Ban Treaty (CTBT), as it is aimed primarily at stopping countries (with or without nuclear weapons) from testing and modifying their weapons. Enforcing CTBT is more plausible, since regional countries do not possess nuclear weapons and are signatory to the NPT (with the exception of Israel). Interestingly, Israel is also a signatory to the CTBT and is more likely to ratify it within a broader agreement on the WMDFZ.

The second step entails the few remaining regional countries—Djibouti, Israel, Mauritania, and Syria—signing and/or ratifying the BWC. The most compelling argument to achieve universalization of the BWC in the region is that biological weapons have limited military use, but ease of acquisition by non-state actors or terrorists has heightened the need for stronger regulation and oversight. The WMDFZ could achieve increased security measures by enforcing a region-wide ban on the acquisition, development, or use of biological weapons. With increased transparency, verification, and oversight, the prospects will become stronger for a regional collaboration in the legitimate peaceful uses of biological field.[4]

The third step requires regional states become part of the CWC. Once again, most states in the Middle East have signed and ratified the convention, including the 2013 Syrian accession (excluding Comoros, Egypt, and Somalia, with Israel needing to ratify).[5] The most important impetus for the remaining countries to join and ratify the convention is the fact that the Middle East is the only region since World War II where chemical weapons have been used, and with devastating human cost (Iran, Iraq, Yemen, Libya, and Syria).[6] With such historical precedents, there is a willingness on the part of all regional countries to see an end to chemical weapons use, production, and stockpiling. Matters have become even more urgent due to the risk of Syrian chemical weapons landing in the hands of extremists or terrorists in the ongoing turmoil in that country.

The fourth step is to counter WMD trafficking and terrorism by having firm commitments from and implementation by regional countries of a series of UNSC resolutions (UNSCR), conventions, and treaties. These include the following: (1) UNSCR 1373, which criminalizes any form of support (financial, material, or safe haven) for terrorists;[7] (2) UNSCR 1540, which is the first universal resolution to counter WMD acquisition by non-state actors and strengthen existing nonproliferation treaties;[8] (3) the Convention on the Physical Protection of Nuclear Material (CPPNM), which aims to safeguard radioactive materials and mitigate accidents or malicious use;[9] (4) the International Convention for the Suppression of Acts of Nuclear Terrorism (ICSANT), which encourages states to prosecute offenders that commit acts of sabotage or damage to nuclear facilities;[10] and (5) strengthening already established infrastructures aimed at regional cooperation on biological threats, such as the Middle East Consortium on Infectious Disease Surveillance (MECIDS).[11] It goes without saying that the Middle East is rife with conditions for terrorists to take advantage of its instability to acquire, develop, and use WMD. Terrorism is a common enemy of the region and can be the catalyst to bring all regional countries to proactively implement these resolutions and conventions.

The fifth and final step requires Israel sign and ratify the NPT, as all other regional countries have already done so. The two main obstacles to regional universalization of the NPT are concerns over Iran's nuclear program and the presence of Israel's nuclear weapons arsenal. The former obstacle was removed with the landmark Iran nuclear accord in 2015; however, the current status quo of maintaining Israel's nuclear monopoly in the midst of the Arab Awakening and Iran's mastery of the nuclear fuel cycle is no longer sustainable. We have discussed in an earlier chapter the genesis and development of the Israeli nuclear weapons program and the need for concerted international political pressure for Israel to disarm.

We have also proposed technical steps Israel could take to relinquish its nuclear arsenal and join nonproliferation efforts. These steps require Israel to (1) shut down its Dimona plutonium-production reactor and reprocessing plant; (2) place all nuclear materials and facilities under the IAEA safeguards agreement; (3) dismantle stockpiles of nuclear weapons and fissile materials (separated plutonium and HEU) in collaboration with IAEA and in accordance with an agreed schedule; (4) limit the level of uranium enrichment; and (5) begin the official process of joining the NPT as a nonnuclear weapons state.

Iran nuclear accord: advancing the global nuclear weapons ban

The Iranian nuclear accord, or JCPOA, is one of the most important nonproliferation agreements in decades, and provides a building block that could contribute to the overall progress toward the WMDFZ in the Middle East. It also removed a key justification (by regional and international players) for the slow pace of progress on the zone. The success and realization of the zone will rely heavily on the sustainability of the Iranian nuclear accord. The comprehensive agreement has established transparency for Iran's nuclear program, eased sanctions, and guaranteed the rights of Iran under the NPT, ultimately strengthening nuclear nonproliferation efforts. As discussed in an earlier chapter, the regionalization of key components of transparency, verification, and monitoring of the JCPOA not only will strengthen nonproliferation but also will bring the region a step closer to realizing the zone.

Since the JCPOA was agreed on by all permanent members of the UNSC—which is an achievement on its own—it could be expanded to be incorporated into a regional nonproliferation regime. The other regional benefits from the JCPOA include (1) a reduction in international and, more important, regional concerns about the nature of Iran's nuclear program and a strengthening of the WMDFZ initiative; (2) cooperation among regional countries in the field of peaceful nuclear energy as stipulated in Article IV of NPT;[12] (3) the easing of tensions within the international community over Iran's nuclear program to, hopefully, shift the focus toward calls for increased pressure on Israel—the sole nuclear weapons state and non-party to the NPT in the region—to forego its nuclear arsenal and join all other nations in the region by adopting the NPT; and (4) encourage other regional countries to proactively advance the zone while highlighting the benefits of a peaceful nuclear energy program. This vantage point will enable Iran to become the hub for regional cooperation on peaceful nuclear technologies.

The benefits of the Iran nuclear accord are not bound by the borders of the Middle East. Rather, this historic agreement can serve as the blueprint toward strengthening global nonproliferation with the ultimate aim of reaching zero nuclear weapons.[13] As former U.S. President Barack Obama stated in the aftermath of the Iran nuclear accord, "every pathway to a nuclear weapon is cut off."[14] In a sense, globalizing the contours of the Iran nuclear accord would "cut off" the means for nuclear weapons proliferation by other countries. It would also spearhead the major incentive of the NPT, one that was the central bargain for the treaty to function, whereby, in exchange for remaining a nonnuclear weapons state, signatories would gain access to peaceful nuclear technology and cooperation. Furthermore, it would provide momentum to Article VI of the NPT, which requires disarmament by nuclear weapon members. These measures would foster a stronger and more effective nonproliferation effort and, in doing so, strengthen the NPT and its credibility.

The crux of the concerns over Iran's nuclear program was the production and stockpiling of HEU and plutonium reprocessing—both a major proliferation risk. The nuclear deal, though, addressed these concerns by placing limits on enrichment levels and production, capping the number of centrifuges, and prohibiting plutonium reprocessing. The nuclear deal also put in place the most stringent inspection, monitoring, and verification requirements. The Iran nuclear accord provides for the first time the mechanisms to close the gaps within the NPT by enhancing IAEA inspection arrangements and setting limits on enrichment and plutonium separation. As former U.S. and U.K. ambassadors to the United Nations Thomas Pickering and Lord Hannay penned in an article, "the Iran Agreement completes the work of the Non-Proliferation Treaty (NPT) for the first time . . . [and] to draw on that agreement to use its standards by applying them to all countries seeking to enrich uranium for any purpose or attempting to use plutonium for reactor fuel."[15]

In the same article, the ambassadors outline the major benefits of globalizing the principles of the Iran nuclear accord: (1) strengthen global nonproliferation efforts and, in doing so, remove some of President Trump's reservations about the Iran nuclear accord; (2) serve as a confidence-building measure between global powers, specifically the United States and Russia; (3) set an international standard and limits on uranium enrichment and plutonium separation; (4) transform the commitments by Iran as part of the nuclear deal to become the norm and apply to all states; and (5) remove the sunset clauses in the Iran nuclear accord, as by doing so, the new "Global Nuclear Accord" will have no time limitation and Iran, too, will be part of it.[16]

Global religious support for WMD nonproliferation

Countering WMD proliferation requires proactive efforts, including obtaining religious support for the WMDFZ in the Middle East by bringing Islamic leaders to endorse Iranian Supreme Leader Ayatollah Khamenei's Fatwa banning all WMD. Such an initiative will contribute positively on two fronts. First, it places a religious obligation on the majority Muslim population of the region and their respective governments to support the realization of the zone and commit to WMD nonproliferation. Second, since the dominant religion in the region is Islam, it sets a common foundation to facilitate regional cooperation on an array of issues, including tackling terrorism and extremism; addressing social and economic needs; and enhancing civil society engagement.

If successful, this initiative can serve as the basis to expand the religious commitment by the Islamic world to include other major religions. Toward this aim, the Permanent Representative of the Islamic Republic of Iran registered Ayatollah Khamenei's Fatwa banning all WMD as an official UN document

(A/64/752—S/2010/203) with the UNSG.[17] As a follow-up step, the UNSG might propose establishing a forum where religious leaders of all faiths could discuss and collectively endorse a ban on production, stockpile, and the use of WMD. This would have a profound effect, since the endorsement would be an agreement with religious leaders representing billions of followers from major religions. Such a measure would also receive the endorsement of other minority religious groups in the Middle East, including Christians and Jews.

The head of the Roman Catholic Church, Pope Francis, representing 1.27 billion followers worldwide, has also voiced his support for the eradication of WMD, specifically nuclear weapons.[18] During the 2014 Vienna Conference on the Humanitarian Impact of Nuclear Weapons, he stated, "Nuclear deterrence and the threat of mutually assured destruction cannot be the basis for an ethics of fraternity and peaceful coexistence among peoples and states," adding, "A world without nuclear weapons is a goal shared by all nations and echoed by world leaders, as well as the aspiration of millions of men and women. The future and the survival of the human family hinges on moving beyond this ideal and ensuring that it becomes a reality . . . to ensure nuclear weapons are banned once and for all."[19]

Regional security arrangement

A regional security arrangement is fundamental in achieving the WMDFZ in the Middle East. The creation of the zone in one of the world's most volatile regions requires collective security assurances. Each regional country, while facing unique security challenges, can address them more effectively in the context of a regional security arrangement. Yet, there is no region-wide security arrangement to mitigate the eruption of violence and no regional mechanism to resolve grievances. This has led to instability, insecurity, and heightened mistrust, which impedes progress on security cooperation. The situation is made worse by the petrodollars that have funded over-militarization of the region and by interventions by foreign powers that disrupt any natural power equilibrium.

The regional security arrangement is envisioned as an independent and parallel track to the WMDFZ, with proposed sets of actions to resolve pressing regional security issues. The key will be to ensure that if a regional security arrangement fails it does not derail efforts to realize the WMDFZ. However, progress on either the regional security arrangement or the zone should be used to build bridges between regional states and strengthen the chances for further cooperation.[20]

A subregional security apparatus known as the Persian Gulf Cooperative Security Arrangement (PGCSA) can serve as the basis for a wider regional security apparatus. Elements of the PGCSA include (1) the six members of the Persian Gulf Cooperation Council (Bahrain, Kuwait, Oman, Qatar, Saudi Arabia, and the UAE) plus Iran and Iraq, based on Article 8 of UNSCR 598; (2) preservation of territorial integrity, political independence, international boundaries of all states in the region, and assured noninterference in internal affairs of other member states, similar to the Organization for Security and Cooperation in Europe (OSCE); (3) gradual removal of various limitations on political, security, economic, and cultural relations; (4) a joint security committee to deal with common security concerns, including terrorism, extremism, sectarianism, organized crime, asymmetric threats/warfare, and drug smuggling; (5) establishment of a free trade bloc between regional countries, similar to the EU; (6) a guarantee of the production and export of energy in the region to safeguard the interests of regional and external states and stabilize the international energy market; (7) a joint consortium on nuclear cooperation between the regional countries for confidence-building and producing nuclear fuel and other peaceful uses of nuclear energy under the supervision of the IAEA; (8) joint military exercises in the Persian Gulf and open lines of communication between respective militaries; (9) cooperation on maritime security and combating piracy, as the Persian Gulf's waterways are vital to international maritime trade and to key economies of the region; (10) a plan to end the regional conventional arms race to free up funds for economic development in the region; (11) a plan for gradual withdrawal of foreign military forces from the region and the establishment of a system in which regional countries would provide full security in the Persian Gulf region;[21] (12) a collective mechanism for the peaceful settlement of disputes among member states, avoiding the use of force; (13) a task force to deal with regional crises, such as Syria, Iraq, Arab Spring, and Afghanistan, through regional and multilateral diplomacy and cooperation with influential foreign and regional players such as the United States, the EU, China, Russia, India, Japan, Turkey, and the UN;[22] (14) constructive engagement with the same regional and international players to safeguard their national security and economic interests in the region and to create incentives for them to be cooperative; and (15) a regional push for the establishment of a WMDFZ in the Middle East and the Persian Gulf.[23]

In addition to the points just mentioned, which can be expanded into a region-wide security arrangement, there are two interlinked issues that were omitted from the subregional security arrangement. These include the Palestinian–Israeli peace process and Israeli nuclear weapons. The latter issue has been discussed extensively, with technical and political prescriptions provided to rid Israel of its nuclear arsenal. Here, we will touch on the positive impact a regional security arrangement will have on ending the decades-old Palestinian–Israeli conflict. Resolving both these issues will be crucial in the path toward realizing the zone and the regional security arrangement.

A major obstacle to the realization of the zone has been the precondition set by Israel for progress on the Palestinian–Israeli peace process. Lumping all security and stability issues facing each nation in the region into the formal efforts of reaching the zone will not be conducive to the process, and the wide scope will inherently derail it. Therefore, the peace process should be separated from the formal discussions and process for the zone and, instead, be incorporated into efforts to establish a regional security arrangement. Any progress on the Palestinian–Israeli peace process will inevitably provide positive momentum toward the zone, but should not be held hostage to it.

The Palestinian–Israeli peace process has remained stagnant, and there are no indications the situation will change in the near future. This stalemate has a long history, littered with grievances on both sides and short-lived episodes of hope for reaching a compromise.[24] Progress toward establishing a regional security arrangement will advance the Palestinian–Israeli peace process, as it will reduce tensions in the region and create a more conducive space for constructive roles to be played by regional and international communities. This would likely result in a more robust regional initiative based on a just peace, assuring the legitimate rights of both sides, respecting the UNSC resolutions, and reducing unconstructive interference in the peace process. This will lend itself toward constructive steps for a lasting peaceful resolution to the Israeli–Palestinian conflict whereby security guarantees are provided to all regional countries as part of the regional security arrangement.

The onus rests with both Palestinians and Israelis; they must decide to achieve a just resolution to their decades-old conflict. It will require Israel to shift away from policies such as settlement expansion, undermining the rights of Palestinian refugees, excessive military force in urban Palestinian areas, collective punishment of Palestinians as showcased in the blockade over the Gaza Strip, and stemming efforts for the legitimate right of Palestinians to a state. At the same time, Palestinians should speak with a united voice on the parameters for a final settlement with Israel, denounce terrorist acts, advance the cause of the Palestinians through robust nonviolent activism, and enhance their governance capability to provide better socioeconomic services to their population. However, there will be increased responsibility placed on other regional countries to play a constructive role in achieving a lasting peace and bringing an end to decades of Palestinian suffering.

More broadly, the United States, Russia, and other world powers, as the providers of the lion's share of security guarantees to select countries in the region, can leverage those security assurances to provide sustained and necessary backing for both a regional security arrangement and a WMDFZ. The regional security arrangement will require member states to increasingly shoulder the burden of security while reducing their reliance on foreign powers. Security and stability in the region will inevitably bolster trust among nations and contribute to sustained peace and socioeconomic development in the region.

Promoting socioeconomic development

The Middle East is flooded with conventional arms from leading arms exporters (the United States, the EU, China, and Russia), a testament to the sustained conflicts raging in the region.[25] The advancement of the WMDFZ in the region, however, will remove some security concerns of regional countries and, in doing so, facilitate a reduction in the conventional arms race in the Middle East. It will also shift government focus toward increasing intrastate conflicts that render sophisticated weaponries, in addition to nuclear or any other WMD arsenal, useless. Rather, there would be increasing interest in region-wide security guarantees and mechanisms to cooperate on curbing illicit trade in arms and incitement by extremists.

While security concerns will continue to dominate government priorities, the deep-rooted conflicts in the region cannot be addressed without dealing with other "soft security" issues. These issues include regional cooperation under a UN umbrella on environmental issues; curbing drug trafficking; immigration and refugee issues; and discussions on civil society matters pertaining to gender equality, political representation, educational reform, and health care.

Another key activity that could facilitate establishment of the WMDFZ is to address economic cooperation among regional states to foster closer relations and build trust. This could include technology transfer, transnational transport, water and energy infrastructure, as well as job creation programs to boost employment. These areas are less contentious, and bringing regional countries on board could tremendously improve bilateral relations as well as national economies. This strategy will be a long-lasting and least-expensive one for effective cooperation among regional and international partners. Confidence-building measures would play a critical role in aligning socioeconomic and political factors more favorably for a WMDFZ. Regional countries will be able to shift their focus from reactive policies to ones that address the root causes of domestic turmoil and popular grievances. This will have profound policy consequences for regional states and not only strengthen security cooperation but also attend to the dismal social record of the governments. In effect, a WMDFZ will give voice to the masses and ensure the wealth of countries goes toward fundamental socioeconomic and political development instead of toward procuring or stockpiling weapons.

Notes

1 "Communication Dated 12 September 2012 Received from the Resident Representative of the Islamic Republic of Iran Concerning 'Facts on Iran's Nuclear Policy'," September 12, 2012, www.iaea.org/sites/default/files/publications/documents/infcircs/2012/infcirc842.pdf.
2 "Trump: Cut Sanctions on Russia for Nuclear Arms Deal," *Al Jazeera*, January 16, 2017, www.aljazeera.com/news/2017/01/trump-cut-sanctions-russia-nuclear-arms-deal-170116033107521.html.
3 "2010 Review Conference of the Parties to the Treaty on the Non-Proliferation of Nuclear Weapons, Final Document," United Nations, 2010, www.un.org/ga/search/view_doc.asp?symbol=NPT/CONF.2010/50%20(VOL.I).
4 David Friedman, "Towards WMDFZ in the Middle East: Biological Confidence-Building Measures," EU Non-Proliferation Consortium, November 6, 2012, www.nonproliferation.eu/web/documents/backgroundpapers/friedman.pdf.
5 Dina Esfandiary, "Building Confidence Towards a MEWMDFZ via a Chemical Weapons Ban," EU Non-Proliferation Consortium, November 6, 2012, www.nonproliferation.eu/web/documents/backgroundpapers/becker.pdf.
6 "Chemical and Biological Weapons Status at a Glance," Arms Control Association, accessed September 1, 2016, www.armscontrol.org/factsheets/cbwprolif.
7 "Security Council Unanimously Adopts Wide-Ranging Anti-Terrorism Resolution," United Nations, September 28, 2001, www.un.org/press/en/2001/sc7158.doc.htm.
8 "Resolution 1540 (2004)," United Nations Security Council, April 28, 2004, www.un.org/ga/search/view_doc.asp?symbol=S/RES/1540%282004%29.
9 "Code of Conduct on the Safety and Security of Radioactive Sources and the Supplementary Guidance on the Import and Export of Radioactive Sources," IAEA,

December 29, 2005, www.iaea.org/sites/default/files/publications/documents/infcircs/2005/infcirc663.pdf.

10 "The International Convention for the Suppression of Acts of Nuclear Terrorism (ICSANT)," United Nations, 2005, https://treaties.un.org/doc/db/Terrorism/english-18-15.pdf.

11 "Background," MECIDS, accessed September 1, 2016, www.mecidsnetwork.org/content/background.

12 "NPT Treaty," United Nations, accessed September 1, 2016, http://www.un.org/en/conf/npt/2005/npttreaty.html.

13 Thomas Pickering, "4 Ways Trump Can Keep Relations Steady with Iran | Commentary," *Dallas News*, December 2, 2016, www.dallasnews.com/opinion/commentary/2016/12/02/4-ways-trump-can-keep-relations-steady-iran.

14 Gardiner Harris, " 'Every Pathway to a Nuclear Weapon Is Cut Off,' Obama Says," *New York Times*, July 14, 2015, http://www.nytimes.com/live/iran-nuclear-deal-live-updates/obama-says-every-pathway-to-a-nuclear-weapon-is-cut-off/.

15 Lord Hannay and Thomas Pickering, "Trumping Proliferation: From a One-Off Deal to a Global Standard," December 6, 2016, www.europeanleadershipnetwork.org/trumping-proliferation-from-a-one-off-deal-to-a-global-standard_4301.html.

16 Ibid.

17 "Identical Letters Dated 20 April 2010 from the Permanent Representative of the Islamic Republic of Iran to the United Nations Addressed to the Secretary-General and the President of the Security Council," United Nations Security Council, April 22, 2010.

18 "Pontifical Yearbook 2016 and the Annuarium Statisticum Ecclesiae 2014: Dynamics of a Church in Transformation," *Vatican*, March 5, 2016, https://press.vatican.va/content/salastampa/en/bollettino/pubblico/2016/03/05/160305b.html.

19 "President of the Conference on the Humanitarian Impact of Nuclear Weapons," n.d., www.bmeia.gv.at/fileadmin/user_upload/Zentrale/Aussenpolitik/Abruestung/HINW14/HINW14_Message_from_His_Holiness_Pope_Francis.pdf.

20 Sinan Ülgen, "A Think Piece on Confidence-Building Measures in the Middle East," Carnegie Europe, November 1, 2012, http://carnegieeurope.eu/2012/11/01/think-piece-on-confidence-building-measures-in-middle-east.

21 Frederic Wehrey and Richard Sokolsky, "Imagining a New Security Order in the Persian Gulf," Carnegie Endowment for International Peace, accessed August 31, 2016, http://carnegieendowment.org/2015/10/14/imagining-new-security-order-in-persian-gulf-pub-61618.

22 Robert E. Hunter, "Building Security in the Persian Gulf," Rand Corporation, 2010, www.rand.org/pubs/monographs/MG944.html.

23 Ibid.

24 "Timeline: Middle East Peace Talks," *The Guardian*, January 23, 2011, sec. World News, www.theguardian.com/world/2011/jan/23/timeline-middle-east-peace-talks.

25 Catherine A. Theohary, "Conventional Arms Transfers to Developing Nations, 2004–2011," Congressional Research Service, December 21, 2015.

Index

Note: Surnames starting with "al-" are alphabetized by remaining portion of the name.

For Product Safety Concerns and Information please contact our EU
representative GPSR@taylorandfrancis.com
Taylor & Francis Verlag GmbH, Kaufingerstraße 24, 80331 München, Germany

www.ingramcontent.com/pod-product-compliance
Ingram Content Group UK Ltd.
Pitfield, Milton Keynes, MK11 3LW, UK
UKHW011018180926
475701UK00004B/806

* 9 7 8 0 3 6 7 5 0 0 0 2 3 *